LEGAL ISSUES IN MEDICINE

This book is dedicated to Beth,
Bill and Douglas, with love and
thanks for their encouragement
and affection over the years.

Legal Issues in Medicine

Edited by
SHEILA A. M. McLEAN
University of Glasgow

Gower

Published by Gower Publishing Co. Ltd, Gower House,
Croft Road, Aldershot, Hampshire GU11 3HR, England.

British Library Cataloguing in Publication Data

Legal issues in medicine.
   1. Medical laws and legislation - Great Britain
   2. Medical jurisprudence - Great Britain
   I. McLean, Sheila A.M.
   344.104'41   RA241

ISBN 0 566 00428 3

Printed in Great Britain by Biddles Ltd, Guildford, Surrey

Contents

The Contributors

J. Douglas Bell M.B.Ch.B.,
M.R.C.P.(E), M.F.O.M. (R.C.P.),
D.I.H.

Occupational Physician.

Tom Campbell M.A., Ph.D.

Professor of Jurisprudence,
University of Glasgow.

Douglas Cusine Ll.B.

Lecturer, Department of Private
Law, University of Aberdeen.

Robin Downie M.A., B.Phil.

Professor of Moral Philosophy,
University of Glasgow.

Malcolm Ferguson-Smith M.B.Ch.B.,
F.R.C.P.(Glas.), F.R.C.Path.,
F.R.S.E.

Professor of Medical Genetics,
University of Glasgow.

Angelo Forte M.A., LL.B.

Lecturer, Department of Private
Law, University of Dundee.

Alan Gamble LL.B., LL.M.

Lecturer, Department of Private
Law, University of Glasgow.

Gerald Gordon Q.C., LL.D.

Sheriff of Glasgow and
Strathkelvin, Sometime Professor
of Scots Law, University of
Edinburgh.

Robin Leake M.A., D.Phil.

Lecturer, Department of
Biochemistry, University of
Glasgow.

Angus McKay M.A.

Lecturer, Department of Moral
Philosophy, University of Glasgow.

Sheila McLean LL.B., M.Litt.

Lecturer, Department of Forensic
Medicine and Science, University
of Glasgow.

Gerry Maher LL.B., B.Litt.(Oxon)

Lecturer, Department of
Jurisprudence, University of
Glasgow.

Sami Shubber Lic. en Dr.,
Dip. in Law, LL.M., Ph.D.(Cantab)
Of Gray's Inn, Barrister-at-Law.

Senior Legal Officer, World Health
Organization, Geneva.

David Soutar M.B.Ch.B., F.R.C.S.

Senior Registrar, Canniesburn
Hospital, Glasgow.

Gordon Stewart B.Sc., M.D.,
F.F.C.M., F.R.C.Path.,
F.R.C.P.(Glas.), D.T.M.& H.

Professor of Public Health,
University of Glasgow.

Foreword

Forensic Medicine has been taught to both medical students and law students at the University of Glasgow for over 140 years, and these courses continue to the present day. The course for medical students has remained much the same over the years, with considerable emphasis being given to what is now called forensic pathology. This subject still forms the basis of lectures to students of law, but the subject matter of the law course has been greatly extended to include an examination of a wide variety of medico-legal problems, and is now taught over three years to the Honours level. This expansion has been necessary because of the progressive introduction of new techniques in medicine, and the emergence of a huge volume of new law in the form of both case law and statutes which have profoundly changed the practice of medicine.

Some of these problems form the subject matter of this multi-author book, which will prove extremely valuable to all those concerned with medico-legal issues. Its value lies not simply in the fact that the approach taken is analytical rather than purely descriptive, but also in that it adopts a comparative approach to the problems considered by discussing both Scots and English Law and, where available, American and European cases and regulations. Mrs. McLean is to be congratulated for presenting this collection of essays, which will form a valuable basis for continuing debate on these difficult problems.

W. Arthur Harland,   30 April, 1981.
M.D.,Ph.D.,F.R.C.Path.,F.R.C.P.,F.R.S.E.,
Regius Professor of Forensic Medicine,
The University of Glasgow.

Introduction

In recent years medicine and its practitioners have come under increasing scrutiny from the media and the law. Public interest has been aroused in respect of the ethics of medical practice and research. Equally, the medical profession has become increasingly concerned about a variety of ethical problems and about potential legal intervention in the practice of medicine.

Although much of the interest, both in litigation and research, has been concentrated in the United States of America, there has been increasing debate concerning various aspects of medical practice in a European context. It is our hope that this book will contribute something to this debate by analysing the structure of medical practice, primarily in the United Kingdom, and by examining some of the fundamental assumptions which have tended to underlie the traditional legal and community responses to dilemmas in medicine. It is impossible to deal with these matters in a completely comprehensive manner, and therefore I have omitted consideration of some popular medico-legal issues, such as abortion and the termination of medical treatment. Rather, the present authors have attempted to deal with those problems which seem to be either so fundamental that their omission would be a gross deficiency in any work of this sort, or those which have traditionally received less attention but which seem to be of major importance.

In compiling this collection of essays, I have sought to bring together the diverse talents and interests of several disciplines - law, medicine, science and philosophy - and thereby to present a rounded view of the dilemmas facing patients, doctors and medical science.

Some issues considered in this book are predominately legal, but they are nonetheless of considerable interest to the medical profession, for example the law relating to products liability has clear implications for those involved in the production or prescription of drugs. The imputation of responsibility in this area is highly problematic for patient, doctor and the law, and the inference of lack of care which is an essential part of the present system of liability based on tort/delict, causes some considerable concern for those who may be held to have failed in their professional duties. The role of medicine in the criminal law also cannot be discounted, neither in terms of the evidence provided to courts and tribunals by medical science and medical experts, nor in terms of the development of legal doctrines concerning responsibility for behaviour, which purport to be based on medical principles and which require medical evidence in order to be established.

Equally, not all the issues considered in this book are obviously legal at first sight, for example some are predominately scientific or philosophical, but they have, nonetheless, clear implications which are necessarily at least partly legal. For example, the question of who is responsible in the provision of health care is not simply a philosophical issue. It has been of considerable interest to the law since, in any attempt at litigation, it is essential to identify the party who is appropriately sued. Further, international law has created a supra-national organisation with regulatory powers, which makes the wide-spread sharing of responsibility fundamental to world health.

In compiling this book, I owe debts of gratitude to many colleagues, friends and relatives who have been helpful and encouraging throughout. To my husband Alan I owe a great debt for his long-suffering patience throughout the many frenetic hours of work and for his valuable comments on the chapters as they came in. I am also indebted to Mrs G. Robertson for her speedy and accurate typing and her patience and good-humour throughout. Mrs. M.Harrison and the late Mrs. N.McCulloch also contributed greatly to the preparation of this book. I am particularly grateful to Dr. R. Anderson, who fought the Departmental word-processor and won! His contribution to the final preparation of the manuscript cannot be underestimated. He gave freely of his time and expertise, and for this I am most grateful.

I must also express my sincere thanks to the contributors who have made this book what it is, and to the law students specialising in Forensic Medicine at the University of Glasgow, whose alert and lively comments and questions throughout the last five years have contributed much to the final document. Finally, I wish to express my thanks to Professor W.A.Harland, Regius Professor of Forensic Medicine at the University of Glasgow, who has not only prepared the Foreword for this book, but who has also devoted much time and energy to reading and commenting on each chapter, and who has given generously of his and his department's time.

Sheila A.M.McLean,

Department of Forensic Medicine
and Science, University of Glasgow.

30 April 1981.

Table of Cases

TABLE OF CASES

1 Collective Responsibility in Health Care

R. S. Downie

There is a widespread assumption that responsibility in health care is vested in the last resort in the individual doctor who is caring for a given patient. In the first section of this chapter the plausibility of this assumption will be considered, and the concept of collective responsibility which it allows will be examined. The second and third sections will try to show the fatal weaknesses of the assumption in its unmodified form, and argue that if the nature of health care at the present time is to be understood the norm must be taken to be collective and not individual responsibility. The two relevant senses of collective responsibility will be discussed, and it will be shown how they can be reconciled with what is acceptable in the widespread assumption of individual responsibility.

There are two connected arguments which can be urged in favour of the assumption that individual responsibility should be the norm in health care. The first argument turns on two premises: a premise expressing the conceptual point that the nature of any skill is determined by the object of the skill, by what the skill is intended to bring about, and a premise expressing a contingent or substantial point about medical skill. The substantial point is that medical skill, the practice of medicine, is directed towards the preservation of life by the treatment of illness, disease, injury or disability. If disease or injury are thought of in terms of measles or a broken leg it is easy to think of the skills for their treatment as being such as can be vested in the individual doctor. Moreover, we are encouraged to think in this way by the mystique of medical education; doctors themselves seem to believe, and have encouraged generations of the general public to believe, that prolonged medical education gives the individual doctor the knowledge and skills which enable him as an individual to treat disease and injury. The community has become accustomed to believe that for a wide variety of ills (and nowadays these ills include the mental as well as the physical) the doctor is the appropriate person to consult. But this belief could not be rational unless we also believed that he as an individual had the requisite skills or expertise to help us, and that, having the skills, he would be responsible for our care.

The second argument is a much wider one since it concerns the grounds of moral responsibility. It is plausible to maintain that since the practice of medicine can profoundly benefit or harm us, the practice of medicine must necessarily be the practice of morality. Let us therefore concede this, and examine the individualist's thesis that the conditions for moral responsibility are realised only in an individual consciousness.

Is this the view that it is a <u>sufficient</u> condition of an action's being the appropriate target of a moral judgment that it be performed by an individual person? This is a strong thesis the investigation of which produces many arguments of relevance to moral philosophy. But as far as present interest in the premise is concerned we need attribute to the individualist only the weaker thesis that it is a <u>necessary</u> condition of an action's being suitable for moral judgement that it be performed by an individual. It is not yet clear, however,

1

whether, when the individualist says that it is suitable or legitimate to make moral judgements only about the actions of individuals, he means that it is _logically_ suitable, or whether he means that it is _morally_ suitable.

The answer to this question depends on the nature of the arguments used to defend the premise.

One argument might be what is often called the '"ought" implies "can" argument': that if there is anything a person categorically or morally ought to do then he must unconditionally be able to do it, although he may or may not in fact do it. This argument can be criticised on various counts, but from the present point of view its defect is that by itself it does not succeed in establishing the required necessary connection between individual action and moral predicates. It would surely be possible for a group to have this freedom to act otherwise. Only if freedom is analysed (as Kant perhaps does) in such a way that the necessary conditions for possessing it can be found only in an individual person does the argument succeed, and in that case it has succeeded at the price of begging the question. To say this is not, of course, to reject the '"ought" implies "can" argument' as such, nor even to reject the Kantian analysis of freedom, but simply to reject the argument as an independent basis for establishing the major premise of the individualist's position.

A second line might be called the 'pragmatists' argument': that it is socially desirable to connect moral responsibility with individual action because the establishment of such a connection provides a social atmosphere friendly towards law and order. There is clearly a close connection between moral responsibility and legal responsibility, particularly criminal responsibility,[1] and it is therefore useful and desirable to assume that when it is legitimate to think of blame for some action it is necessary to look for particular individuals on whom to pin the blame. The trouble with the pragmatists' argument here, however, is that, like many other pragmatic arguments, it does not bear on the question of the _truth_ of the individualist's major premise. It establishes only (what is no doubt plausible as far as it goes) that it makes for stability in society to assume that behind any moral or criminal failing there is always some one individual or individuals on whom the blame can be pinned. No doubt it would also be desirable as a means of social control if we all assented to the proposition 'God exists', but the usefulness of the belief would not establish its truth.

It is in fact probable that there is no argument which would independently establish the individualist's major premise. Any argument which seems plausible will turn out to be presupposing the premise. The conclusion must therefore be reached that in the major premise there is a fundamental assumption of the moral point of view. In other words, if blame is logically to count as _moral_ blame the actions concerned logically must have been performed by individual persons. It might be objected at this point that whereas what I say may be true of certain moral points of view, it is not true of everything that might be called a 'moral point of view'. But is this really so? Certainly, there may be sets of beliefs which do not make this assumption, and those beliefs may have many resemblances to what might be called moral beliefs. It is arguable, however, that what has come to be known as 'morality' in civilised nations (say, those which signed the U.N. Declaration of Human Rights) is necessarily connected with the free decisions of individuals. The position then is that it is <u>logically</u> appropriate to look for individuals on whom to pin moral blame, although this logical truth may be based on a foundation of the contingent historical development of a set of assumptions about the individual and his actions.

If these arguments for individual responsibility in health care are granted, there is a problem as to whether there can in any sense at all be such a thing as collective responsibility in health care. This problem can indeed seem insoluble if the premise is assumed that the actions of collectives are not the actions of individuals, for in that case collective responsibility logically could not be moral responsibility, whereas health care according to the individualist clearly entails the moral responsibility of individuals. And the defence of the premise could be that it is simply a matter of definition that if collectives are acting we cannot also say that individuals are acting.

But this defence is simplistic. If a voice at the end of the telephone says 'This is the Newtown Health Centre' we do not imagine that the voice proceeds from anything other than an individual person (unless, of course, a telephone answering machine!). This suggests that there is a misleading disjunction between individual action and responsibility and collective action and responsibility, that it does not follow from the fact that a collective is acting that some individual person or persons are not also acting and responsible.

Why then would the individualist want to speak at all of 'collective' action and responsibility? One answer might be that it is convenient to do so - that it can be useful to use the idea of a collective to refer to the sum total of the actions and responsibilities of some group of associated individuals. For example, in medicine doctors are often part of a group practice. There are obvious advantages in this for doctors and patients in the provision of continuous patient-care throughout the year, the sharing of expensive equipment, and so on. A group practice in this sense is a collective, but there is no incompatibility with the doctrine of individual moral responsibility. In this sense of collective responsibility the actions of the collective, the group practice, are divisible into the actions of the individual doctors, who are each independently responsible for what they do. There is an analogy here with a dandelion which is itself a flower but consists of a number of florets each of which is also a flower. Collective responsibility in this sense is the responsibility of aggregates.

Doctors also work in teams involving nurses, radiographers, physiotherapists, and so on. Each of these health workers is individually responsible for his own contribution to a different aspect of health care, but insofar as they are part of one team, there will be one individual who has overall responsibility. This is the collective responsibility of a hierarchy, and it is another sort of collective responsibility which is compatible with individual responsibility, to the extent that there is one person who has ultimate authority to take decisions. Aggregative and hierarchical responsibility together or separately might be thought conceptually sufficient to enable us to make sense of hospitals and all other apparent collectives in medical care without at all forcing us to abandon or modify the strong doctrine of individual responsibility.

There are, however, fatal limitations to this simplistic model of responsibility in health care. Take first the basic idea of the practice of medicine, and grant that when a doctor acts an individual acts. The important point which is obscured by this truism is that

3

he is not acting as an individual, but rather as a doctor, viz. as an individual who has not only certain skills but also certain statutory and professional rights and duties.

It is possible to approach this point in another way. In the first section of this paper the doctor was characterised as an individual who necessarily aims at health and has the expertise relevant to promoting health, or at least to removing impediments to health. It follows from that that the doctor's activities intimately bear on human good and harm. But it can now be stressed that, insofar as the doctor's activities bear intimately on human good and harm, the State will take an interest in them, and lay down broad conditions for the qualifications of doctors and the running of the medical profession. In other words, the doctor's activities are governed by legal statute. For example, there will be legislation laying down in general or specific terms when a patient has a legal right to medical care, to hospitalisation and so on. There may even be cases, perhaps of certain infectious disorders or certain phychiatric disorders, where the doctor has a duty to commit the patient to care against his wishes. In the latter case, the authority by which a person may be compulsorily detained in a hospital obtains legally in Britain from an Act of Parliament. Medical practitioners and mental welfare officers have to be properly trained and duly authorised. Indeed, the mental welfare officer is specifically given protection in case of civil or criminal proceedings arising from the carrying out of any of these compulsory duties, provided he has not acted 'in bad faith or without reasonable care'. Whatever the details of legislation, however, it is clear that the bond which holds doctor and patient together is at least a legal one.

The bond is constituted, secondly, by rather vaguer sets of rules, or even of expectations, which doctors and patients have of each other. Doctors often refer to this as the 'ethics' of their profession. There are many different facets to this. For example, a patient has the assurance that a doctor will not take advantage of him with respect to any information about his private life which emerges, and there will be no gossip about medical conditions, social predicaments and so on.[2] The medical profession is very strict about enforcing its own discipline on these matters. Reciprocally a doctor would expect a patient to tell the truth, to try to carry out prescribed treatment and so on. Social workers indeed to as far as to speak of a 'contract' between themselves and their clients.[3]

It is important that the doctor/patient relationship should be constituted, at least partly, by these legal and quasi-legal institutional bonds, for at least the following reasons. Firstly, because doctors and all health and welfare workers, by the nature of their job, intervene in existentially crucial ways in the lives of others. This is a serious matter and its consequences for a patient can be major. It is therefore in the interest of patients that there should be some sort of professional entitlement to intervene. In other words, if he is not simply to be a busybody, a doctor must have the right to intervene, and if he has the right to intervene he must have duties and responsibilities; the concept of an institution encapsulates these ideas of rights, duties and responsibilities. A second reason is that doctors must ask about many intimate details of people's lives, for example, about their marriages; and they also may conduct examinations of people's bodies. Questioning of this sort, far less physical examination, can create situations in which people can be exploited, or which could be embarrassing even to doctors themselves.   The fact that it is an institutional bond which brings the doctor together with his patient provides emotional insulation for both parties in such situations.   Moreover, since it is important that the doctor should know these intimate details there must be some assurance that no untoward use will be made of the information, that it will not be passed on, for example, to neighbours.   But the idea of an institution entails rules, and the rules can, thirdly, impose confidentiality on the doctor and provide security for the patient. Fourthly, doctors are given a measure of security by virtue of the fact that they work inside an institutional framework.   There are various aspects to this.   For instance, it is good for all professions to have ways and means whereby new skills and knowledge can be shared, and members of a profession can support and encourage each other.   Again, doctors require legal or similar professional protection from exploitation, unfair criticism or legal action against them by their patients.   Reciprocally there must be some institutional mechanism whereby the professions can criticise themselves and look for ways of improving their services to the public.   These then are some of the reasons why a complex legal and institutional structure has grown up governing directly and indirectly the relationships between health and welfare workers and their patients.

There are various desirable and undesirable aspects to this, but the relevant point for present purposes is that when the doctor or nurse or other health worker appears to be acting as an individual he is also acting as a representative of his profession, and to a lesser extent also of his State.   In other words, the individual action of a doctor or other health worker expresses also the collective values of his profession;   individual responsibility becomes collective responsibility since it is through the individual that the profession is represented.   We might say that the individual health worker represents his profession in two senses.   First, he is the ascriptive representative, in that the profession authorises his actions, having sanctioned his training.   Second, he represents the values of the profession insofar as he acts in terms of its ethics, and its ethics are all-pervasive in the actions and attitudes of the individual health worker.

But if the individual actions of the doctor or nurse are also the actions of collectives, what remains of the doctrine that individuals and only they can be held morally responsible for their actions? Helpful here is the concept of a social role, understood for this purpose as being a set of rights and duties to be analysed in terms of institutional concepts.   An individual person is able to act not only in a private capacity but in a social role, and this concept, understood institutionally, enables justice to be done to the valid points in the collectivist's case, for it is logically unanalysable in purely individualistic terms;   its adequate specification must be in logically irreducible institutional terms.   Yet the concept of social role, so understood, also enables us to do justice to the individualist's insistence that moral responsibility must remain with the individual person, for we can say that, insofar as an individual consents to act in a role, he or she thereby becomes morally responsible for the actions which are done in its name.   In accepting the role, he adds to his share of rights and duties those which go with the role;   if he feels unable to accept the rights and duties of the role he can refuse to accept the role.   Here, then are the beginnings of a theory which will enable agreement with the

5

individualist that moral responsibility belongs ultimately to individuals, while also agreeing with the collectivist that there is much more to collective action than can be explained in terms of individuals acting in a purely private capacity. We can call this first dimension of collective responsibility 'the morality of role-acceptance'. The problems in this dimension are those of when an individual should accept a given role, when he should resign, or, if resignation is for some reason inappropriate or impossible, when he should refuse to carry out the apparent duties of the role. What is here called the 'morality of role-acceptance' has of course been discussed traditionally under headings such as 'a sense of vocation', or 'a calling'.

When collectives act, individuals act, but those individuals act in roles whose capacities are defined by the nature of the collective. To put it another way, we can say that the individuals are authorised by their collectives to act in certain ways, depending on the function of the collective. Or the matter could be put in yet another way if we say that an individual could be made the representative of the collective. However, the terms of the authorisation will vary a great deal. For example, at one extreme a junior clerk may be authorised to stamp certain documents if and only if certain conditions hold; at the other extreme a teacher may be authorised to teach a certain historical period and given no directive as to how he must do this. In the latter case there is clearly room for a new dimension of moral responsibility which we can call the 'morality of role-enactment'. Indeed, even in the former case there is some, although very little, scope for variation in role-enactment. For example, questions of speed, neatness, and courtesy might be raised in respect of the role-enacting of the clerk; but the enactment of the rights and duties which constitute roles of the latter type characteristically leaves much greater scope for the initiative of individuals, and the greater the scope, the more room there is for moral judgments about the enactment of the roles. Clearly, the doctor is at the same end of this spectrum as the teacher, in that there is enormous scope for individual initiative and the exercise of a whole range of skills and moral qualities in the enactment of the medical role.

The third dimension to the morality of collective action can be called the morality of the role as such. We can and often do pass moral judgments about certain roles or offices on the grounds that they are likely to lead to good or bad actions, irrespective of who occupies them. To take an obvious and melodramatic example, it might be said that the role of secret policemen is evil in that if it is operated it will lead to evil action no matter who the secret policeman is. If a society is characterised in total abstraction from its members, this concept generally suggests the morality of the system of roles. This point is illustrated by Gandhi who, when speaking of the British Government in India, said:

> ... an Englishman in office is different from an Englishman
> outside... Here in India you belong to a system which is
> vile beyond description. It is possible, therefore, for me
> to condemn the system in the strongest terms, without
> considering you to be bad and without imputing bad motives to
> every Englishman.[4]

This is a characterisation of a system of roles conceived in abstraction from its operators.

It should be noted that the justification for using the language of moral, as distinct from natural, good and evil in speaking of a system of roles does not lie merely in the fact that the roles, if operated, will lead to morally good or evil actions. The roles themselves are connected with human decisions in a manner such as will justify their assessment in moral language. The connection lies in the fact that society is a human artefact; it has been built up as a result of innumerable human judgments, decisions and acceptances in the past. Of course, not all the judgements and decisions which have led to the creation and development of social institutions are to be assessed in moral language: many will simply be the result of the mistakes or happy chances which inevitably follow from limited human knowledge, and honest mistake of fact is hardly to be assessed in moral terms.

Moreover, some institutions can less properly be said to have been built up by judgment and decision, rather they have grown up by custom: we did not so much create them as find ourselves in possession of them. Nevertheless, among the judgments and decisions which have created our social institutions are some to which both praise and blame can be attached, and those institutions which have grown up by custom are at least accepted by us; even if we did not make them we do consent to their presence. Our institutions, then, are images of ourselves as moral creatures. It is society, rather than the individuals now acting in their roles, which is responsible in this sense, because the individual does not necessarily choose the actions to which his role commits him. What is true of society as a whole is <u>a fortiori</u> true of the medical institutions within it. Over the years they grow and are developed by decisions, some taken by the medical profession, some by the State, some deliberately taken, some forced by public opinion or the law, but as a whole moulding the roles and therefore influencing the moral decisions taken by members of the health professions. This is a dimension of collective moral responsibility because there remains a connection, although an oblique one, between the actions resulting from the nature of the medical role and individual human decision. But is is only one dimension of collective moral responsibility, since clearly room must be made for the first and second dimensions as well.

We have, then, three dimensions of moral responsibility in collective medical action as medical action is affected by its institutional structure - the morality of the role, the role-enactment, and the role-acceptance - and the complex nature of judgments of collective responsibility in health care is due to the fact that all three dimensions may be relevant. The earlier account of the collective responsibility of group practices and medical teams would require to be made more complex to take into account the institutional side to medical action.

In the first section of this paper it was claimed that there were two arguments for regarding individual responsibility as the norm in medical practice. One, which was based on the assumption that moral responsibility must be vested in the individual, has been modified in the preceding section to make it compatible with the collective responsibility of the medical profession for patient care. It is now appropriate to consider the other argument.

This is concerned with the skill of the doctor and with his aim. The general premise was that skills have an end, aim or point which determines the nature of the skill, and the specific premise was that in the case of medicine the aim is to try to treat any illness or disease, malfunction or injury which might interfere with human

good.   Being thus encouraged to think of health care in terms of the
removal of specific impairments or impediments, society is likewise
encouraged to think of the requisite skills as being in the possession
of the individual doctor who has responsibility for a given patient.
The acceptability of this argument depends on the acceptability of the
account of the aim of the doctor.

The weakness in this account is that it adopts a narrow, even a
negative, view of the aim of medicine;   it conceives the aim as being
that of the removal of impediments to health.   But there can also be
a positive aspect to health: not merely absence of discomfort and
incapacity, but the positive feelings of a sense of fitness and
energy, and a supple and well tuned body - the condition in which
someone is said to glow with health, be bursting with health and so
on.   What may be seen as a luxury from the point of view of the
negative aspect of health, such as the promotion of vigour in old age,
is central from the point of view of the positive aspect.   Medical
concern with contraception can perhaps also be classified as the
promotion of positive health;   in general, at any rate, neither
pregnancy nor abstinence constitutes or produces ill-health, but any
doctor who says his patients must choose between them is ignoring one
element of physical pleasure and well-being.   The aim of the doctor
should therefore be seen not just negatively, as the attempt to free
people from unwanted or abnormal conditions, but also positively.
Indeed, it must further be said that the aim of the doctor is not just
that of promoting health, but should be even more broadly conceived as
the promotion of 'wholeness'.   Or, if it is thought that 'the
promotion of wholeness' is too ambitious an aim then the old-fashioned
or religious-sounding noun 'healing', which covers more of the ground
required for an adequate characterisation of the aim of medicine than
our common modern word 'health', could be employed.

If it is granted that the aim of medicine should thus be broadly
conceived as the promotion of the wholeness of a person, his
'healing',[5] what follows about the nature of the skills and
expertise required to promote it?   The obvious implication is that
the skills and expertise will be so varied that no one individual
would be able to possess them all.   Of course, the aim of the doctor
could be re-stated in a way which would make it possible for the
necessary skills to be in the possession of individual doctors, at
least in many cases.   Thus, thinking in terms of the earlier-stated
negative aim - the removing of impediments to normal functioning -
then, in many cases at least, an individual doctor will have the
skills necessary to promote that aim.

And, of course, a large part of medical work is concerned with
just that.   But if the aim of medicine is thought of more positively,
as the promotion of wholeness, of total well-being, then it is clear
that what is required is a co-operative or collective exercise.

It will be a co-operative exercise moreover of considerable
width.   In other words, it will not be simply the collective action
of associated teams of health workers mentioned above.   To illustrate
this point, consider the connections between health and welfare.
First of all, health is clearly one very important part of welfare, in
that it is reasonably wanted for its own sake and in that possession
of it is a necessary condition for pursuing very many other goals.
For this reason part of the social worker's job will be to promote the
health of his client: to encourage him to seek medical advice and to
take it, and to help him battle with, for example, inefficient
National Health or other similar bureaucracy for free spectacles and

8

the like.   This is not of course to say that the social worker may usurp the doctor's function of bringing his unique skill to bear on the patient's medical problems.   But the social worker has an overall responsibility for the patient, which makes it quite reasonable that he should want to know what is going on medically.   He will often also be the best person to defend the patient against the medical profession, where that is necessary: not where a legal defence is needed (for that he would have to call in another specialist!) but where what is needed is firm speaking by someone who has the confidence to address the doctor on equal terms as a fellow professional: about, say, overpersuasion by the doctor to undergo some experimental or controversial treatment, or about a refusal to allow parents of young children to visit them in hospital.

It has been said that the possession of health is a necessary condition for the pursuit of many other goals.   The vital importance of this point will be clear when it is remembered how often a person becomes a 'case' because he is unable to 'hold down' a job through chronic ill-health or alcoholism or mental illness;   the immediate problem may be his lack of financial means, but the underlying cause of the problem is a medical one, even if the client thinks of himself as a social work rather than a medical case.   It is also often for such medical reasons, that a person (for example a neglectful parent or violent spouse) damages the interests of others to the extent that social workers become involved.   In such cases the social worker needs to be able to consult the doctor on questions which are partly, but not wholly, medical: e.g. is this man sufficiently recovered from his depression to be encouraged to look for a job, or is this woman likely to recover quickly from her mental illness and be able to look after her children again, or must long-term plans be made for them?

The second connection between health and welfare is of course the dependence of health, mental and physical, on other aspects of welfare, both material and non-material.   To take an obvious example, an old person's health may be impaired because his house is damp, or up too many stairs, or because he cannot afford proper clothes or food or heating, or because he is not sufficiently able-bodied to look after himself.   In all these situations, the expertise in specifying what is needed may be the doctor's, but the expertise in getting it, through statutory or voluntary services, is that of the social worker.   And the skill required to thread the maze of regulations and to persuade officialdom of the urgency of need can be considerable. There are also, of course, cases where the dependence of health on welfare is at a deeper level, as in those cases of phychiatric or indeed physical illnesses which seem to be bound up with family or personal problems, and here the doctor may need social work help not only in alleviating the problem but also in understanding it.

It should emerge from these fairly obvious considerations that health and welfare are inextricably bound up together and that the doctor and the social worker can each be - must each be - ancillary workers to the other, rather than mutually antagonistic, if these twin aims are to be achieved.   The thrust of this line of argument will be to break up the idea that doctors, social workers, and other similar professionals ought to have their own separately indentifiable aims of health, welfare, etc.   It seems preferable to minimise the differences in the specific aims of these professions rather than to see them all as 'caring' professions aiming at 'wholeness'.   Indeed, if we consider the importance in contemporary life of health education, of legislation to control pollution and in general to maintain the environment, it becomes evident that responsibility for 'wholeness' must be widely distributed.

The conclusion can be drawn from this section of the argument that responsibility for health care must be collective in a second sense. The first sense of collective responsibility was concerned with the institutional side to health care. It brought out the point that even if the health worker was acting as an individual he was also acting as a representative of a profession with the rights, duties and values of the profession. This sort of collective responsibility could be thought of as 'vertical'. The second sort, by contrast, is horizontal, in the sense that responsibility for 'wholeness' (of which 'health' is a component) is shared by a wide variety of professionals, and in the last resort by each one of us. The first sense is a reminder that health makers are members of professions, the second sense reminds us that they are members of a community. Collective responsibility for health care in the second sense is clearly compatible with the doctrine of individual responsibility stated in the first section. It makes the point that for adequate health care, for wholeness, it is required not just that we should be served by a collectively responsible health profession in the first sense, but that we should be a collectively responsible society.[6] Membership of a health profession, however broadly conceived, must be supplemented by our being members one of another.

R.S. Downie

*Some of the material in this paper appears in The Journal of Medicine and Philosophy, January 1982, and I am grateful to the Editor for permission to make use of it here.

NOTES.

1.   For further discussion, see infra ch. 14.
2.   The importance of confidentiality was originally expounded in the Hippocratic Oath, by which doctors still consider themselves bound. This code was restated in the Declaration of Geneva in 1947, and the Declaration of Sydney in 1968, which states that the medical practitioner will 'respect the secrets which are confided in [him]...even after the patient has died.' For further discussion on confidentiality, see infra pp. 19-21.
3.   c.f. 'Values of Social Work', paras, 3.13 - 3.19, Central Council for Education and Training in Social Work, Paper 13, 1976; Pincus, A., and Minahan, A., Social Work Practice: Model and Method, F.E. Peacock, 1973; Cheetham, J. and Hills, M., 'Community Work : Social Realities and Ethical Dilemmas' British Journal of Social Work, 1973.
4.   Quoted by C.F. Andrews, Mahatma Gandhi's Ideas, at p. 241 London : Allen and Unwin, 1929.
5.   These points are developed in Downie, R.S. and Telfer, E., Caring and Curing, Methuen and Co., London and New York, 1980.
6.   For discussion of the organisation of collective

reponsibility on an international basis, see infra ch. 4.

2 The Occupational Physician and the Law

J. D. Bell

Into whatever House I enter, I will enter to help the sick.
And whatever I shall see or hear in the course of my
profession, as well as outside my profession, in my
intercourse with Man, I will never divulge, holding such
things to be holy secrets.

Hippocrates

The Hippocratic Oath was adopted in 1947 by the World Medical
Association in the Declaration of Geneva. This modernised version of
the Hippocratic Oath includes, amongst others, commitments which
medical graduates acknowledge at the time of being admitted as members
of the medical profession:

I solemnly pledge to consecrate my life to the service of
humanity.

I will practice my profession with conscience and dignity.

The health of my patient will be my first consideration.

I will respect the secrets which are confided in me.

My colleagues will be my brothers.

I will not permit considerations of religion, nationality,
race, party politics or social standing to intervene between
my duty and my patient.

I make these promises solemnly, freely and upon my honour.[1]

These undertakings remain the transcending code under which the
occupational physician, as all his medical colleagues, conducts his
profession. In this, the term 'occupational physician' must be
liberally interpreted since it includes all those medical
practitioners who are employed in an organisation in order to provide
medical advice, opinion or service to, or in respect of, employees in
the course of their work.

Recent developments in the discipline of occupational medicine
have conferred different connotations upon the terms occupational
physician, occupational health doctor, works medical officer and
medical adviser or even company doctor but, by whatever title he is
known, it is probable that he is being paid by the employer to provide
some level of medical service in respect of, or to some or all of, the
employees. In this sense, it is convenient to refer to this doctor
in general terms as an occupational physician but neither such a
title, nor the source of his financial reward, frees him of any of the
obligations to which he committed himself in taking the Hippocratic
Oath in either the ancient version or its modern counterpart.

The range of services and expertise provided by medical practitioners in the occupational setting varies considerably. In part, it is the size, nature and complexity of the undertaking and the policy and attitude of the employer, which determine the need for some form of medical service within, or associated in some way with, the employer's organisation.

In the United Kingdom, the law does not place any obligation upon employers to provide a medical service. Recent developments in the law have, however, placed on the employer a much heavier onus of responsibility to ensure the health, safety and welfare of all employees while at work.[2] Many employers do provide medical services, despite their voluntary nature, ranging from highly developed, sophisticated and multi-disciplinary occupational health services, to the retention of a local medical practitioner, generally a family doctor, on an occasional part-time or even on-call basis.

To some extent, the provision of such services may have been stimulated originally by earlier government action and legislation. The Workman's Compensation Act 1897 led many employers to retain physicians for reasons largely, if not totally, unconnected with altruism. The motive was rather to protect the employer against claims by workers than to protect workers against hazards at work which might give rise to claims for compensation. The physician, then, was the employer's man, a belief which is not without its adherents even in the second half of the twentieth century.[3]

During the second world war, by government order, factories employing more than a specified number of persons, who were almost by definition drawn from the less fit members of the community, were obliged to employ a medical practitioner in order to supervise the health of their employees. This too may not have been entirely altruistic on the part of government, as its fundamental purpose was to maintain the production of essential war time supplies rather than necessarily being evidence of concern for the health of such workers. However, this move did implicitly recognise that production and productivity are to some extent, perhaps even to a great extent, dependent on the health and welfare of those on the shop floor.[4] Both the 1897 Act and the war time order, in their respective ways, gave rise to an increasing awareness of the importance of the medical practitioner in industry.

The Association of Industrial Medical Officers was formed in 1953 by a number of founder members. A change of title in 1965 to the Society of Occupational Medicine, evidenced the understanding that the benefits of the 'application of medicine at the inter-face between man and his work in order to promote efficiency'[5] need not be limited to 'industry' but may be relevant in all occupations.

Occupational health services increased in number after the second world war, and nationalisation of the coal mines, steel industry and the railways gave rise to medical and nursing services being developed by the National Coal Board, the British Steel Corporation and by British Rail. Large private organisations, such as Imperial Chemical Industries, the Ford Motor Company and Unilever, amongst others, also mirrored this trend by establishing or expanding their own in-house medical services. Further, thanks to finance being made available by the Nuffield Foundation, Group Occupational Health Services developed in such places as Slough, Harlow New Town, Newcastle Upon Tyne and Dundee. These Group Services made occupational health facilities available on a fee paying basis to firms which were perhaps not large enough to justify their own in-house medical service.

Increasing numbers of employers began to retain their own occupational physicians and nurses on either a full or a part time basis, although it is probably true that, in the case of the latter, a majority practised general medicine in a work setting, rather than specialising in occupational medicine per se. The specialist occupational physician is primarily concerned with the working environment and the possible influences which that environment may have on the health of workers. He is rather less concerned with the management of non-occupationally induced disease which is more appropriately within the remit of the National Health Service as a whole.[6] In this connection, the occupational physician must engender the best working relationships with his professional colleagues in general and hospital practice, in order to generate a free exchange of ideas and information and to safeguard the health of those to whom he has a responsibility.

FUNCTIONS OF THE OCCUPATIONAL PHYSICIAN

The functions of the occupational physician can broadly be divided into two main categories:
1. Advice to management in respect of:
    (i)   Employees' health, including the prevention of ill health, especially that which is occupationally induced.
    (ii)   Analysis of sickness absence patterns amongst employees.
    (iii)   The medical aspects of government legislation, particularly in the interpretation of new legislation.

2. Clinical responsibility in respect of:
    (i)   Pre-employment medical screening and/or examination of applicants for employment.
    (ii)   Organisation of the primary medical care of those injured or becoming ill at work. This includes responsibility for the organisation of the medical department and first aid services.
    (iii)   In-service medical surveillance of selected employees, for example those in hazardous trades and those returning to work after a period of absence on account of illness or injury.

These functions as outlined are not exhaustive, since an occupational health service must be capable of flexibility in order that it may be so constructed as to meet the needs of particular employers or industries, and that it may take account of any special circumstances pertaining to a particular occupation or industry. In this respect, the occupational physician is concerned with the health and welfare of the enterprise as a whole in addition to his medical responsibility for the work force. Medically, there is no distinction made by the occupational physician between the most senior and the most junior of personnel, and in this respect also he fulfills the undertakings of the Hippocratic Oath.[7] He must act, and be seen as acting, without favour or bias either towards management or workforce, and it is only by achieving his objective of impartiality that he can hope to obtain the respect, confidence and cooperation of all.

THE EVOLUTION OF HEALTH AT WORK LEGISLATION IN THE UNITED KINGDOM

The Factories Act 1844 granted powers to Factory Inspectors to appoint 'Certifying Surgeons' whose main function was to provide certificates to the effect that children applying for work in the textile mills, to which the application of the Act was confined, had the appearance and development of one of eight years of age or more,[8] since this was the minimum age for entering such work. However, few children at that time possessed birth certificates since the compulsory registration of birth did not become fully effective until the late 1850's,[9] and some other means of establishing age was necessary.
The Certifying Surgeon, later re-titled the Examining Surgeon in keeping with the change in his main function, was the fore-runner of the Appointed Factory Doctor (A.F.D.) who continued to provide service to government and industry until 1973, by which time there were some 1,500 A.F.D.s in England, Scotland and Wales.
    The establishment of the National Health Service and developments in the School Health Service, both in 1948, made health care provision and medical supervision available to all.[10] The National Insurance (Industrial Injuries) Act 1948 established a scheme for the compensation of industrial injury and certain industrial diseases.
In the latter case, government, through the Department of Health and Social Security (previously the Ministry of Health) identified and listed a number of prescribed diseases (including the various pneumoconioses), a list to which additions continue to be made from time to time. There are, in addition to the pneumoconioses, 52 precribed diseases on this list in 1981.[11] Increasingly, legislation was introduced to govern employment in factories, ship-yards, coal mines and quarries, agriculture and most, if not all, heavy and light industry, and in some cases, for example the Offices, Shops and Railway Premises Act 1963, supervision became the responsibility of local authorities rather than central government.
    The International Labour Office Convention of 1961 committed the signatory governments, of which the United Kingdom was one, to the provision of occupational health care. Under this agreement there was allowance for flexible implementation depending upon the requirements of each country, existing provisions for general health care as well as relevant legislation pertaining to industry in the widest sense. The existence in the United Kingdom of the National Health Service[12] and an effective workman's compensation scheme, together with reasonably effective, relevant, if rather complex, legislation rendered the need for a national occupational health service much less necessary although there were many, especially in the trade union movement, who disputed this, and some who still do.
    In 1972, the government introduced the Employment Medical Advisory Service Act which revoked legislation giving effect to the medical inspectorate of factories and the appointed factory doctor scheme.
This Act established, in 1973, the Employment Medical Advisory Service (E.M.A.S.) which recruited full time or part time[13] medical practitioners with experience, training and qualifications,[14] to a total of about 100 full time equivalent practitioners, who are designated Employment Medical Advisers (E.M.A.s). Initially, nine Employment Nursing Advisers who had occupational nursing experience were recruited. This number has since been trebled, evidence that the properly trained and qualified nurse possessing the occupational health nursing certificate has a major contribution to make in promoting health at work.

The service was set up as part of the Department of Employment, and its functions were essentially advisory, consultative and investigative. Employment Medical Advisers also assumed the statutory functions previously performed by A.F.D.s. The service is available to all interested parties from the Secretary of State for Employment to Factory Inspectors, employers, trade unions and individual employees, as well as to medical and nursing colleagues in the N.H.S. and in industry. E.M.A.S. was in effect the government's response to the I.L.O. covention agreement of 1961.

Following the report of the Committee on Safety and Health at Work, (Robens Report)[15] the government acted to introduce the Health and Safety at Work Etc. Act 1974. This established the Health and Safety Commission, comprising a chairman and nine members, all of whom are appointed by government after consultation with both sides of industry and with local authorities. The Commission comprises three representatives of trade unions, three from the Confederation of British Industries and three from local authorities. The operational arm of the Commission is the Health and Safety Executive, comprising three members, which now governs the functions of:

Factory Inspectorate; Mines and Quarries Inspectorate; Alkali Inspectorate; Nuclear Installations Inspectorate; Explosives Inspectorate; Agricultural Safety Inspectorate; Railway Inspectorate and the Employment Medical Advisory Service.

In Scotland, the Industrial Pollution Inspectorate, part of the Scottish Home and Health Department, acts as the Alkali Inspectorate on an agency basis for the Health and Safety Executive and, throughout England, Scotland and Wales, the Petroleum Engineering Inspectorate of the Department of Energy acts on a similar basis in respect of oil and natural gas exploration and production activity on, and in relation to, off-shore installations. The 1974 Act was further extended by an Order in Council in October 1978 to include work on off-shore installations along the Continental Shelf.

The Health and Safety at Work Act is a general enabling Act which confers duties on the Health and Safety Commission, the Health and Safety Executive and its officers and also upon employers, employees, manufacturers and importers.[16] It was designed to have immediate effect by endorsing existing relevant legislation, in relation to the various Inspectorates listed supra, but with powers to repeal, revise or replace it.[17] The original Employment Medical Advisory Service Act 1972 was effectively repealed and replaced by Part 2 of the 1974 Act, which embraced all employers, the self-employed and employees with the solitary exception of the household domestic servant.[18] Immediately, some 8 million people, who had been previously unprotected by legislation, came under the umbrella of the Health and Safety at Work Act which conferred on employers a duty to take such action, as far as is reasonably practicable, to ensure the health, safety and welfare of all employees while at work. Similar injunctions were placed on manufacturers, designers and importers in respect of materials, plant, machinery, equipment and so on, for use in the work place. The far reaching effects of the Act were also to confer protection for the employees of other employers, for example contract workers, as well as to visitors to employment premises, members of the general public and to the community as a whole under certain circumstances.[19]

STATUTORY MEDICAL EXAMINATIONS

Under the Factories Acts, at various times throughout this century, specific trades have been identified as possessing certain hazards which merit pre-employment and periodic medical examinations of employees. These are statutory examinations required by a number of special regulations:

a) Manufacture of paints and colours; Yarn (dyed by lead compounds) Heading; Vitreous enamelling; Tinning of metal hollow-ware,etc.; Lead smelting; Lead compounds; Women and young persons involved in processes involving lead compounds; Electric accumulator; Pottery; the Lead Processes; Indiarubber;

b) Chemical Works; Patent fuel; Mule spinning; Work in compressed air; Diving operations; Carcinogenic substances; Ionising Substances (unsealed radioactive substances); Ionising radiations (sealed sources).

The regulations in a) supra will be revoked in whole or in part on 18 August 1981, on which date the Health and Safety Control of Lead at Work Regulations 1980 will be implemented. Simultaneously, the Approved Code of Practice - Control of Lead at Work - will also take effect. One effect of the new regulations will be to extend specific requirements to certain industries, for example to ship-breaking and demolition work, which are not presently covered by specific legislation. Prior to 1973, statutory medical examinations were conducted by appointed factory doctors, but since the establishment of E.M.A.S. this responsibility (for which fees are payable) has become that of employment medical advisers.[20]

Appointed Doctors   Employers retaining their own medical adviser may apply to the Health and Safety Executive to have him 'Appointed' for the special purpose of conducting these statutory examinations under any one or more specified regulation(s). Such 'appointments' are made by the senior employment medical adviser for the area in consultation with the E.M.A. responsible for the area in which the employer's premises are located, and the area director of the factory inspectorate of H.S.E. It is the responsibility of the employer, to whose premises such special regulations may apply, to ensure that employees subject to Regulation are not so employed unless declared 'fit' for that purpose by the E.M.A. or the appointed doctor (A.D.), and the appropriate entry made in the special register. 'Unfitness' for a particular job or trade, subject to statutory provision, may be temporary or permanent. In either case, the employer may not employ that individual in the trade to which the regulation applies unless or until an appropriate entry of 'fitness' is made in the register. Enforcement of this provision is the responsibility of the Health and Safety Inspector and not that of either the E.M.A. or the A.D. Under the terms of his employment, the A.D. is required to submit a quarterly return to the senior employment medical adviser (S.E.M.A.) detailing the number of medical examinations, together with the results of these examinations, performed by him under each statutory regulation under which he has been appointed. Appointments of A.D.s are subject to quinquennial review by the S.E.M.A., but may be terminated, at any time, after notice by either party.

Approved Doctors   Medical practitioners wishing to undertake medical examinations of divers operating under any of the appropriate regulations[21] must be specially approved by the Director of Medical Services of H.S.E. In order to be considered for approval, a number of criteria must be satisfied including attendance by the applicant at a recognised course of training in underwater medicine. A diver certified as unfit to dive by an approved doctor has a right to appeal against that decision to the Director of Medical Services who may confirm or reverse the decision. 'Certificates of Approval' are issued for periods of 3 years, and renewals of such certificates are made by H.S.E. on the recommendations of senior employment medical advisers without further application being necessary. Changes in the regulations will be made on 1 July 1981 in line with the Health and Safety at Work (Diving Operations) Regulations 1980[22] under the terms of which all medical practitioners wishing to undertake medical examinations of this sort, will require to be specially approved for the purpose.

NOTIFICATION OF INDUSTRIAL DISEASE

1. 'Every medical practitioner attending or called in to visit a patient who he believes to be suffering from poisoning by: lead, arsenicals, phosphorous, mercury, from infection by anthrax, must send forthwith to the Health and Safety Executive....details, etc.'[23] The employer is also required to notify the local factory inspector and the employment medical adviser about each case.

2. By various Statutory Regulations and Orders (S.R. and O's) made prior to the 1961 Factories Act, the following notifiable conditions continued in force:

Toxic Jaundice	S.R. and O.	1915	No. 1170
Epitheliomatous and Chrome Ulceration	S.R. and O.	1919	No. 1175
Poisoning by Carbon Bisulphide and Anilene and Chronic Benzene Poisoning	S.R. and O. (as amended by S.I. 1966	1924	No. 1505 No. 1400
Compressed Air Illness	S.R. and O.	1938	No. 1386
Toxic Anaemia	S.R. and O.	1942	No. 196

3. The Factories (Notification of Diseases) Regulations 1966[24] confirmed the requirement of notification in respect of the conditions outlined in 1. and 2. supra. They also made certain additions relating to poisoning by beryllium; cadmium; organic compounds of lead, mercury and arsenic; triphenyl phosphate; tricresyl phosphate and certain effects from organic phosphorous compounds.

4. Extensive exposure to ionising radiations also carries similar requirements for notification in terms of the Ionising Radiations (Sealed Sources) Regulations 1969 and (Unsealed Sources) Regulations 1968.[25]

5. Following receipt of notification, investigations are conducted by both the factory inspector and the employment medical adviser. It is the function of the latter, after due consideration of all the circumstances, to confirm or refute the diagnosis, to so report to the Health and Safety Executive and, if the diagnosis is confirmed, to state that the condition arose as the result of an occupational

exposure.

NOTIFICATION OF ACCIDENTS

Similarly to the notification of industrial diseases, accidents
involving loss of life or requiring absence from work for more than
three working days must be notified the the Chief Inspector of
Factories of H.S.E. by the employer. These too are investigated by
the factory inspector and, in the case of gassings, by the employment
medical adviser. The latter considers all the circumstances,
including occupational exposures, clinical effects and relevant
observations by attending physicians and reports his conclusions to
the investigating factory inspector. Similar investigations are made
by the E.M.A. in respect of poisonings, suspected poisonings and
gassings reported to the agricultural safety inspectors of the Health
and Safety Executive.
   The Health and Safety at Work Act not only places on employers the
responsibility for the health, safety and welfare of employees at
work, it also creates the means for the introduction of new
legislation in this respect. In addition to the 1981 Regulations
mentioned supra, during 1981-1982 revised legislation in respect of
ionising radiations and first aid will also be implemented. It is an
intrinsic function of an occupational health physician to be
conversant with the medical aspects of legislation relating to health
at work, and only by being so informed can he fully discharge his
responsibility to his employer and his duties in respect of the
employees. Perhaps more importantly, the occupational physician, by
being well informed, may be in a position to influence the attitudes
of both management and labour force in order that they conduct their
activities within the spirit of the law. In this way, he may also
satisfy his committment to the ethic of Hippocrates.

CONCLUSION

The relationship between the occupational physician and an employee is
assumed to be bound by the same professional and legal obligations as
that between the general practitioner or hospital doctor and his
patient. However, at first sight, the occupational physician is in a
somewhat different position from that of the ordinary doctor, since by
and large his committment may be diagnostic and preventive rather than
therapeutic. For those doctors employed by a company to safeguard
the health of the employees and to treat illness as it occurs, there
is no such problem. As the British Medical Association have pointed
out 'He [the occupational physician] deals constantly with other
doctor's patients. But these considerations do not alter the
doctor-patient relationship...'.[26] However, for those employed on
an ad hoc or statutory basis for the purpose of pre-employment or
statutory examinations the position is less simple.
   The legal duties of any physician basically mirror those which he
accepts on an ethical basis in terms of the Hippocratic Oath, and they
are generally deemed to flow from an offer to treat. This
relationship is personal to the doctor and his patient and exists
independently of other factors. Martin[27] indicates that, in
assessing whether or not such a relationship exists, extraneous
matters, such as who the actual employer is and so on, have no major

19

relevance in assessing the duty of care owed by the doctor in question. Rather, he claims, 'His duty is independent of contract and rests upon the fact of a medical practitioner undertaking the care and treatment of a patient...'.[28] Although in some situations, for example private medicine, the relationship between doctor and patient may be contractually based, the duty of care owed to the patient arises also, and more fundamentally, from delict or tort and is thus independent of the contracting parties.

Thus, in Edgar v. Lamont,[29] a suggestion that a claim raised by Mrs. Edgar against her doctor in respect of negligence would fall because it was not she but her husband who employed the doctor, was dismissed on the grounds that, regardless of who employed him, he nonetheless owed a duty of care to whomever he offered to treat. Of course, in many situations, the doctor in occupational medicine offers not to treat but merely to diagnose. However, logic would suggest that an 'offer to treat' must be inclusive of examination and diagnosis,[30] since, by implication if this were not the case, the doctor who was unable to treat by the nature of the illness would not be deemed to have entered into the same relationship with his patient as the doctor who diagnoses an illness which is treatable. Nor does it seem to be relevant to the nature of the doctor's duties towards his patient that he is employed, for example, by the government or by a particular employer, rather than being summoned by the patient himself.[31]

However, one major cornerstone of the committments undertaken by doctors, both legally and in terms of the Hippocratic Oath, is the duty of confidentiality.[32] In the standard consultation, there will be little conflict in this undertaking, and it is generally regarded as essential to the doctor/patient relationship that the patient has confidence that the doctor will not divulge confidential, and perhaps embarrasssing, information to anyone else. The duty of confidentiality is a moral or ethical as well as a legal one,[33] and in some ways this is the reflection of the fact that a doctor has only the right to claim a qualified privilege in matters which he does disclose, i.e. he is not protected from the raising of a legal action against him in respect of comments made regarding a patient except in certain circumstances.[34] These circumstances may vary,[35] but from the point of view of the occupational physician there are two main areas of concern.

First it is clear that in many situations, the occupational physician has a statutory duty to make certain information available to employers in respect of an employee's fitness for work or his apparent over-exposure to harmful substances. Thus, although bound to the person whom he examines or treats, he also has statutory duties which infringe on the basic concept of confidentiality.[36] Occupational disease and the general consequences of an injury sustained in the course of work are, or should be, the concern of the employer. Information in respect of such matters, in addition to that which may be statutorily required, will generally therefore be passed on to the employer, without necessarily obtaining the consent of the employee, and such information as the doctor does pass on to the employer will normally be of a general rather than a specific nature.[37]

It is normally regarded as being part of the general duties of the doctor as a citizen to protect others,[38] and the occupational physician may occasionally come into possession of information which he may regard as potentially affecting the health, safety or well-being of others. In the uncommon situation of information of this sort being available, limited disclosure may be made on the basis of the greater good and such action by the physician will be a matter for his conscience. In such circumstances, it is unlikely that he would be held legally liable for such an apparent breach of confidence, always assuming that the disclosure made is made to an appropriate person, e.g. the employer.[39] In these circumstances, disclosure without consent, where the person refuses to make such consent available, but if at all possible with due notice to the individual concerned and appropriate entries in the medical records, is unlikely to reflect adversely on the professional or legal position of the physician in question.

The responsibilities and duties of the occupational physician may, therefore, be seen to be those of the standard medical practitioner, although the physician concerned in employment may seem to have two masters to serve. On the one hand, he has a duty to his employers, to whom he is accountable for the use he makes of his time and resources placed at his disposal. Professionally, however, he remains independent, and although the employer is responsible for the organisation and operational conduct of the occupational health service, the physician remains personally responsible for the standard of the care which he personally delivers to any given client.

Generally, the occupational physician will surmount any apparent problems in relation to disclosure of information regarding an employee by requiring his consent both to examination and to subsequent disclosure to an employer of information in respect of work-related diseases which he may identify. However, the situatioon may be more problematic when the occupational physician, who may be required to carry out extensive examination of an employeee or prospective employee, discovers or diagnoses an illness which is not work-related and in respect of which neither he nor the employer has any particular remit.

It is clear that generally no disclosure should be made of such information unless it is potentially harmful to others, since the patient's rights to privacy and self-determination may seem to be more important in these situations.[40] The occupational physician may attempt to obtain the consent of the client to make such disclosure, or to ensure that the person consults his/her own doctor, but if theco attempts are unsuccessful, then this decision must be respected although the doctor would be well advised to note on the medical records, which are generally also confidential,[41] that such an attempt was made. Although good medical practice might dictate that communication is made to the patient's own doctor that such a diagnosis has been made or is likely, in order to fulfill the general obligation to the patient to do the best for him, there would seem to be no legal duty on a doctor to communicate with a client's own doctor, even where treatment, rather than simple diagnosis, is involved.[42] In general, however, doctors are likely to feel that good practice would dictate that such information should be passed on, particularly in view of the dissenting judgement of Lord Denning in the case of Chapman v. Rix.[43]

The occupational physician is then, although bound by statutory guidelines and limitations, and required to carry out particular or even unusual types of duties nonetheless equally bound by the ethical codes of his profession, by the legal rules which have grown up around these and by his general duties to the community as a whole, and the working community in particular.

J.D. Bell

NOTES

1.   Reproduced in Handbook of Medical Ethics, British Medical Association, 1980, ch. 11, where the text of the other major ethical codes governing medical practice may also be found.
2.   The Health and Safety at Work Etc. Act 1974.
3.   Handbook of Medical Ethics, supra, at p. 21 where it is stated that 'An occupational physician has to be particularly careful. He holds his appointment from the management, but his duties concern the health and welfare of the workers, individually and collectively.'
4.   This recognition parallels the development of community medicine; see infra ch. 3.
5.   This definition of occupational medicine is attributed to Prof. A. Mair, University of Dundee.
6.   For discussion of the remit of the National Health Service, see infra ch. 3.
7.   'I will not permit considerations of religion, nationality, race, party politics or social standing to intervene between my duty and my patient.'; see infra p. 12.
8.   The 1833 Act specified a minimum age of 9 years, under s. 11. The 1844 Act reduced the age from nine years to eight years, s. 29, and medical certificates to prove age were required to be provided by a Certifying Surgeon appointed by the Factory Inspector in terms of s. 8.
9.   Births and Deaths Registration Act 1836; Registration of Births, Deaths and Marriages (Scotland) Act 1854.
10.   For further discussion, see infra ch. 3.
11.   Notes on the Diagnosis of Occupational Diseases, Department of Health and Social Security, London, H.M.S.O., 1980.
12.   Which specifically excludes occupational health from its remit, see infra ch. 3.
13.   Usually for not less than 20 hours per week.
14.   The qualifications are as follows:-

Diploma in Industrial Health	D.I.H.
Master of Science (Occupational Medicine	M.Sc.(O.M.)
Fellow, Member or Associate of the	F.M. or A.F.O.M.
Faculty of Occupational Medicine.	

15.   Report on Safety and Health at Work, London, H.M.S.O., 1972.
16.   ss. 2 - 7.
17.   s. 15.
18.   s. 53.
19.   ss. 5 and 6.
20.   Health and Safety at Work Etc. Act 1974 s. 57(1).
21.   Offshore Installations (Diving Operations) Regulations 1974; The Merchant Shipping (Diving Operations) Regulations 1975; The Submarine Pipe-Lines (Diving Operations) Regulations 1976.
22.   These regulations will replace those outlined in note 21 supra, and also the Diving Operations (Special Examinations) Regulations 1960.

23. Factories Act 1961 s. 82.
24. S.I. 1966 No. 1400.
25. 1969 Regulations s. 20; 1968 Regulations s. 23.
26. Handbook of Medical Ethics, supra at p. 22.
27. Martin, C.R.A., Law Relating to Medical Practice, (2nd Ed.), Pitman Medical, 1979.
28. ibid., at p. 361.
29. Edgar v. Lamont 1914 S.C. 277.
30. It is implicit in many important cases that diagnosis does create the duty of care between doctor and patient which is necessary before an action in negligence is competent; c.f. Hunter v. Hanley 1955 S.C. 200.
31. Edgar v. Lamont, supra.
32. For discussion, see Mason, J.K., Forensic Medicine for Lawyers, Bristol, John Wright and Son, 1978, at pp. 383-386, and Knight, B., Legal Aspects of Medical Practice, London, Churchill Livingstone, 1976, at pp. 4-8.
33. For further discussion, see Samuels, A., 'The duty of the Doctor to Respect the Confidence of the Patient', 20, Med.Sci. & Law, 58 (1980). See also, infra ch.1.
34. The only professional group to whom an absolute privilege applies in respect of refusing to disclose information in a court of law, is to lawyers, and even then the privilege is actually that of the client rather than the lawyer himself; c.f. A.-.G. v. Mulholland, A.-G. v. Foster [1963] 1 All E.R. 767, Schneider v. Leigh [1955] 2 Q.B. 195. Protection will of course be offered to the doctor when such disclosure as he makes is in pursuance of a statutory duty (as often with the occupational physician), or, for example, in terms of the Abortion Act 1967, or in pursuance of a general duty imposed on all, for example under the Road Traffic Act 1972, to disclose certain information in the interests of justice; c.f. Hunter v. Mann [1974] 2 All E.R. 414.
35. It is important if the doctor is to be protected that any disclosure which is made is made to the appropriate person or authority, c.f. AB v. CD (1851) 14D 177, and that it is not made maliciously, c.f. Kitson v. Playfair 'The Times' 28 March 1896.
36. i.e which require disclosure by their very nature.
37. See Handbook of Medical Ethics, supra, where it is pointed out at p.23 that 'Individual clinical findings are confidential, though their significance may be conveyed to a third party.'
38. c.f. H.M.A. v. Pritchard (1865) 5 Irv. 88, where the court indicated that the doctor's duty as a citizen always overrides his duties in terms of his 'professional ettiquette'. The decision as to which type of information should be disclosed on 'social' grounds is clearly often difficult for the doctor, and in the long run it is his conscience which will dictate his behaviour in this respect. In these cases, he should of course attempt to encourage the patient in question to make the disclosure himself.
39. c.f. AB v. CD, supra.
40. For general discussion of rights to self-determination, see infra ch. 13. ; with particular reference to the provision or witholding of consent in medicine, see infra ch. 8.

41.   Medical records may be disclosed, to the litigant himself, on the order of a court, in terms of the Administration of Justice Act 1970 s.32(1) (where someone who is not a party to the proceedings may have valuable information); c.f. McIvor v. Southern Health [1978] 2 All E.R. 625. Also disclosure may be made in terms of s. 31 which relates to the production of documents before proceedings are commenced; Deistung v. South West Metropolitan Regional Health Board [1975] 1 All E.R. 573. In Scotland, similar provision is made under the Administration of Justice (Scotland) Act 1972 s. 1(1) and (2); c.f. McGown v. Erskine & Ors. 1978 S.L.T. (Notes) 4, disagreeing with Baxter v. Lothian Health Board 1976 S.L.T. (Notes) 37.

42.   Chapman v. Rix (1959) B.M.J., 2, 1190.

43.   In this case the doctor, who had treated a patient in an emergency resulting from an accident at work, was held not to have been negligent in failing subsequently to communicate his diagnosis and the fact of the contact, with the patient's own doctor, although Lord Denning indicated that in his opinion, this was a breach of professional duty and should amount to negligence.

3 Medicine and the Community
G. T. Stewart

The practice of medicine, whether in hospital, clinic or household, is conventionally geared to a transaction between one or more doctors and a patient. In seeking or receiving medical advice and treatment, the individual assumes what Parsons[1] has called the 'Sick Role' and becomes that doctor's patient. The relationship between them, for the time being, is personal, the ratio one-to-one. In the case of consultation with, or treatment by, a specialist, this one-to-one relationship lasts for the duration of the episode of illness, short or long as it may be. Before and after referral to a specialist, the patient theoretically is in a continuous one-to-one relationship with his general practitioner. In the U.K. every citizen is entitled to be registered with a general medical practitioner (G.P.) in such a way as to receive free and continuing medical advice and treatment under the terms of the National Health Service (N.H.S.). The G.P. receives for every patient on his list a standard capitation fee weighted for age and location in such a way as to provide extra remuneration for the additional work entailed in looking after children, old persons and communities in remote areas or in scattered dwellings. Under the N.H.S. patients cannot obtain the services of a specialist except on referral to hospital by a G.P. or request for a domiciliary consultation. Patients may, however, and often do, refer themselves (self-referral) to the emergency rooms or casualty departments of hospitals for example when their own doctor is unavailable or after accidents. The N.H.S. is comprehensive in that it provides a complete diagnostic, consultative and therapeutic service for all ailments in all age groups. The only fees required at present, apart from statutory deductions from the earnings of employed persons, are small charges for prescriptions, spectacles, wigs and certain optional appliances.

There is also in Britain a small but rapidly growing independent private sector with its own hospitals, clinics and laboratories. This private sector overlaps with the N.H.S. in some cases by using private wings and out-patient suites in certain hospitals. Doctors serving N.H.S. hospitals can have part-time contracts to enable them to see and treat private patients but other hospital staff do not have this privilege. G.Ps. are in contract with the N.H.S. to provide directly or by deputies a 24 hour service for patients on their lists; they may also have private patients and hold contracts - unspecified in nature and number - with other bodies. G.Ps. are expected under the terms of their contract to provide certain preventive services - for example, immunisation and family planning - and to maintain liaison with the community medical and social services. For this purpose, practice nurses and health visitors are assigned to them directly or in Health Centres.

Community medicine is that branch of medicine which looks beyond the individual patient and episodic illness to the state of health of the community as a whole.[2] The specialist in community medicine in the U.K. is the descendant and successor of the Medical Officer of Health and his medically-qualified assistants who, prior to reorganisation of the N.H.S. in 1974,[3] were responsible for public health under the Acts of 1867, 1897 and 1925.[4]. The transition from one system (pre-1974) to the other has led to considerable shifts in responsibilities for hygiene, disease-control, social and preventive aspects of medicine. To understand this and to explain the complexities of the present system, it is necessary to review briefly the origins of public health, community and preventive medicine which began, in the U.K., on social grounds arising out of the condition of the poor and the employment of young children in factories and mines in the first half of the 19th century.

History.

Every society, and almost every cultural group within any society, has a need and a place for medicine men as healers and counsellors. Medicine as a profession began when it adopted the ethical standards of Hippocrates around 500 B.C.[5] This provided not only a code of practice but also a philosophy in which the environmental and ecological aspects of medical practice were regarded as inseparable from diagnosis, prevention and treatment. Disease was seen as the outcome of personal and environmental factors and it was bad practice to separate the patient and his illness from these background factors which were seen as clues to prevention. The aim of the physician was to try to understand the interaction of all relevant factors and to do his best for his patient according to the prevailing circumstances. It was recognised that disease was often inevitable and incurable, in which case the physician was expected to do his best to alleviate suffering and, above all, to do no harm to his patient and community. This admirable philosophy is enshrined in the Hippocratic Oath, which is still taken by medical graduates in many countries.

This oath, and much of the underlying ethic, has prevailed and is still a major guideline for doctors at all levels today. Unfortunately, the associated philosophy which linked preventive and environmental medicine with curative medicine has never since then been fully honoured in practice. It became unusual for doctors – with some very notable exceptions – to take notice of environmental hygiene and ecology even when, in the 19th century, the international public health movement arose and prospered.[6]

The Emergence of Public Health as a Discipline.

The industrial revolution of the late 18th and 19th centuries stimulated the growth of population in towns and cities on a scale which led to unmanageable herding and crowding, with consequent squalor and lack of hygiene. The diseases caused by this then spread to such an extent that they began to resemble the plagues of mediaeval days, threatening entire communities with epidemics of cholera, smallpox, dysentery and numerous other infections, especially of children. The public health movement arose out of the kind of concern which Charles Dickens and Lord Shaftesbury expressed and, equally, out of some elementary statistics collected by Edwin Chadwick (1842) and William Farr (1851) showing the relationship between poverty, crowding and disease. Chadwick's work led to the Poor Law Amendment Act of 1845 which provided public funds to supplement charities in the case of the sick poor. The first Public Health Act of 1848 followed, under which local authorities were required to appoint Health Boards and doctors commissioned to prevent and control disease, at first only in large cities, and then in the community as a whole.   The doctors - drawn usually from general practice - gradually emerged as a cadre of public health.   Under the stimulus of the next Public Health Act of 1867, the cities and counties appointed full-time or part-time medical officers of health, public health nurses and sanitary personnel.   The medical schools of universities, starting with Cambridge in 1876, introduced training courses and by 1900 several were offering diplomas or degrees for doctors specialising in public health.   In the provincial medical schools, though not in London, Public Health was also included in the undergraduate medical curriculum.

All this activity was linked to regulations governing sanitation in a series of bye-laws culminating in the Public Health Acts of 1895 and 1897.   These Acts laid down standards in respect of hygiene, disposal and slaughtering of animals, maintenance of parks and recreational areas, inspection of food, purity of water and numerous other matters.   They gave powers to local authorities to appoint personnel to oversee and enforce compliance with the law as set out in these Acts, and in preceding statutes, bye-laws and amendments. Special regulations were drawn up for ports so that quarantine measures could be applied to ships and persons or materials thought to be carrying disease.   A preventive medical service for schools and school children was introduced under a further Act of 1908.

The Public Health Acts, together with regulations passed before 1897, also required Local Authorities to provide accommodation for isolating and treating the major communicable diseases.   Sea ports were required to set up Port Health Authorities for examining ships to ensure that persons or cargoes with scheduled infections, such as anthrax or typhoid, were not allowed to land.   The Acts also made some provision for institutional treatment of infectious disease and, under extensions of the Poor Law (1834), for accommodation for the homeless and destitute in hostels and institutions, and for the mentally disordered in asylums, but did not otherwise provide for treatment of the sick.   Patients were expected to pay a fee for services rendered by their doctors, although there were a number of prepaid medical insurance schemes run by various private companies, voluntary societies and trade unions.   Various hospitals provided medical and surgical treatment on the basis of voluntary local support and contributions from patients and insurance schemes.   Poor persons received treatment free but the number of beds and facilities generally were far below requirements and demands.   Private hospitals, or private wings in Voluntary Hospitals, were built to cater for those who could afford to pay.   For the remainder, if there was no bed in a voluntary hospital, the only alternatives to home care were the institutions, built under the Poor Laws, which gradually began to serve as comprehensive hospitals.   The first proposals for a unified state medical service came from public health doctors in a series of recommendations to the Royal Commission on the Poor Law in 1906.   This was followed by an Education Act 1907, the School Medical Service Act 1907, the Old Age Pensions Act 1908, the National Health Insurance Act 1911 and the Maternity and Child Welfare Act 1918, All of these were landmarks in the social and political movements which led to these enactments and underlay the establishment of a comprehensive health service.

The National Health Insurance Act 1911 was the first major attempt to provide medical care eliminating various social and geographic anomalies, and irregularities in facilities for treatment and in standards.   Under this Act, small deductions were made from the wages of lower paid workers and used to fund a 'Panel' of general practitioners to provide medical advice, consultation and treatment to subscribers but not to their dependents. The fund was bolstered by substantial contributions from general taxation, and gradually extended to include workers with higher earnings so that, by 1938, some 20 million people, i.e., the greater part of the working population, were covered. The 'Panel' scheme was so arranged as to incorporate all the various voluntary and charitable schemes of industrial insurance then existing, and to preserve the additional benefits which some of these schemes offered to their subscribers.

The Public Health Act 1867 required all local authorities to appoint a Medical Officer of Health who was required under Regulations added in 1925 to acquire the Diploma in Public Health. The individual appointed was required to administer the Health Department of the Authority, including not only preventive services and sanitation but also such domiciliary and therapeutic services as were not provided by the voluntary or private hospitals or by general practitioners. There was great growth of municipally-based public health services in the period between 1925 and the outbreak of World War II in 1939, borne largely by local taxation but with growing support from central funds for certain services, such as slum clearance and free milk for school children.[7]

From Public Health to National Health Service.

Philosophically, the idea of a comprehensive Health Service had various origins in social and humanitarian issues, as described supra; politically, it was motivated by egalitarianism and by the unemployment of the 1930s, resulting in massive overdrawing of unemployment and sickness benefits from the friendly societies; legally, it was the outcome of a combination of these factors plus an attempt to weld together in a single Act all the diverse parts of preceding statutes and regulations.

Political action started with the abolition of the Poor Law by the creation of the unemployment Assistance Board in 1934. This provided extensions of unemployment benefit and enabled central funds to be used for relief of hardship in areas of economic depression. The legal position and range of services were greatly improved by the original Amendment Act of 1845 and by subsequent enactments and regulations mentioned supra, but the administration of the service remained cumbersome because of the piecemeal nature of the legislation and the many authorities involved. Gaps in provisions for assistance to dependents, and for medical care, became wider with the outbreak of World War II in 1939. The Coalition Government appointed a Committee in 1941 to survey 'existing national schemes of social insurance and allied services, including workmen's compensation',[8] and to make special reference to interrelationships between schemes.

The Report of this Committee (Beveridge Report) is an historic document in the evolution of services for health and welfare because it identified five prime causes of social decay, namely: Want, Disease, Ignorance, Squalor and Idleness; and formulated a comprehensive policy for dealing with them. The principle was that working individuals should contribute to a fund which would provide them with health care and pay them when unemployed or when unable to work because of sickness, injury, handicap or old age. This called for a flat rate of contribution and of benefit, scaled to be adequate without being so attractive as to encourage idleness. It was the first version of the social contract between citizen and state and it was the foundation of the National Health Service to which the Government of the day and its successor were committed.[9]

The National Health Service Acts.

The Beveridge Report, the proposals for implementation by the wartime coalition Government (Willink Report)[10] and the initiative of Mr. Aneurin Bevan, Minister of Health in the post-war socialist Government, all contributed to the formulation of the National Health Service Act 1948 in respect of England and Wales, and the corresponding Act for Scotland. The underlying principle which was a further landmark in welfare legislation was that prevention, diagnosis and treatment of disease were the responsibility of the State, and that every citizen was entitled to full medical or surgical treatment and hospital care for each and every sickness, disability or injury, irrespective of cost.

It will be recalled that responsibility for health care prior to 1948 was in a variety of hands - private doctors and hospitals, charities, voluntary hospitals, local authority hospitals and clinics. The Ministry of Health had certain marginal responsibilities for administering the National Health Insurance and other Acts, and for overseeing some services such as the Public Health Laboratory Service and wartime Emergency Medical Service, but it had not been developed or staffed in a manner which made it able to organise and administer a comprehensive health service throughout the country. The Acts of 1948 recognised this, and accepted also the desirability of retaining local responsibility where practicable. The N.H.S. was therefore developed as a regionally-based service with local Executive Councils to serve General Medical Practice and Regional Boards to manage the hospitals, most of which became, under the Acts, the property of the State overnight.

There were two serious omissions. Paradoxically, public health and the large sector of preventive medicine which belonged to it, were not included in the National Health Service. The Medical Officer of Health and his large staff of assistant medical officers, health visitors, sanitarians and social workers were left under the authority of the Counties, Cities and Municipalities, as they were under the Acts of 1925 and before. This meant that maternal and child welfare, school health and environmental health remained apart from the Health Service. Occupational health and the factory medical inspectorate were likewise excluded.

The second omission was the failure to provide Health Centres and to integrate general practice into the Service. G.Ps. remained as private contractors, using and providing their own surgeries. The State provided them with salaries, based on capitation fees for persons registered with them, but no facilities or other support. Dental practitioners, similarly, remained as independent contractors, reimbursed by a fee for service - which did not include preventive work or advice.

Hospital doctors were all invited to join the N.H.S. and were graded, according to their seniority and experience, as consultants, assistants, or in various training ranks (registrar, house-officer). Consultants were eligible for options, according to their location and speciality, of full-time or part-time contracts with one or more hospital boards. Nurses and most of the other professionals, including laboratory and radiographic technicians, were all given full-time contracts. Part-time contracts were available for opticians, physiotherapists and certain other auxiliary health personnel.

To administer the Service under the general supervision of the Ministry of Health (subsequently renamed the Department of Health and Social Security, D.H.S.S.), the country was divided into regions, each with a Hospital Board and subservient Hospital Management Committees. Hospital Boards were appointed by the Minister after consultation with local authorities and other interested parties. Hospital Management Committees were appointed by Hospital Boards, and doctors and nurses were eligible to be appointed as members of these committees, or to attend as representatives of their colleagues. In Scotland, a similar administration was operated, independently, under the general supervision of the Scottish Office (later renamed the Scottish Home and Health Department) which had responsibility to Parliament for home affairs in Scotland. Separate arrangements, with minor administrative differences, were also made for the operation of the N.H.S. in Wales and Northern Ireland. Coroners and industrial medical officers were not included in the N.H.S. Acts.

Despite its name, the National Health Service was essentially a sickness service. It grew rapidly in size and expenditure, but it became obvious that it could not undertake comprehensive health care unless steps were taken to rectify the omissions described above. This required a new Act of Parliament and a greater measure of central control to ensure that responsibilities which formerly belonged to the local authorities could be maintained. Other professional groups - notably nurses, sanitarians and social workers - also wanted a greater degree of freedom from medical supervision, and their claims were upheld in the reports of various working parties and commissions in the period 1965-72,[11] when the principle of reorganisation was accepted by the main political parties and by two Governments. All this, together with the geographic review of local authority domains, led to the reorganisation of the Health Service in 1974.

Reorganisation of the N.H.S. in the U.K.

The legislative basis of reorganisation is set out in two Acts of Parliament namely, the National Health Service (Scotland) Act 1972 and for England and Wales, the National Health Service Reorganisation Act 1973.

There were two main aims in reorganisation:
1) to intregrate general practice and medical aspects of public health into the N.H.S.
2) to make health areas administratively coterminous with the new local authority areas as defined in the Local Government Reorganisation Act 1974.

Neither aim was fully achieved. Environmental health became the responsibility of non-medical officers working for local authorities. Medical participation was reduced to permissive consultation between sanitarians (environmental health officers) and community medicine personnel whose authority became 'sapiential' instead of executive as heretofore. The fact that the Health Areas were established before the legislation and reorganisation affecting local government had been agreed by Parliament led to some errors and discrepancies in boundaries. The reorganisation of health services became effective in 1974 but in local government it was delayed until 1975.

Central Organisation.

Overall responsibility for policy, planning and finance is in the hands of the Secretary of State in the Department of Health and Social Security (D.H.S.S.). This Department also controls certain common services, such as the Public Health Laboratory Services, negotiations with professional bodies and trade unions, conditions of employment and pensions, and purchase of equipment and supplies. As its name implies, and unlike the peripheral operation of the N.H.S. (except in Northern Ireland), the D.H.S.S. deals with personal social services and social security. It also has responsibility for international aspects of health, including liaison with the World Health Organisation,[12] for food hygiene and for licensing and monitoring the use of medicines and vaccines. For these purposes, the Secretary of State receives advice from a number of specialist committees containing representatives of all parts of the United Kingdom.

England   The N.H.S. in England is divided into fourteen Regional Health Authorities, subdivided in turn into 72 areas. To facilitate conversion, each region corresponds to that of the former Hospital Boards created by the 1948 Act, and each district corresponds to an administrative district of the reorganised local authorities.
    The regions have responsibility for implementing national policies and, independently, for planning, coordination and supervising all general medical and hospital services. The Regional Authority is exercised by a team of officers which includes the executive, medical, nursing and financial officers, and is advised by a medical advisory committee of general practitioners, consultants and others. Services which are highly specialised, such as neurosurgery and radiotherapy, are usually regional responsibilities, as are reference laboratories, information services and postgraduate training of professional staff. Chairmen and members of Regional Authorities are appointed by the Secretary of State, after consultation with appropriate interested organisations within the region - universities, local authorities, professional groups and trade unions.
    Area Health Authorities were appointed by the Secretary of State in consultation with representatives of the region and others, including universities, local professional and other organisations. Certain areas with appropriate facilities were designated as 'teaching' areas. In each area there is at present a Joint Consultative Committee with the local authority to ensure coordination in activities of mutual interest, such as social and environmental services, housing and education.
    Day-to-day management in the Areas has two essential components:
    a) The Area Executive Group, comprising the executive officer, area medical officer, nursing officer and finance officer. These, together with an Area Medical Committee and other committees, provide advice, and implement the decisions of the Authority but in so doing they rely largely upon,
    b) District Management Teams, consisting of a consultant, general practitioner, nursing officer, finance officer, administrator and community physician. Their function is linked with district medical committees representative of all general practitioners, dentists and specialists in the district.
The Areas correspond to borough boundaries, or groups of boroughs, but the districts do not. The postgraduate teaching hospitals are

administered by their own Boards of Governors, which are directly responsible to the D.H.S.S. and are therefore largely independent of the Regional and Area Authorities. Under a recent amendment to the 1972 Act,[13] Area Health Authorities will be abolished in 1982, and their functions as outlined in a) supra, will be transferred to Regions although their District functions, outlined in b) supra, will remain. After-care services and rehabilitation are organised at present on an Area basis, but in future responsibility will be devolved to Regions and Districts. However, since there is a considerable overlap between health, social work and employment, there is a need, not by any means answered yet, for coordination of these various activities for which there is no single authority at present.

Scotland, Wales and Northern Ireland   Although the aims and methods of reorganisation were applicable to all parts of the United Kingdom, the administrative instruments were different in so far as the service is mediated by three other government departments.[14]   The organisation in Northern Ireland provides a useful model for the rest of the country, since its main - and important - difference is that health and social services are fully integrated at both Area and District level.   At a time when the social and behavioural aspects of illness and disability are increasingly inseparable from the medical aspects, such integration has obvious advantages.

Responsibilities of the reorganised N.H.S.

Reorganisation in 1974 brought together the following services:
    (a)   All hospital and specialist services,
    (b)   General and family practitioner services: domiciliary consultations between general practitioners and specialists,
    (c)   Services formerly managed by local authorities:-
ambulances;   family planning;   health centres;   welfare clinics;   assessment centres;   health visiting;   home nursing;   maternal and child care including midwifery; notifications of infectious diseases;   vaccination;   home nursing and supplementary care,
    (d)   The school health service.

It should be noted that the N.H.S. is not responsible for:
    measures for prevention and spread of infectious diseases (other than vaccination, epidemiological work, if any, and treatment);   food safety and hygiene;   port health;   diseases of animals which affect human health at work and in the home;   occupational and industrial health.
In a so-called National Health Service these must be seen as serious omissions.

Administration of the Service

Policy, planning and expenditure are the responsibility of the Regional and Area Health Authorities referred to supra, or of the corresponding Area Health Boards in Scotland, Wales and Northern Ireland, under the general authority of the appropriate Secretary of State.   Great importance is attached to the concept of local control based on districts whose number and size depend upon local conditions.   Each district was planned to contain or develop a District General Hospital and to be run by a local Management Team and medical committee.[15]

Community Health Councils.   The views and needs of the public are
represented by these Councils which are elected in each district and
have a statutory right to obtain information about the local services,
to visit Hospitals and Health Centres, and to have access to officials
at District and Area level.

Specialists in Community Medicine.   This term is used to describe the
medically-qualified administrators and others whose functions are to
run the medical side of the service for the welfare of the community
as a whole.   Apart from their general role in Committees at Area and
District level, they are responsible for three main aspects of the
service[16]:
     1) As managers of arrangements for medical staffing,
     planning and evaluation of services, and certain aspects of
     preventive medicine such as vaccination and notification,
     2) Information services and epidemiology,
     3) Liaison with local authorities in matters of
     environmental health.
Most of the medical administrators in the N.H.S. and in central
government are affiliated with Community Medicine, and it is customary
for trainees to work for accreditation as specialists by obtaining by
examination the Diploma of Membership of the Faculty of Community
Medicine of the Royal Colleges of Physicians.   This requires some
five years of postgraduate study and service in epidemiology,
statistics, social science, environmental health and organisation of
health care.   Those who are interested in occupational health follow
a similar track under the aegis of the Faculty of Occupational
Medicine, and are usually employed, separately from the N.H.S., by the
Employment Medical Advisory Service[17] or by individual industrial
firms.   Specialist degrees and diplomas in community and occupational
medicine are also available.

Labour relations in the N.H.S.

In an organisation as complex as the N.H.S., the range of services,
personnel and skills is very wide indeed.   Terms and conditions of
service vary accordingly.   It was necessary at the inception of the
Service in 1948 to make provision for new employment with pension
rights and reasonable security for large numbers of essential
personnel who were previously self-employed.   Most doctors were in
this category and, since the Service could not be established without
their collaboration, it was no easy matter to provide them with
incentives while allowing them to retain their professional
independence and other privileges.   General practitioners elected to
participate as 'independent contractors' whereby, in theory, they
remained self-employed, although the bulk of their income came from
the State.   Senior hospital staff were given the option of whole-time
or part-time employment but junior hospital staff were usually
required to take whole-time posts with limited tenure.   Most
opticians and pharmacists remained outside the N.H.S., providing
services as required at agreed rates.   Nurses, administrative staff,
engineers and others were generally employed on a full-time basis.
     To meet these diverse occupational demands the Government of the
day established various negotiating bodies.   The best-known is the
Whitley Council, which negotiates and arbitrates terms of service for

various professional groups. Alterations in terms of service and hearing of complaints are handled by this Council and its decision is final. Consultative machinery was also established with the appropriate trade unions or professional associations, including the British Medical and Dental Associations and the General Nursing Council. Settlement of disputes in respect of the care of non-professional staff is usually agreed with the appropriate unions.

Although the Service is national it is also diverse, resembling a loose aggregation of collaborating professional groups who enjoy a large measure of autonomy and professional discretion in their daily work and loyalties. This ensures, above all, that doctors and dentists enjoy a remarkable degree of freedom of decision and choice in clinical matters.[18] It is written into the Act of 1948 that this freedom shall be maintained and shall include the right to criticise and to publish criticism of the N.H.S. itself.

Legal aspects of nationalised medicine.

As part of the price of retaining their clinical freedom, doctors are required in their contracts to maintain a type of insurance indemnifying them against litigation for negligence. A patient who considers that he has suffered as a result of medical or surgical treatment, directly or indirectly, can sue the Health Authority or the doctor or both for negligence. Damages and costs, if awarded, may be apportioned by the court proportionately to both parties. The medical defence unions are therefore, increasingly, an important if unofficial part of the N.H.S.[19]

It is becoming increasingly recognised that injury resulting from medical treatment - what is sometimes called 'iatrogenic disease' - has to be accepted as an inevitable consequence of technology, and of advances in medical science. Lord Scarman, in a recent lecture to the Royal Society of Medicine, has referred to the possible need for 'no fault' settlements in such cases.[20] The point is a difficult one. Under the Hippocratic ethic, the doctor is instructed, above all else, to 'do no harm', but to follow this admirable injunction to the limit may also mean that the doctor must take no risk of exposing the patient to new or speculative procedures which by definition carry risks.[21] It is accepted in law that a patient, in accepting treatment, accepts the principle that he might have to take the rough with the smooth,[22] but it is equally accepted that, in so doing, he must be protected against experimentation or excess of therapeutic zeal. The difficulty is to find a legal formula which protects the patient while not discouraging the doctor or the advance of medical science. For the present, the matter rests with the law as it stands, and the undoubted discretion of the Courts.

There are certain statutory safeguards, the most notable of which is the Committee on Safety of Medicines,[23] and the Medicines Commission, established under the Medicines Act 1968. These committees, together with previous enactments concerning dangerous drugs, poisonous substances and certain appliances, lay down standards of usage and issue warnings to doctors, nurses and pharmacists about side effects and adverse reactions to treatment. The Committee on Safety of Medicines maintains a register of adverse reactions, notified confidentially and voluntarily by doctors on yellow cards. It has a Secretariat which has the right to investigaste any reaction reported to it, to obtain information from manufacturers and to organise working parties and contracts to investigate special problems. A warning notice issued by this Committee usually has a salutory effect on prescribing.

A manufacturer offering any new medicine for sale must first satisfy the Committee that it is therapeutically justifiable and reasonably safe, in so far as it can be tested in laboratory animals[24] and human volunteers. The new medicine is then licensed, as appropriate, for clinical trial on a limited or extended scale and finally, all being well, for general use, with or without restrictions as to the type of case in which it may be used. Any adverse reactions then occurring are supposed to be detected by the yellow card system but, since this is voluntary and in many ways misunderstood, the response rate is poor.[25] It is not surprising but it is nonetheless disappointing, to find that 'No serious adverse reactions have yet been detected'[26] by this system although, during the period of its existence, many such reactions, some of them serious and life-threatening, have been detected by unofficial methods and independent observers. There would seem to be room for improvement, and possibly legislation in this respect, in order to ensure that corrective action can be taken to safeguard the community and to provide compensation on grounds other than negligence in an individual case.[27]

Unique medico-legal and ethical problems arise when procedures are applied to individuals, not primarily for their own safety, but for that of the community. This happens in various circumstances as for instance when passengers from a ship or aircraft are placed in quarantine because of the presence or suspicion of infectious disease among them. This may cause not only inconvenience, but also loss of earnings or other financial or personal difficulties. Vaccination of healthy individuals may come into this category when performed, not at the request or with the consent of the party to be vaccinated, but because of policies adopted by local or national health authorities. This may happen in two ways:

1. routine vaccination in childhood;
2. periodic vaccinations in special situations.

1. Vaccination in Childhood It is routine practice in the United Kingdom as in most other developed countries, to give infants three injections of 'Triple vaccine' and three oral doses of attenuated poliomyelitis virus vaccine during the first year of life, beginning usually at three months. Vaccination against measles, with a live, attenuated viral vaccine, is given once by injection during the second year of life. Girls aged 11-13 years are given one injection of rubella vaccine. Boosters, especially of polio vaccine, are recommended if there is additional risk of exposure to disease, e.g. when travelling.

Any of these vaccines - indeed any vaccine - can cause adverse reactions, but these are generally mild and transient. However, severe reactions can occasionally occur which are sometimes life-threatening or, very rarely indeed, fatal. In practice, reactions are most frequent after triple vaccine, i.e. a combined vaccine containing diphtheria toxoid, tetanus toxoid and a killed bacterial suspension of Bordetella pertussis, the organism associated with common forms of whooping cough. This suspension contains all the main toxins of the bacteria and is responsible for most of he adverse reactions observed after the injection of triple vaccine. In their most serious forms - about once in every thousand children vaccinated - these reactions affect the central nervous system causing

shock, screaming fits or convulsions. More rarely, perhaps in about
1: 20,000 - 1: 50,000 children, there is permanent brain damage, with
crippling mental or physical defect or both. Because of this
possibility, it is universally recommended that infants or children
with a history of convulsions or other disorders of the nervous
system, or family history of same, should not receive pertussis
vaccination, and that anyone reacting in this way to a first or second
dose should not receive a second or third.

To meet this need, a 'double' vaccine containing diphtheria and
tetanus toxoids, but omitting the pertussis component, is available.
Some parents and doctors prefer this vaccine to the standard triple
vaccine, for obvious reasons. The difficulty of making a decision as
to whether or not to give the pertussis vaccine is accentuated by the
fact that, unlike the other vaccines listed it is relatively
ineffective in preventing or lessening the target disease. The use
of vaccines is further complicated by changes in the target diseases
themselves; mortality from measles and whooping cough is now almost
nil, and severe infections are unusual. This brings closer a
situation where the risk of severe infection might be less than the
risk of a severe reaction to the vaccine. Against this, it is argued
by some health authorities that the risk of recurrence of epidemics in
the absence of high levels of vaccination in the community might lead
to recrudescence of severe forms of the disease and mortality.
Evidence on these matters is conflicting, but it is a fact, often
forgotten, that most major infectious diseases like smallpox, plague,
cholera and scarlet fever have diminished, or even disappeared, in the
past without vaccination programmes, and that mortality from measles
and whooping cough was approaching zero before national vaccination
programmes were instituted.[28]

2. Periodic Vaccinations These are performed on the recommendation
of health authorities, or at the request of individuals, to confer
protection against actual or potential outbreaks of disease, or
because a susceptible individual or group is visiting a foreign
country where they might encounter an infection which is absent in
their domestic setting. Many individuals experience uncomfortable
sequelae to these vaccinations and occasionally a severe reaction
occurs, raising again the question of what level of risk is acceptable
for the vaccine vis-a-vis the disease itself.

Legal Aspects of Vaccination

The legal situation is obviously complex, not only because of the
difficulties in assessing relative risks of vaccine and disease, but
also for other reasons: for example it may be problematic to assess
whether a reaction is attributable to the vaccine and not to some
extraneous or coincidental factor, and the apportionment of
responsibility between client, doctor health authority and
manufacturer. In the case of a child, decisions are made by parents,
guardians or health personnel in what is deemed to be the child's best
interests,[29] but such decisions are encumbered by recommendations,
regulations and computer-controlled call-ups which reduce the personal
element. If a person considers himself damaged by vaccination, the
onus is on him or his representative to provide proof of such damage
before compensation can be obtained from the State under the terms of
the Vaccine Damage Payments Act 1979, which provides that compensation
of £10,000 may be obtained on an all-or-none, once only basis if it

can be shown that a person has suffered 80 per cent disability as a result of vaccination.[30] Normally such applications would be made by parents on behalf of their children. Decisions are made in the first instance by the medical officers of the D.H.S.S. but applicants have a right of appeal to a tribunal of three, including two independent doctors appointed by the Department. Similar schemes now operate in other Western countires and in Japan. In the United Kingdom payment of an award does not prejudice the right of a damaged party to seek additional redress through the courts,[31] but in fact few cases come to court because of expense and of the problems of proof, even in those cases which appear to be straightforward. Theoretically, responsibility for vaccination rests with general practitioners, but they may delegate this responsibility to clinic nurses and in any event they can claim legitimately to be following the recommendations of central health authorities, which in turn are probably following the advice of independent experts or committees which frame national and international policies. Equally, manufacturers can claim that they are offering vaccine in response to national and international regulations in accordance with specifications attaching to these regulations. There are clearly, therefore, considerable problems in assessing who is the appropriate party to sue in such cases, and in attempting to assess who, if anyone, is at fault - a necessary constituent of any action for damages based on tort or delict.[32]

Protection of the Community against Medical Injury

It is clear that many of the complaints and injuries resulting from health-related procedures cannot satisfactorily be dealt with through normal legal channels which require a complainer to identify a person or party against whom a suit for negligence can be raised. Problems arise when there is no obvious negligence by any one party, but where the deficiency is in the system itself. To meet these difficulties, the Ombudsman was appointed as Parliamentary Commissioner for the Health Service, and any individual wishing to lodge a complaint or oook non-legal redress for negligence or injury may seek the advice and intervention of the Ombudsman through a Member of Parliament. The Ombudsman is then required to examine the complaint and, if it is within his terms of reference, to investigate it. Matters involving clinical or purely medical decisions are outwith his terms of reference[33] which are, somewhat vaguely, defined as the investigation of problems arising from the administration of the Health Service. He may, for instance, criticise doctors for not bringing the risks of a given medical or surgical procedure to the attention of a patient,[34] but may not investigate or comment on the procedure itself, even if it is known to be injurious. Because of the increasing complexity of high-technology medicine there has been strong criticism of the limitations of the present sanctions in respect of health-related procedures. Community Health Councils are now viewed as general clearing houses for complaints which cannot be resolved by direct dealings with the Health Authorities. This machinery does not, however, seem to be adequate to deal with borderline cases where the discretionary powers of administrators are being questioned, since there is no right of access to officials or documents, or to the Ombudsman.

Client and Community

It will be apparent that the N.H.S. in the United Kingdom has many imperfections, some of which stem from false premises, others from faulty structure. The belief that extension of medical care would lead to a reduction in demand, as envisaged by Lord Beveridge, has been shown to be false: demand has increased continuously and shows no sign of abating. The premise that a comprehensive service could be funded by pre-paid contributions was also false and led to gross fiscal miscalculations and commitments. The structure, which remains faulty despite review and reorganisation, is cumbersome because it is an amalgam of new with pre-existing institutions and activities of varying nature and efficiency. The fragmentation of the Child Health and School Medical Services, the omission of responsibility for environmental and occupational health, and hence for major segments of preventive medicine, are serious defects. The condition that open-ended demands shall be met with a fixed budget and negligible fund-raising capacity, except by taxation, is unrealistic. There is little incentive to initiative except in clinical matters, and even less to economy and internal reform. Management is weak, in some respects amateurish, and often subject to political appointments and expediencies. Audit and evaluation are patchy and often absent when most needed.

These and other faults lay the N.H.S. open to continuous criticism and may also lower morale and efficiency. Yet the abiding fact remains that the N.H.S. provides a remarkably comprehensive domiciliary and institutional care system. Within its limited resources it strives sincerely to meet the enormous demands of keeping pace with the rapid and costly advances in all branches of health care. Above all, it achieved in 1948 what no other medical care system had up to that point attempted, namely, the removal overnight of the worry which absence from work and medical costs could cause to sick persons. This total commitment remains and, even for those who are not sick, is a reassurance in itself and a significant factor in national morale and welfare. In this way, the N.H.S. achieves its dual objective of serving client and community and, in all essentials, of serving them about as well as can be expected of any complex human institution.

G.T. Stewart

NOTES

1. Parsons, T., The Social System, London, Routledge and Kegan Paul, 1951.
2. See Nelson, A.M., Handbook of Community Medicine, Bristol, John Wright & Son, 1975.
3. National Health Service (Scotland) Act 1972 and National Health Service Act 1972.
4. For discussion, see McKeown, T., Lowe, C.R., An Introduction to Social Medicine, (2nd Ed.), Oxford, Blackwell Scientific Publications, 1974.
5. For the text of this Oath, see infra p. 12.
6. See McKeown and Lowe, op.cit.
7. For further discussion, see Mackintosh, J.M., Trends of

Opinion about the Public Health 1901-51, Oxford University Press, 1953.

8. Social Insurance and Allied Services, (Beveridge Report), Cmnd 6404/1942.

9. See, Davies, J.B.M., Community Health, Preventive Medicine and Social Service, (3rd Ed.), London, Bailliere, Tindall & Cox, 1975.

10. A National Health Service, (Willink Report), Cmnd 6502/1944.

11. For example, National Health Service: Twentieth Anniversary Conference, Report, H.M.S.O., 1968; Health and Welfare; the development of community care: plans for the health and welfare services of the local authorities in England and Wales, Cmnd. 1973/1963; The Administrative structure of the medical and related srevices in England and Wales, H.M.S.O. 1970; Report of the Committee on Nursing, Cmnd. 5115/1972; Health Services in Britain, C.O.I. Pamphlet No. 10, 1974; Community Medicine in Scotland: Report of Joint Working Party on the Integration of Medical Work, H.M.S.O., 1973.

12. For an explanation and discussion of the organisation and powers of the World Health Organisation, see infra ch. 4.

13. Reference for recent amendment to 1972 Act.

14. Scotland Health services, like other domestic affairs, are the responsibility of the Secretary of State for Scotland, as head of the Scottish Home and Health Department. He is advised by a Health Services Planning Council formed from two representatives of each Health Board, Medical School and from his own nominees. For certain purposes where central organisation and expertise are required, there is a Common Services Agency handling such matters as information and statistics, building and blood transfusion. A Chief Scientist, with his own secretariat, has responsibility for research and intelligence, as in England and Wales. Scotland is divided into 15 areas, each served by its own Health Board which has responsibility for hospital and general medical services and for liaison in matters of environmental health with the regional authority, which is not necessarily co-terminous. Because of the geographic and deomographic variation within Scotland, the Boards serve areas which are vastly different in their needs and resources. The senior officers of each Board form an Area Executive Group.
Wales. As in Scotland, there is no Regional Health Authority. The Area Health Authorities are responsible to the Secretary of State in the Welsh Office, who is advised by committees representing the medical and nursing professions, social services and environmental health officers. For specialised services and advice, there is a Technical Services Organisation corresponding approximately to the Scottish Common Services Agency. Administrative channels are otherwise as in England.
Northern Ireland. The N.H.S. Act of 1972 is applied to Northern Ireland in the form of the Health and Personal Social Services (Northern Ireland) Order of 1972. This created four Area Boards, each corresponding to a local government district boundary. As in Scotland and Wales, there is no additional regional authority, so each Board is directly responsible to the Secretary of State for Northern

Ireland.   Each Board has four standing committees advising respectively on health service, social service, administration and policy.   Day-to-day administration is carried out by Area and District Executive Teams.   There is provision for consumer interest and some degree of intervention in the form of District Committees appointed by the Area Boards, but including local councillors and members of voluntary organisations.   The Secretary of State is advised by a Health and Social Services Council composed of Chairmen of the Health Boards and various Advisory Committees.   There is also a Central Services Agency with responsibility for payments to general practitioners, dentists, pharmacists and opticians as well as for legal services and contracts.

15.   Rogers Report.   <u>Management Arrangements for the Reorganised Health Service</u>, London, H.M.S.O., 1972

16.   See Nelson, op.cit.

17.   For discussion of this organisation, see infra ch. 2.

18.   This right to clinical freedom is jealously guarded by doctors, and generally protected by the law.   For a discussion of the implications of this, see McLean, S.A.M., 'Negligence - A Dagger at the Doctor's Back?', in Robson, P., and Watchman, P., (eds), <u>Justice, Lord Denning and the Constitution</u>, Gower Publishing Co., 1981; see also infra ch. 7.

19.   For a brief discussion of the function of Defence Unions, see McLean, loc.cit.; see also Wood, C., (ed), <u>The Influence of Litigation on Medical Practice</u>, London, Scolar Press, 1978.

20.   Scarman, 'Legal Liability and Medicine', <u>J. Roy.Soc.Med.</u>, <u>74</u>, at pp.11-15.   'No fault' liability is seen by some as offering a means of increasing the availability of compensation, since it requires, as its name suggests, no proof of fault.   For further discussion of the various forms of liability, see infra ch. 6.

21.   For discussion, see infra ch. 9.

22.   For discussion, see infra ch. 8.

23.   The predecessor of this Committee, the Committee on Safety of Drugs, was formed in 1964.

24.   For discussion of the use of animals for experimental purposes, see infra ch. 5.

25.   For discussion of the importance of this voluntary reporting system, see infra ch. 11.

26.   See Editorial, <u>Brit.Med.J.</u>, <u>282</u>, 342, (1981).

27.   See infra ch. 6.

28.   See Stewart, G.T., 'Infection and Immunization', <u>24</u>, <u>Scott.Med.J.</u>, 47.

29.   Nonetheless, the provision of proxy consent can cause both ethical and legal problems. See infra ch. 8.

30.   The question of what amounts to 80% disability is clearly one which contains a substantial subjective element, and which may leave any individual whose claim to be 80% disabled is not successful, with only the option of an action in negligence which is probably unlikely to succeed.   This is much the same position as was adopted by the Royal Commission on Civil Laibility and Compensation for Personal Injury, (Pearson Commission), Cmnd 7054/1978, (whose recommendations led to the passing of the Vaccine Damage Payments Act), in

respect of children born with congenital defects. In this case, they recommended that increased allowances should be payable to those suffering from 'severe handicap', without proof of fault. For further discussion, see infra ch. 11.

31. This residual right of action remains also in the case of children suffering from congenital defects. In the case of vaccine damage, it would be available also to those whose injuries were not assessed as amounting to 80%.

32. For discussion, see infra ch. 6.

33. Recent suggestions that such matters should be included in his terms of reference have been met with hostility from some parts of the medical profession. See Editorial, 'The Guardian' 6 January 1981.

34. Even although the law may ultimately not criticise the doctor. For further discussion, see infra ch. 7.

4 World Health and WHO

S. Shubber

The World Health Organisation is an international, inter-governmental organisation.[1] It is one of the Specialised Agencies brought into relation with the United nations (UN), in accordance with Article 69 of its Constitution,[2] and also with Article 57 of the UN Charter. In the agreement bringing WHO into relation with the UN, the latter recognises WHO '... as the specialized agency responsible for taking such action as may be appropriate under its Constitution for the accomplishment of the objectives set forth therein.'[3]

WHO came into existence on 7 April 1948, when its Constitution received the twenty-sixth ratification required for bringing it into force.[4] The establishment of an international health organisation was in the consideration of States which took part in the United Nations Conference on International Organisations at San Francisco in 1945. The Brazilian delegation submitted a memorandum in which it quoted a statement by Cardinal (then Archbishop) Spellman that 'medicine is one of the pillars of peace.'[5] It was this memorandum which led to the insertion in the United Nations Charter of health as one of the problems to be considered by the United Nations, and later to the joint declaration by the Brazilian and Chinese delegations calling for the early convocation of a general conference for the purpose of establishing an international health organisation.[6] The San Francisco Conference approved unanimously the joint declaration, and after the UN came into existence, the Economic and Social Council decided:

> to call an international conference to consider the scope of, and the appropriate machinery for, international action in the field of public health and proposals for the establishment of a single international health organisation of the United Nations.[7]

The International Health Conference was held in New York from 19 June to 22 July 1946 and at the end of its deliberations adopted the Constitution of WHO.[8]

THE STRUCTURE OF WHO

The work of WHO is carried out by three organs,[9] each of which has certain functions laid down in the Constitution of the Organisation. These organs are:

        (1)   the World Health Assembly,
        (2)   the Executive Board, and
        (3)   the Secretariat.

The World Health Assembly is the plenary organ of WHO and is composed of delegates representing Members.[10] The Assembly is the policy-making organ and therefore has a very important role to play in the achievement of the objective of the organisation, and in working towards international co-operation in the field of health. In the words of the Director-General of WHO, Dr. H. Mahler, the Assembly's policies '... represent the collective views on health of the

governments of by far the greater part of the world.'[11]   The
Executive Board is the executive organ of WHO and consists of thirty
persons designated by thirty Member States.[12]   They are elected by
the World Health Assembly, taking into account an equitable
georgraphical distribution.   Members of the Executive Board do not
represent the Member States which designate them, and they are
therefore considered as individuals who possess the appropriate
technical qualifications in the field of health.   It may be
worthwhile to note that in other international organisations, e.g. the
Food and Agriculture Organisation of the United Nations (FAO), and the
United Nations Educational, Scientific and Cultural Organisation
(UNESCO), members of the executive organs do represent States.[13]
The private status of Members of the Executive Board can be considered
as one of the special features of the WHO.[14]

The Secretariat of WHO comprises the Director-General and such
technical and administrative staff as the Organisation may need.[15]
The staff of the Secretariat are appointed by the Director-General in
accordance with staff regulations established by the World Health
Assembly.[16]   There are certain criteria which have to be met in the
recruitment of the staff, namely the highest level of efficiency,
integrity, and internationally representative character, as well as
geographical distribution.[17]

Measures to ensure the widest possible acceptance of international health standards

In order to achieve its objective, namely 'the attainment by all
peoples of the highest possible level of health',[18] and to fulfil
its functions,[19] WHO has the authority under its Constitution to
take certain measures.[20]   These are the adoption of treaties,
regulations, recommendations and international standards, which, when
adopted and accepted or ratified by Member States, would create a
large measure of uniformity in the areas of health covered by these
instruments.   For, a treaty or regulations adopted by the World
Health Assembly and ratified or accepted by Members will create a
special regime and lay down certain rules and standards.   Such rules
and standards, for example, in the field of environmental health, will
lead to the creation of uniform requirements, procedures and perhaps
national legislation, within the territories of Member States which
have accepted or ratified such instruments.   The uniformity thus
created should assist the various health authorities in the States
Parties to such instruments in their dealings with each other, their
mutual co-operation in the achievement of the objectives of such
instruments and the promotion of the health of their peoples.

There are a number of measures which WHO may take under its
Constitution in seeking to achieve its objective.[21]

1.   **Treaties**   One of the functions of WHO in terms of its
Constitution is 'to propose conventions, agreements ... with respect
to international health matters ...'.[22]   Furthermore, Article 19 of
the Constitution of WHO provides that 'the Health Assembly shall have
authority to adopt conventions or agreements with respect to any
matter within the competence of the Organisation.'   Accordingly, WHO
possesses the authority to adopt treaties[23] on any question within
its competence, be it a treaty regulating the question of smoking,
production of certain drugs, advertisement of breastmilk substitutes
or environmental pollution.   The World Health Assembly possesses a

wide power in this respect and the only limitation which exists on this power is that its exercise should be related to the competence of WHO, i.e. pertaining to health. A treaty lays down certain rights and obligations with respect to the parties to it. Therefore, the treaty provides a means of ensuring a wide acceptance of the rules, standards and other requirements contained in it. For instance, if the World Health Assembly adopts a treaty on the prevention of the discharge of polluted waters into internatonal rivers or the sea, the parties to the treaty would be under the same obligations, and would have to conduct themselves in the same way so far as this area of public health is concerned. Consequently, any practices which are not compatible with the terms of the treaty would be illegal, and pre-existing practices which may differ from the terms of the treaty would have to be altered to come into line with it. Therefore, it could be said that the treaty would create a uniform regime, with uniform practices and standards.

Hitherto, WHO has not adopted any treaty under Article 19 of its Constitution and this source of providing international acceptance of health standards and creating uniform rules remains untapped. There is no impediment, from a legal point of view, which may prevent the World Health Assembly from using treaties to regulate internatonal health matters. Perhaps the Assembly might have been influenced by the fact that in some cases it may take a long time to bring a treaty into operation. But this is not an inherent feature of treaties, for States, if so minded, can bring a treaty into operation in a short period of time.

2.   Regulations   Another possibility exists under Article 21 of the constitution of WHO, for the purpose of achieving the widest possible acceptance of international health standards. This is the adoption of regulations. Article 21 read as follows:

The Health Assembly shall have authority to adopt regulations concerning:

(a) sanitary and quarantine requirements and other procedures designed to prevent the international spread of disease;

(b) nomenclatures with respect to diseases, causes of death and public health practices;

(c) standards with respect to diagnostic procedures for international use;

(d) standards with respect to the safety, purity and potency of biological, pharmaceutical and similar products moving in international commerce;

(e) advertising and labelling of biological, pharmaceutical and similar products moving in international commerce.

Accordingly, the World Health Assembly could adopt standards on any of the subject-matters mentioned in Article 21, e.g. with respect to diagnostic procedures, and the safety or purity of biological and pharmaceutical products. The exercise of this authority by the World Health Assembly will create uniform international standards in the field of health, vis-a-vis Member States which have not rejected, or made reservations to, the regulations in question. For, in accordance with Article 22 of the WHO Constitution, regulations adopted under Article 21 come into force for all Members after due notice has been given of their adoption by the Health Assembly, except for such Members as may notify the Director-General of rejection or reservations within the period stated in the notice. In the absence of rejection or reservation, the regulations adopted under Article 21 of the WHO Constitution bind all Members of the Organisation. This power may be called the quasi-legislative power of WHO.[24]

The measures required by the International Health Regulations 1969, may serve to illustrate the point regarding the international standards and their uniformity in this respect. The Regulations require the health authorities of Member States to take all practical measures, at ports or airports:

... (a) to prevent the departure of any infected person or suspect; (b) to prevent the introduction on board a ship, an aircraft, a train, a road vehicle, other means of transport, or container, of possible agents of infection or vectors of a disease subject to the Regulations.[25]

Such measures are designed to prevent the spread of disease and protect the health of the peoples in the States through which the means of transport mentioned in the provisions may pass. Thus, a uniform regime has been created in this area of public health by the International Health Regulations, binding on all Members of WHO, except those which have rejected the latter Regulations or made reservations to them.[26]

WHO has so far adopted two instruments under Article 21, namely, the WHO Nomenclature Regulations 1967[27] and the International Health Regulations 1969.[28] In addition, the World Health Assembly has requested the Director-General of WHO to prepare an international code of marketing in respect of breastmilk substitutes, either as a regulation in the sense of Article 21 of the WHO Constitution, or a recommendation in the sense of Article 23 thereof.[29] The Director-General has prepared the said code and it will be placed before the Thirty-fourth World Health Assembly in May 1981. The latter will decide whether or not this code will be adopted as a regulation or a recommendation.

3. Recommendations   Another means available to WHO of ensuring the widest possible acceptance of international health standards is the adoption of recommendations on matters of health. According to Article 23 of the WHO Constitution 'the Health Assembly shall have authority to make recommendations to Members with respect to any matter within the competence of the Organisation.' The normal description of a recommendation is:

... to describe as recommendations only the acts that the great majority of their authors have characterised as such. From this point of view, there is no doubt that the prevailing meaning is that of "invitation", hence recommendations are only the resolutions adopted with no intention of binding their addressees.[30]

WHO could, in a recommendation, call on its Members to adopt certain measures on a health issue, e.g. immunisation, pollution control. It could also adopt a recommendation containing standards, guidelines or codes of practice on health matters, and invite Member States to implement them in national legislation. In fact WHO has recommended to Member States a number of instruments under Article 23, such as the guide to Hygiene and Sanitation in Aviation 1959,[31] the Classification of Pesticides According to Hazards[32] and guiding principles on essential drugs.[33] The international code of breastmilk substitutes could also be adopted as a recommendation. Indeed, the Executive Board adopted a resolution in January 1981, recommending to the World Health Assembly the adoption of the latter code as a recommendation.[34]

It is worthy of note that WHO has authority to make recommendations under two international conventions, namely, the Single Convention on Narcotic Drugs, 1961,[35] and the Convention on Psychotropic Substances, 1971.[36] According to the former, WHO has the right to evaluate the safety and efficacy of drugs and to recommend control measures if it finds that a given substance is liable to abuse and may produce ill effects similar to those produced by drugs covered by Schedule I or II of the Convention.[37] On the other hand, according to the latter, WHO has the right to evaluate the safety and efficacy of psycotropic substances and to recommend control measures, if it finds that the substance has the capacity to produce a state of dependence, and central nervous system stimulation or depression, resulting in hallucinations or disturbance in thinking or behaviour; or that there is sufficient evidence that the substance is being, or is likely to be, abused so as to constitute a public health and social problem.[38]

WHO makes such recommendations to the UN Commission on Narcotic Drugs. The recommendations are based on the evaluation of the substance in question by WHO expert group, which examines the relevant data and makes its determination. Such evaluation is communicated by the Director-General of WHO to the Secretary-General of the U.N. It will be seen that such recommendations are not made by the World Health Assembly itself, though they constitute the recommendations of the Organisation. It would appear that the Director-General has been given a mandate by the World Health Assembly to take decisions as to the scheduling of substances in accordance with existing international agreements and upon receipt of the appropriate expert advice, and to forward to the U.N. Secretary-General such notifications and assessments as WHO is called upon to make under the above-mentioned Conventions.[39] This mandate may be considered as the legal basis for the communication of the evaluation of substances covered by these Conventions, and as representing the views of WHO and its recommendations in this respect.[40]

While recommendations of WHO are not binding, they may nevertheless lead to uniform practices in the field of health among Members of the Organisation, and would at least help to create awareness of the risks to health to which such recommendations may be addressed, which might eventually lead to the formulation of national legislation or regulations. However, WHO recommendations must carry some persuasive authority, for they are the expression of the views of the collective membership of an organisation whose objective is the attainment by all people of the highest possible level of health.

4. International standards   WHO has the means of adopting international standards for the purpose of protecting health and in the fulfilment of its functions. According to Article 2, paragraph (u), of the WHO Constitution, it is a function of the Organisation 'to develop, establish and promote international standards with respect to food, biological, pharmaceutical and similar products.'

WHO, in co-operation with FAO, has established the Codex Alimentarius Commission, which is the plenary organ of the FAO/WHO Joint Food Standaros Programme.[41] One of the Commission's functions is the preparation of food standards aimed at the protection of the health of the consumer.[42] Further examples of standards under this heading are the WHO European Standards for Drinking-Water, 1970 and the WHO International Standards for Drinking-Water 1971.[43]

These standards lay down certain uniform requirements designed to protect the health of people in the Member States and promote the development of hygienic conditions, sound and proper food production, the provision of safe and adequate water supplies and so on.

These international standards are recommended to Member States by the Codex Alimentarius Commission and the WHO Expert Committee.[44] They are not binding per se, but may become binding when accepted by Member States, and when accepted, they may be given effect to, or implemented, in national legislation or regulations. It might be interesting to point out that the Codex Alimentarius Commission has, so far, recommended some one hundred and thirty international food standards covering a wide range of foodstuffs.

Scrutinisation of action taken on treaties, regulations and recommendations

WHO possesses no machinery for scrutinising the national actions of Member States with respect to treaties, regulations and recommendations adopted by the World Health Assembly. However, in accordance with Article 62 of the WHO Constitution 'each Member shall report annually on the action taken with respect to recommendations made to it by the Organisation and with respect to conventions, agreements and regulations.' This provision could be considered as a means of measuring the compliance with, and the implementation of, treaties, regulations or recommendations by Members of the Organisation. Of course, the provision is silent with respect to the question of which organ of WHO should consider these reports; nor does it state what could be done by the Organisation in this respect. Therefore, it might be argued that the World Health Assembly could consider such reports and perhaps call upon Members to give effect to such instruments, thus, perhaps, providing a means of putting moral pressure on Members to do so. It would, however, appear that Article 62 has not been used for this purpose.[45]

International liaison on health care

While WHO is the specialised agency concerned with health matters, it also co-operates with other international organisations and national institutions in Member States on health matters. Indeed, the WHO Constitution makes the direction and co-ordination of international health work one of the functions of the Organisation.[46] The Organisation carries out, in co-operation with the UN, other Specialised Agencies, and scientific and professional groups, programmes for the advancement of health, improvement of nutrition, economic or working conditions and so on. [47] In fact, WHO has co-operation agreement with many international organisations and bodies and, to name but a few, the Food and Agricultural Organisation, the International Labour Organisation, UNICEF, and the United Nations. WHO has also made arrangements with a large number of national institutions, such as universities and laboratories. These are called 'Collaborating Centres'[48] in the jargon of the Organisation, and their purpose is the carrying out of research, studies, surveys and so on. WHO has also relations with a large number of non-governmental organisations which are concerned with health and health issues.[49] Such liaison helps to avoid duplication of effort, enables WHO to make better use of its resources and makes the advance in technical and scientific knowledge in Member

States easily accessible to WHO through the contribution of these 'Collaborating Centres'.

Impact of WHO on World Health

WHO has been in existence for over 33 years and can claim to have made some significant contributions in the field of health. For example, through the efforts of WHO, and with the co-operation of Members, WHO can claim the credit for the eradication from the whole world of smallpox. It may be appropriate to quote the relevant resolution:

The Thirty-third World Health Assembly, on this the eighth day of May 1980;

Having considered the development and results of the global programme on smallpox eradication initiated by WHO in 1958 and intensified since 1967;

1.
DECLARES SOLEMNLY THAT THE WORLD AND ALL ITS PEOPLES HAVE WON FREEDOM FROM SMALLPOX, WHICH WAS A MOST DEVASTATING DISEASE SWEEPING IN EPIDEMIC FORM THROUGH MANY COUNTRIES SINCE EARLIEST TIMES, LEAVING DEATH, BLINDNESS AND DISFIGUREMENT IN ITS WAKE, AND WHICH ONLY A DECADE AGO WAS RAMPANT IN AFRICA, ASIA AND SOUTH AMERICA;

2.
EXPRESSES ITS DEEP GRATITUDE TO ALL NATIONS AND INDIVIDUALS WHO CONTRIBUTED TO THE SUCCESS OF THIS NOBLE AND HISTORIC ENDEAVOUR;

3.
CALLS THIS UNPRECEDENTED ACHIEVEMENT IN THE HISTORY OF PUBLIC HEALTH TO THE ATTENTION OF ALL NATIONS, WHICH BY THEIR COLLECTIVE ACTION HAVE FREED MANKIND OF THIS ANCIENT SCOURGE AND, IN SO DOING, HAVE DEMONSTRATED HOW NATIONS WORKING TOGETHER IN A COMMON CAUSE MAY FURTHER HUMAN PROGRESS.[50]

WHO has carried out, and is still carrying out, many projects in Member States, for example in the fields of medical research, training, water supply, family health, onchocerciasis control, and tropical diseases.[51] Furthermore, the organisation has very ambitious programmes, such as 'Health for All by the Year 2000',[52] which could have far-reaching consequences for humanity. Meetings of the Organisation, its seminars and conferences on health matters, e.g. the International Conference on Primary Health Care at Alma-Ata, USSR in September 1978, and the debates of the World Health Assembly could, to say the least, draw attention to, and create awareness of, the existence of risks to health and the need for action on national and international levels.[53] All this must have contributed, directly or indirectly, to the improvement of health in members of the Organisation and the attainment of its objective.

S. Shubber

* The views expressed in this chapter are those of the author alone.

NOTES

1. For further discussion, see Berkov, R., The World Health Organization, Geneva, Librairie E. Droz, 1957.
2. The Constitution of WHO is to be found in World Health Organization, Basic Documents, (30th Ed.), Geneva, WHO, 1980, at pp. 1-18.
3. see Article 1 of the Agreement between the UN and WHO, 1948, ibid., at p. 41.
4. Article 80 of the WHO Constitution. See also, The First Ten Years of the World Health Organization, Geneva, WHO, 1958,. at p. 453.
5. ibid., at p. 38.
6. id.
7. See resolution of the Economic and Social Council dated 15 February 1946: the text of this resolution is reproduced in Official Records of the World Health Organization, (hereinafter referred to as WHO Off. Rec.), 1, Geneva, WHO, at pp. 39-40.
8. See Final Acts of the International Health Conference, New York, 19 June - 22 July 1946.
9. See article 9 of the WHO Constitution.
10. See ibid., Article 10.
11. Introducing WHO, Geneva, WHO, 1976, Foreword, at p. 6. The membership of WHO is now 156 Members and Associate Members.
12. See Article 24 of WHO Constitution. The functions of the Executive Board are laid down in Article 28 of the WHO Constitution.
13. See Article V, para. 1, of the Constitution of FAO, and Article V (A), para. 1, of the Constitution of UNESCO.
14. Another special feature of WHO is its regional structure. The Organisation has six regional organisations: the Regional Office for Africa (AFRO), the Regional Office for the Americas (AMRO), the Regional Office for the Eastern Mediterranean (EMRO), the Regional Office for Europe (EURO), the Regional Office for South-East Asia (SEARO), and the Regional Office for the Western Pacific (WPRO). On the regional structure of WHO, see Vignes, C.-H., 'La Regionalisation de l'Organisation Mondiale de la Sante', in Podone, A., (ed), Regionalisme et universalisme dans le droit international contemporain, Paris, 1977 at pp. 189 et seq. See also Articles 44-54 of WHO Constitution.
15. See Article 30 of WHO Constitution.
16. ibid., Article 35.
17. The WHO Secretariat comprises 112 nationalities at the moment; see Executive Board Document EB67/26, 3 December 1980, Annex 3 at pp. 18-20.
18. See Article 1 of the WHO Constitution.
19. The functions of WHO are laid down in Article 2 of the WHO Constitution.
20. On the competence of WHO to take measures against pollution, see Shubber, S., 'The Role of WHO in Environmental Pollution Control', 2 Earth Law Journal, 363, (1976).
21. For discussion, see Alexandrowicz, C.H., The law-making functions of the Specialised Agencies of the United Nations, Sydney and London, Angus and Robertson, 1973.
22. See Article 2, para. (K).

23. Lord McNair, The Law of Treaties, London, O.U.P., 1961, at p. 4, defines a treaty as 'a written agreement by which two or more States or international organizations create or intend to create a relation between themselves operating within the sphere of international law.' According to Article 2, para. 1(a) of the draft articles on treaties concluded between States and international organizations or between two or more international organizations, prepared by the International Law Commission (ILC), 'a "treaty" means an international agreement governed by international law and concluded in written form:
(i) between one or more States, and one or more international organizations, or
(ii) between international organizations,
whether that agreement is embodied in a single instrument or in two or more related instruments and whatever its particular designation.' See Report of the ILC on the work of its thirty-first session, 14 May - 3 August 1979; General Assembly, Official Records, Thirty-fourth Session, Supplement No. 10 (A/34/10) (1979), at p. 374. See also Article 2, para. 1(a) of the Vienna Convention on the Law of Treaties 1969, reproduced in 63 American Journal of International Law, at pp. 875 et seq. (1969).

24. See Shubber, S., 'The Legal Structure of the World Health Organization - A Brief Note', 67 WHO Dialogue, 14, (1979).

25. See Article 31, para. 1.

26. The International Health Regulations are binding on some 150 Member States of WHO.

27. See Resolution WHA20.18, WHO Handbook of Resolutions and Decisions of the World Health Assembly and the Executive Board, Vol. I, Geneva, WHO, 1948 - 1972, (1973), at pp. 175-6.

28. See International Health Regulations, second annotated edition, 1974.

29. See Resolution WHA33.32, para. 6(4) and (5). See also WHO Report by the Director-General on Infant and Young Child Feeding - Draft International Code of Marketing of Breastmilk Substitutes, Executive Board Sixty-seventh Session, EB67/20 (10 December 1980).

30. See Castaneda, J. Legal Effects of United Nations Resolutions, New York, Columbia U.P., 1969, at pp. 8-9.

31. See Resolution WHA12.18, note 27, supra, at p. 154.

32. See Resolution WHA28.62, 226 WHO Off. Rec., at p. 33.

33. See Resolution WHA31.32, WHO Handbook of Resolutions and Decisions of the World Health Assembly and the Executive Board, Vol. 2, Geneva, WHO, 1973-1978 (1979), at pp. 53-4.

34. See Resolution EB67.R12 (28 January 1981).

35. For text, see United Nations Treaty Series, Vol. 520. The Convention was amended in 1972; see Protocol amending the Single Convention on Narcotic Drugs, 1961. The text is reproduced in XI International Legal Materials, at pp. 804-810.

36. For text, see ibid., X (1971), at pp. 261-288.

37. see Article 3, para. 3 (iii).

38. see Article 2, para. 4. See also, WHO Expert Committee on Implementation of the Convention on Psychotropic Substances 1971 - Assessment of Public Health and Social Problems Associated with the Use of Psychotropic Drugs, WHO, Geneva,

(1981).

39. see Resolutions WHA7.6, para. 1, WHA18.46, para. 1(b) and WHA30.18, para. 1.   For the text of the first two resolutions see reference in note 27, supra, at pp. 125-6; for the text of the last resolution, see note 33 supra at p. 50.

40. It may be interesting to point out that recently WHO has recommended that four weight-reducing agents, technically called anorectic drugs, be placed under international control.   This recommendation was endorsed by the U.N. Commission on Narcotic Drugs at its 30th. session in Vienna.   The generic names of these drugs are: benzphetamine, mazindol, phendimetrazine and phentermine. See WHO Press Release, WHO/12, 13 March 1981.

41. On the Codex Alimentarius Commission, see Shubber, S., 'The Codex Alimentarius Commission under International Law', 21 International and Comparative Law Quarterly, (1972) 631.

42. See Article 1, paras. (a) and (c) of the Statutes of the Codex Alimentarius Commission.   The Statutes of the Commission and other relevant legal instruments are to be found in the Codex Alimentarius Commission, Procedural Manual, (4th Ed.), Rome, FAO/WHO 1975.

43. The European Standards for Drinking-Water are intended '...to stimulate improvement in drinking-water quality and to encourage countries of advanced economic and technological capability in Europe to attain higher standards than the minimal ones specified in "International Standards for Drinking-Water".' - Preface to the European Standards for Drinking-Water, (3rd. Ed.), 1971, at p. vi.   The first edition was published in 1961 (see The Second Ten Years of the World Health Organisation 1958-1967, at p. 256).   This is the third edition of the International Standards for Drinking -Water, the first edition being proposed in 1958 and the second in 1963.   It is believed that WHO is in the process of combining these two instruments into one.

44. Expert Committees are established by the World Health Assembly, in accordance with Article 18(e) of the WHO Constitution, and by the Executive Board, in accordance with Article 38 of the WHO Constitution.   For the text of the Regulations for Expert Advisory Panels adopted by the World Health Assembly, see reference in note 2, supra, at pp. 89-97.

45. It may be interesting to note the following request to the Director-General, in a resolution proposed by the Executive Board to the Health Assembly in relation to the draft International Code of Marketing of Breastmilk Substitutes. The Thirty-fourth Health Assembly requests the Director-General: (3) to report to the Thirty-sixth World Health Assembly on the status of compliance with and implementation of the Code at country, regional and global levels; (4) based on the conclusions of the status report, to make proposals, if necessary, for revision of the text of the code and for the measures needed for its effective application.' See Resolution EB67.R12, 28 January 1981.

46. see Article 2, para. (a).

47. see ibid., paras. (h), (i) and (j).

48. For details regarding these Collaborating Centres, see WHO

Manual, Part X, Sec. 7, paras. 170-260.

49.   For the criteria for establishing such relationships, see reference in note 2, supra, at pp. 67-69.

50.   See WHO - The Global Eradication of Smallpox - Final Report of the Global Commission for the Certification of Smallpox Eradication, (1980).

51.   See WHO resolution WHA33.3, Thirty-third World Health Assembly, Geneva, 5-23 May 1980, resolutions and Decisions, Annexes, WHA33/1980/REC/1, Geneva, WHO, 1980, at p. 1.

52.   see the Second Ten Years of the World Health Organization (1958-1967), supra cit., at p. 255; see also, Biennial Report of the Director-General - The Work of WHO 1976-1977, WHO Off. Rec., No. 243, at pp. 28-33, 47-55, 70-73; see also WHO Proposed Programme Budget for the Financial Period 1982-1983, PB/82-83, Geneva, WHO, (1980).

53.   See resolution WHA30.43, supra cit., at p. 3, and resolution WHA32.30, Thirty-second World Health Assembly, Geneva, 7-25 May 1979, Resolutions and Decisions, Annexes, WHA 32/1979/REC/1, Geneva, WHO, 1979, at pp. 27-29.

5 Live Animal Studies
R. E. Leake

INTRODUCTION

Although there may be minor exceptions, the use of live animals for experimental purposes is, in the United Kingdom, confined to medical research and the trials of new drugs. The maintenance of animal houses has been carefully monitored for many years and each experimenter must be licensed by the Home Office, and is a) restricted to experiments carefully outlined in his/her licence, and b) required to make a detailed annual return of his/her experiments.[1] Acquisition of a licence requires both demonstration of the necessary practical skills and approval of the overall objectives of the individual worker. This chapter will consider the various types of experiment for which one might apply for a licence, and it is worth noting at this stage that it is the individual who applies for and holds the licence. Universities, for example, cannot get a corporate licence and then decide for themselves who shall do the .work. This discussion is not intended to be all-embracing but will, rather, highlight certain areas of current interest, and hopefully, stimulate the reader to follow up particular points. Equally, it is not intended either to justify or to condemn live animal experiments as a whole, although the final section will consider the extent to which viable alternatives exist to the use of live animals in medical and pharmaceutical research.

The use of live animals for experimental purposes was first referred to in Greek literature,[2] although little is known about the extent to which it occurred. In the scientific revival of the Middle Ages the use of animals was mainly confined to the study of anatomy and physiology and little experimental work on live animals occurred.

As science progressed, the use of live animals for experimental purposes became more frequent. An interesting landmark was the demonstration by Berthold[3] in 1849 that a cockerel loses its secondary male sex character (in particular, atrophy of the comb) after castration, but the character can be restored in full by transplanting the testes from another cockerel. This experiment showed that the male sex hormone is secreted by a particular organ and transported via the bloodstream to act in distant, specific target organs. As the understanding of normal bodily functions became clearer so the need for experimental animals in which to study disease, i.e. abnormal function, became more important. Such studies can be split into two categories. First, there is the study of drugs and other chemicals which might induce or correct abnormal function, and second, there follows the study of the mechanism by which the particular abnormality might arise. These two types of study reflect the twin overall objectives of such experiments - first, of curing existing disease, and second, of eliminating future incidence of the disease.

In more recent years live animals have been used not only for scientific and medical research but also for routine screening of new drugs, food additives and cosmetics in order to comply with government-sponsored safety regulations. This type of experiment must be considered separately, since it additionally highlights the extent to which responses obtained in animals will correspond to those in humans.

In addition to the use of animals in research there is a small but significant use of animals in medical and veterinary education. It is reassuring for any patient or owner to know that the relevant surgeon or vet. has had plenty of experience and has a good understanding of the functions and interactions of the various tissues. However, there clearly are limits to what can be learned from live animal models, either as demonstrations or in personal practical experience.

This chapter will, therefore, be divided into six sub-sections dealing with: the acquisition of animals for experimental purposes and their maintenance during such studies; the use of animals in training and general education; the use of animals in the expansion of fundamental scientific knowledge; the use of animals in specialised applied research, e.g. the clinical search for new contraceptives or anti-cancer drugs; the testing of drugs and related compounds prior to their sale for use on or by humans; the possible alternatives to live animal experiments for each of the purposes discussed and the potential advantages and pitfalls in the use of particular alternatives.

ANIMALS AND ANIMAL HOUSES

Since it appears that animal houses and animal handling are similar in both the Universities and the pharmaceutical industry, the two will be considered together. Many different species of animal have been maintained in animal houses over the years and the Home Office lays down very strict rules on the type of accomodation, amount of exercise area and allowances of food and drink for each species.[4] Commonly found in animal houses are cats, dogs, frogs, guinea pigs, hamsters, mice, rabbits, rats and toads. Specific experiments have involved birds (e.g. hens and pigeons), cattle, fish, goats, horses, sheep and tortoises. This list is not exhaustive but covers most of the species associated with both basic and applied research. The use of domestic animals, e.g. dogs and cats, is perhaps the most emotive, but it should be noted that, in objective terms, an experiment is either necessary or not independent of whether it is a rat or a dog which is being used. Clearly some selection is made because of specific intrinsic characteristics of a particular species, but it is sometimes open to question whether or not enough thought is given to the choice of species.

Before discussing the life of animals in animal houses it is important to consider how the animals are acquired. In fact, the majority of experiments are carried out on animals bred specially for that purpose in the animal house in question. Cats and dogs may be bought in on specific orders, but again these are normally supplied by firms which rear the animals specifically for this purpose. There are several specialist firms from whom specific animals can be obtained, and, for example, one firm also produces corresponding literature on a routine basis[5] so that interested workers can follow the latest work in their own and related fields thus, incidentally, eliminating some unnecessary duplication of experiments.

Conditions in animal houses are extremely carefully monitored, partly to comply with Home Office instructions, but usually the requirements of specific experiments are even more exacting than the general rules dictate. In general, animals are maintained at a constant temperature (usually around 68°F, 20°C) and often have controlled day length (e.g. 14 hours light/10 hours dark). Food (a balanced, appropriate diet) and water are normally supplied ad libitum. Many physiological and biochemical responses are sensitive to changes in environment. Even minor stress can cause marked changes in plasma hormone levels and, therefore, changes in the metabolism of the target tissue for that hormone. For example, if a rat is taken from an animal house to a separate laboratory on a cold day, even a ten minute exposure to cold air will cause marked changes in plasma growth hormone, prolactin and glucocorticoid levels.[6] Thus, in order to ensure that observed responses relate solely to the exeperimental procedure under investigation animals must be cared for in controlled conditions and subject to the minimum amount of extraneous stress.

For the same reasons, conditions in animal house operating theatres are at least as carefully monitored as those in hospitals. Spurious bacterial or viral infections could, of course, greatly influence experimental results. Many of the larger animals are maintained on farms associated with veterinary schools, and these animals are subject to much closer attention than those on normal, independent farms.

In conclusion, animals used for experimental purposes are (in the United Kingdom at least) generally reared specifically for that purpose. They are maintained under constant and favourable conditions. It is perhaps significant that when animal house rabbits, for example, are either let out or escape from their cages they usually return voluntarily to their cages after a few minutes. This is presumably because they lack the experience of the outside world, and enjoy the security of their familiar surroundings. Animals which have been reared specifically would have great difficulty in fending for themselves in the wild. Equally, even if there were a case for using wild animals for selected experimental purposes, inbred laboratory animals show much less inter-animal variation in physiological and biochemical parameters and so are usually better suited to permit easy interpretation of experimental results.

EDUCATION

The use of live animals for teaching purposes is strictly limited by the Home Office. Two principal categories of use will be considered - first, the use of live animals in lecture-demonstrations, and secondly, the use of live animals by individual students. There is no doubt, in general terms, that a live demonstration is more instructive for a group of students than is pure, abstract, theoretical argument. The limited use of live animals in lecturing to medical, dental, and other students, has therefore been considered essential for many years. The types of experiment involved are those which illustrate nervous responses and the relationship between nerve and muscle function,[7] and they tend to be carried out on anaesthetised animals which are not allowed to recover after the demonstration. However, particularly in the case of small groups of students, the possibility must be considered that a colour film of the appropriate experiment would have been adequate.

The use of animals for personal experimental experience by students is probably more difficult to avoid. Anyone who has tried, is well aware that handling tissues in cadavers (preserved or freshly killed) bears no relation to handling the same organs in a live animal. Therefore, whether the student is learning procedures with a view to future practice in medicine or in basic medical research, it is essential that, at some point, first hand experience is gained with live animals. In this case experiments might range from simple injection of conscious animals to surgical procedures, e.g. ovariectomy,[8] adrenalactomy,[9] or partial hepatectomy,[10] on anaesthetised animals which will recover and subsequently be maintained for several days or even weeks. However, this type of experiment can only be carried out under a Home Office licence and such would only be granted to a student working directly under a supervisor competent and well experienced in all aspects of the surgical procedures and in general animal welfare.

There is often a major problem in assisting students to make the transition from handling cadavers to working with live animals, and the manner in which this is handled will depend largely on the individual supervisor. Given that students only make this step if their subsequent work necessarily involves regular use of live animals, it is difficult to see a viable alternative to including work on live animals as part of their training. The Home Office guidelines require that the individual must be competent in all preocedures, using dead animal models, before proceeding to work on live animals.

In conclusion, although some properties of both muscle and nerve are best illustrated using live animals under an anaesthetic, a well-made colour film with commentary by an expert might, to some extent, replace routine use of live animals in lecture demonstrations. On the other hand, specific students, especially veterinary students, must inevitably gain experience with live animals. This also applies to graduate students working in the basic medical sciences, at least until some reliable alternative to whole animal studies is established.[11]

BASIC RESEARCH

Few would argue with the claim that basic medical research has made great progress in the last century, and much of this progress has been possible through the use of live animals in experimental situations. This might involve the animal in very natural behaviour and this type of experiment is generally open to minimal criticism. Equally, simple injection of animals with varying levels of natural products, e.g. hormones, is fairly elementary and uncontentious and induces minimal side-effects. Experiments which might be more readily criticised involve transplantation, immunosuppressence, partial or complete removal of vital organs or glands or induction of specific tumours. Since it is impossible to consider each type of experiment in detail, particular examples will be used.

Simple study of the natural behaviour of animals in controlled conditions can be very meaningful. The particular molecules with which certain (maybe many) species attract a mate are known as pheromones. They are, for example, given off by a male and detected by a female, at a very low concentration, and often a considerable distance away. A typical example involves the change in the habits of a female vole when a corresponding male is nearby. Male and female animals were isolated in separate cages connected only by long, air-tight hoses and it was found that a response occurred, after connecting the hoses, even when the cages were several hundred yards apart. Subsequent chemical analysis of the potential pheromones was then possible.[12] This type of behavioural study has produced much fundamental information with minimal inconvenience to the animals involved. However, this type of experiment can be taken a step further as in the case where rats were trained to run a particular obstacle course. They were then killed and the RNA[13] extracted from their brains, was subsequently injected into the brains of other rats. The intention was to see if memory was stored as RNA, and, if so, if it was transferable.[14]

At the next level, animals simply receive an injection of a natural product at a physiological dose and are subsequently killed prior to analysis of tissue metabolism, Much information on, for example, the mechanism of action of hormones has been achieved in this way. In the case of the immature female rat, levels of circulating sex steroids are low. Injection of oestrogen, in an amount sufficient to give the normal adult plasma oestrogen level, results in growth of the uterus in a manner exactly analogous to that which would normally happen at puberty[15] (i.e. a few days later).[16,17] This means that the effects of the hormone can be compared with an unstimulated, intact control. Studies on many other hormones, which are normally secreted at effective levels throughout life, have to be carried out by first removing the secretory (endocrine) gland from both experimental and control animals and then adding back the hormone to the experimental animal.[18] This latter approach has two main criticisms. First, it is in reality a study of replacement therapy rather than hormonal stimulation above the normal physiological, basal level, and second the stress factor of the operation may induce additional side-effects.

The simple injection approach, which has provided so much information on the fundamental mechanism of action of steroids, can also lend itself to more directly clinical work in the study of treatments of infertility and endocrine cancers.[19] The same approach has also been used to study the pharmacological[20] effects of hormones and some other drugs. In all cases the animals remain in their normal cages, with food and water ad <u>libitum</u> for the interval between injection and sacrifice, prior to the experimental measurements in the target tissue(s). There are no outward signs of stress in animals undergoing this type of experiment and there is no reason to suppose that any discomfort is caused.[21] Although these types of experiment might possibly be done other than in intact animals, there are still several problems to be overcome.[22]

A significant proportion of live animal experiments carried out in basic research involves either the addition of 'foreign' substances or the operative addition and/or removal of cells and tissues. First, there are experiments in which a molecule foreign to a particular species of animal is introduced simply so that the animal's own immune system will produce antibodies to that molecule. A particular example of this type of experiment would involve the isolation of nuclear proteins from a human tumour cell. The proteins themselves, although specific to tumour cells, are in no way carcinogenic.[23] They are injected into an animal, say a rabbit, which simply responds by producing antibodies to proteins which its own immune system recognises as not being native. In the same manner, rabbit proteins can be introduced into goats and the goat produces anti-rabbit antibody. This goat anti-rabbit antibody can be made fluorescent, and then, if one wishes to establish whether or not batches of human cells are normal or tumour cells, the rabbit antibody is added to all the cell types. It should bind only to the tumour cells containing a copy of the original isolated nuclear protein. The fluorescent goat anti-rabbit antibody is then added, but will bind only to those cells which have retained the original rabbit antibody. The fluorescent marker should, therefore, identify selectively those cells which contain the original tumour nuclear marker protein.[24] This type of approach allows both investigation of the fundamental mechanism of antibodies, and also that the experimenter can identify particular types of isolated cell - which cannot always be done morphologically.

The use of experimental animals to generate antibodies is again one which produces very valuable information with minimal inconvenience to the animal. However, in some cases it is necessary to prime the immune system before injecting the foreign molecule. To do this a complicated mixture called Freund's adjuvant is injected with the molecule under study. Such treatment can initially cause the animal to feel sick and, indeed, if inadvertently injected into the experimenter can produce a very inflamed response.

As previously indicated,[25] experiments on regulation of growth and cell division and studies on hormone action often involve the partial or complete removal of the liver or of particular endocrine glands. The operation is, of course, carried out on anaesthetised animals. However, after surgery the animals must be allowed to recover and live for several days or weeks before the final part of the experiment can be carried out. Each of the glands involved in this type of experiment is very important to normal life, and the animal deprived of the appropriate secretions is therefore at a considerable disadvantage. Post-operative animals are therefore sustained very carefully and fed glucose or saline solutions - depending on the particular gland removed. This type of experimentation is illustrated by studies on growth hormone which promotes RNA and protein synthesis in the liver and is secreted from the anterior pituitary at all stages of post partum life. Thus, in order to study the effect of growth hormone on the synthesis of a particular protein (e.g. somatomedin - an essential promoter of long bone growth in childhood and adolescence which may be missing or inadequate in some cases of congenital dwarfism) it is essential to have a control animal with no circulating plasma growth hormone.[26] The anterior pituitary is, therefore, carefully and completely removed (hypophystectomy) and the animal then has to be sustained for some time before the experiment is carried out, to ensure that absolutely all the pituitary was removed since incomplete removal results in a gradual increase of growth hormone secretion from the remaining cells. Unfortunately the anterior pituitary also secretes other hormones of which thyroid stimulating hormone (TSH) and adenocorticotrophic hormone (ACTH) are essential to normal life. Both the thyroid hormones and the glucocorticoids (the principal cortical hormones to be released by ACTH) regulate activity of many tissues including vital organs. It is possible to add back all the hormones, other than growth hormone, to the hypophysectomised animals. However, it is clear that, even so, the animals are not returned to 'normal' life. Such experiments do answer very important questions about the fundamental processes and these answers lead to specific clinical treatments of the hormonal imbalance in humans and

domestic animals.   Nevertheless, there is no doubt that, if
satisfactory in vitro alternatives could be established, this type of
experiment would be one of the first to be dropped.

Some very useful experiments on the nature of tumour cell growth
have been carried out in ascites tumour cells.   Tumour cells usually
grow in culture, but instead of being cultured in glass or plastic
containers as is standard for most cultured cells, ascites cells are
grown in the body cavity of mice which seem able to carry large
quantities of these cells without any apparent pain or distress.
Nonetheless, extreme care must be taken in the maintenance of such
mice.[27]

The close link betweeen fundamental and clinical research is well
illustrated by the case of schistosomiasis or bilharziasis.[28]   This
parasite has a complicated life history and causes very considerable
medical, social and economic damage in parts of Africa where it can be
picked up by humans whilst paddling or swimming.   Proper treatment of
infected individuals and moves to eliminate the parasite have both
stemmed from studies of its life cycle, which studies have been
dependent on live animal experiments using monkeys, rats and mice.
[29, 30, 31]

Our understanding of brain function and nerve/muscle interaction
is firmly based on information from live animal studies.   For
example, recent developments in control of brain abnormalities (e.g.
schizophrenia) and regulation of pain threshold using enkephalins and
endorphins have resulted from studies of the effects of the natural or
synthetic molecules on various metabolic parameters in different
experimental animals.[32, 33]

APPLIED RESEARCH

The line between research to establish fundamental knowledge and that
designed to combat human and domestic animal disease can be seen to be
extremely fine and diffuse.   In this section, discussion of
experiments will be limited to those which bear directly on the
management of selected diseases.

Cancer research now receives as much attention as any other area
of medical research, and it is proposed to discuss here two particular
aspects of recent cancer research which now yield direct benefit to
patients with the relevant cancers.   The most common cancer in
Western women is breast cancer, and about one third of women who
develop this form of cancer have a form of the disease which can be
treated by endocrine therapy.   Initially endocrine therapy of
patients with advanced disease was ablative,[34] and involved the
removal of ovaries in pre-menopausal women and the adrenals and
anterior pituitary in older women.   These procedures are highly
traumatic for the patient and lower her natural resistance to disease
at a time when she needs it most.   The development of synthetic
molecules, which were equally effective when administered as additive
therapy and therefore required no surgical procedures, was welcomed by
patients and surgeons alike.   Much of the development work on these
additive anti-steroids has been done in rats and mice.[35]   Mice of
the strain C3H develop mammary tumours spontaneously with age and
their response to both chemical and radiotherapy has been carefully
monitored.   Much work has been done on the mammary tumours which
develop in Wistar rats after they have had dimethylbenzanthracene
(DMBA) included in their diet.   The mechanism of action of two

anti-steroids now used in treatment of human breast-cancer was partly explained by work on this DMBA tumour.[36]

Recent experiments, again using live animals as experimental models, have confirmed that diet may both cause and prevent particular cancers. Many dietary experiments, particularly those in the U.S.A., have shown that either high levels of a particular foodstuff or prolonged retention of the food bolus in the intestine can lead to gastro-intestinal cancer. More recently it has been found[37] that a diet well supplemented with Vitamin A can lead to resistance to certain tumours, and this information which was initially found in animals, has been successfully transferred to the treatment of human cancer.

Recent experiments on heart and arterial disease have led to the discovery that one of the family of unsaturated fatty acids derived from arachidonic acid,[38] the prostacyclins, may be very useful in treating arterial disease. However, it is again necessary to determine dose response and to look for side-effects of long-term exposure in experimental animals before much more progress can be made in treating humans.[39]

Developmental work on regulation of fertility (both development of new contraceptives and the reversal of apparent infertility) has often been carried out on small animals.[40] However, because the reproductive cycle of small animals is very different from that of humans, it is inevitable that much of the directly relevant clinical work on fertility is carried out on primates. Studies with baboons, marmosets and Rhesus monkeys have led to innovations which are now being tested with controlled groups of humans.[41] These types of experiments cause very little stress to the animals, assuming that failure to conceive is not in itself damaging to the female. Contraceptive drugs being tested do, of course, include male contraceptives but again there is no evidence that the failure to fertilise his partner worries the male since the act of copulation remains identical, and one of the design objectives in such a 'male' pill is that libido should be undiminished. Obviously, one important factor is the determination of long-term effects, if any, of each potential contraceptive,[42] and therefore each pair of experimental animals is maintained on the treatment of choice over a long period and any behavioural, as well as cellular and metabolic, changes noted. It is also important to conclude with the demonstration that the female can become pregnant, i.e. that the contraceptive effect is reversible.

New and improved methods of treatment of well recognised disease may often arise from studies in animals. It is possible, for example, to induce diabetes in rats by feeding them alloxan. In this way some of the less obvious complications found in diabetes were shown to be due directly to withdrawal of insulin rather than to long-term secondary effects of diabetes.[43] Further experiments with silastic implants of hormones in the chemically-induced diabetic rats should relieve the human diabetic of the need to administer daily injections and might overcome the problem that, so far, diabetics are not able to regulate plasma insulin levels in accord with the plasma glucose load at any one time.

In summary, the majority of live animal experiments carried out in the area of applied research are designed to screen drugs which have the potential to combat a particular disease. An experimental animal is found in which the disease runs a similar course to that in humans or the relevant commercially important domestic animal. Colonies of animals are then established so that they have the disease, whether induced or arising spontaneously, in an appropriate stage. Initially, potential drugs may be screened almost at random. Once one drug is found to be partially successful, chemical modifications are made and tested until one is found which is both effective in acceptable doses and has minimal unwanted side-effects. Clearly this process can take several years and may involve a large number of animals.

DRUG SAFETY

All chemicals, whether drugs, cosmetics or food preservatives, which are intended to be in contact with human tissues must first be carefully screened to reduce the risks of side-effects in humans. Tests are carried out over a wide range of concentrations, both within and without the physiological dose range. Since long term exposure might be intended in human treatment, tests must also be carried out over long periods since short-term exposure to a drug may not induce side-effects which could emerge after several months or years useage. Many of these tests are designed, at the moment, to be carried out on selected experimental animals, and only a very small percentage of drugs which reach the test stage are ever subsequently marketed. It is clear, therefore, that testing and launching a new drug is very expensive both in terms of time and experimental animals.[44]

It has already been indicated[45] that it is necessary in the first instance with any new drug to determine the appropriate dose range, including hyper- and hypo- physiological doses, for test. However, even the physiological dose range is not always easy to calculate when analysing tests in animals with a view to potential effects on humans. Before testing a new drug in rats the assumed dose level can be converted from human to rat, or vice versa, in terms of body weight, total surface area or total blood volume. Each reference scale will lead to a different answer. Even the clearance rate of the drug from the bloodstream may, and indeed often does, differ between man and rat. To complicate matters further, the effective plasma concentration of specific drugs may vary from one species to another,[46] and equally some drugs are species significant in their mode of action. For example, Tamoxifen, which is used as an anti-oestrogen in the treatment of human breast cancer, is anti-oestrogenic in rats but a full oestrogen in mice.[47] Testing of potentially marketable drugs must therefore be carried out in more than one species. The case of Thalidomide[48] is a more than adequate reminder that even the most exhaustive testing in experimental animals, including primates, does not completely rule out adverse effects in humans. This adverse effect may not become evident for many years after the drug has been administered. For example, there is, in the United States, an increased incidence of vaginal cancer in young women (about 14 years of age) whose mothers received diethylstilboestrol during pregnancy.[49]

It is now routine to test all new compounds for carcinogenic and mutagenic effects. Mutagenic assays have been devised using bacteria, cultured mammalian cells, yeast, molds, or Drosophila (fruit fly), but none of these satisfactorily replaces tests on live animals.[50] It must be emphasised that these tests must be applied to all new compounds whether they are intended for use as internal or external drugs, cosmetics or food preservatives. For example, carcinogenic nitrosoamines have been found in food on sale in several European countries.[51] Standard tests for carcinogenicity of nitroso compounds using infant mice are available.[52]

One of the areas most open to criticism in the field of live animal experimentation is the testing of new cosmetics. No doubt this is due, at least in part, to the fact that new drugs and food preservatives are seen as essentials whereas cosmetics are considered as luxuries. Nevertheless, cosmetics are used on a very large scale and the cosmetic industry spends a great deal of money on testing new products. However, despite extensive screening, using experimental animals, some women react unfavourably to various cosmetics. This reflects partly the problems of species difference in reaction to particular chemicals,[53] and partly differences in sensitivity between different women to the same chemical. It further raises an important question with regard to the use of live animal tests.

In testing drugs and food preservatives, the experimenter is searching for evidence of unwanted metabolic and/or clinical responses, whereas in testing cosmetics he is principally testing the irritant potential of a given product. Clearly, it is possible to determine the level of inflammatory response in terms of, say, histamine release, but it is much more difficult to establish if an animal feels minor pain. In order to maximise any potential pain response the experimenter may opt to test the product on the most sensitive tissues in the animal, which could involve spraying the product into the animal's eye and which, in the case of a product destined to fail the test, would be extremely painful for the animal concerned. While this type of experiment is highly emotive and often contentious, the experimenter would doubtless argue that the test is essential since future users might also be careless with sprays despite clear warnings to 'avoid all contact with the eyes'.

Until reliable alternatives to animal tests are available, tests of new products on the very sensitive tissues of animals will remain necessary unless human habits, for example in the use of cosmetics, change radically. There are inevitably examples of the experimental use of live animals for which the justification is minimal. Although it is not the object of this chapter to highlight past problems, but rather to review the type of experiments which will continue in the foreseeable future for both legal and scientific reasons, nonetheless it must be mentioned that drug safety experiments can be influenced by the vast amounts of money involved in some industries.[54] For example, experiments were still being carried out on behalf of tobacco firms even after the accumulated evidence that smoking causes lung cancer was virtually irrefutable. Beagles were made to smoke large numbers of cigarettes in an unsuccessful attempt to disprove the direct link between smoking and lung cancer. Related experiments were also carried out in the hope of developing a cigarette which did not cause cancer. Apart from the fact that humans the world over provide pathological data daily which confirm that cigarette smoke causes irreversible damage to lung epithelium, chemical extracts of cigarette smoke can in any event be demonstrated in vitro to be carcinogenic without resort to live animal tests.

In summary, then, the law requires that all new products to be marketed for human use, whether clinically or otherwise, must be tested for potentially harmful side-effects in both the short and the long term.[55] Many of these tests can, at the moment, only be carried out in live animals, and even then differences in species response can lead to problems in humans which were not suspected from the results of the animal tests.

FUTURE PROSPECTS

Those involved in fundamental research and in industrial product assessment would, in general, agree that a good alternative to live animal experimentation would be most useful.[56] Not only would it eliminate any suffering caused to animals, but it would also reduce costs and potentially eliminate the problems which currently arise from species difference. Animal houses would, however, continue to be required since fresh animal tissue would almost certainly still be required as starting material. However, until the time of death, animals would live a carefully monitored and undisturbed life.

The first alternative to live animal experiments is the use of organ culture where tissue is removed from the animal (or patient undergoing surgery) and maintained under conditions as close as possible to those existing in vivo.[57] Unfortunately, tissue does not survive reliably under these conditions and mitochondrial breakdown, for example, can be seen within a few hours even under optimal conditions. Experimental results therefore, tend to reflect relative cell death rates rather than physiological modulations of normal life processes.

The second, and more promising alternative, is the establishment in culture of cells from a particular human tissue,[58] although currently this approach has several drawbacks. In the first place, most human cells do not settle into culture very readily and, if they do, they normally survive only for a relatively short time. Secondly, cells in culture degenerate from the parent cells very rapidly, even to the extent of changing their chromosome number. Thirdly, and perhaps most importantly, different cell types interact with each other in vivo and this interaction is critical to their overall function. For example, epithelial cells from the uterus will grow in culture but, in the intact uterus, they interact closely with stromal cells and their behaviour in the absence of these stromal cells is critically different. It is, however, not yet possible to ensure that the two cell types grow together at the correct relative rates in culture.

Another possible alternative is the use of computer-simulated models. In theory this is an excellent and infinitely flexible approach, but regrettably a computer can only simulate the in vivo situation if it is given all the relevant information, and if this information as to the interaction and interdependence of tissues were already available, many of the experiments which the computer could carry out would automatically became unnecessary. Perhaps, however, when fundamental biological knowledge is adequate, computer simulation will successfully replace live animal experiments.

In many ways, fundamental scientific and medical research requires the continued use of experimental animals, and in the majority of experiments the animal suffers only marginally, if at all. Conditions in animal houses are extremely good and freed animals will often return to their cages of their own accord. However, the use of animals for routine safety testing of new products and, particularly, of new cosmetics is the area in which alternatives can be expected to be adopted in the near future. Indeed, tests for carcinogenicity and mutagenesis are already being carried out routinely in bacterial, yeasts, animal and human cell culture.[59]   The signs are encouraging and as a result of cooperation between the medical/scientific community and the government, there is every chance that unnecessary use of live animals for experiments already is, or shortly will be, virtually eliminated.

R.E. Leake

*Personal work cited has been generously supported by the Cancer Research Campaign and the Medical Research Council.   Many colleagues have contributed useful discussions on this work, particularly Sheila Cowan and John Kusel.

NOTES

1.   Cruelty to Animals Act 1876 ss. 8 and 9.
2.   Galen of Pergamum (2nd. century A.D.) 'Dissection of Experimentation with the Barbary Ape Macaca sylvanus', cited by Valerio, D.A., Macaca mulatta; Management of a Breeding Colony, New York, Academic Press, 1969.
3.   Cited in Hoskins, R.G., The Tides of Life, The Endocrine Glands in Bodily Adjustment, New York, W.W. Norton, 1933.
4.   For discussion, see Lane-Petter, W., and Pearson, A.E.G., The Laboratory Animal - Principles and Practice, London, Academic Press, 1971; see also, Seamer, J., (ed), Safety in Animal Houses, (2nd Ed.), London, Publ. Laboratory Animals Ltd., 1981.
5.   Charles River Digest, published quarterly by the Charles River Breeding Laboratories Inc., Wilmington, Mass., U.S.A.
6.   Goldsworthy, G.J., Robinson, J., Mordue, W., Endocrinology, Glasgow, Blackie, 1981; Archer, J., Animals Under Stress: Studies in Biology No. 108, London, Edward Arnold, 1981.
7.   It is important to note that the brain itself is a collection of neurones.
8.   i.e. removal of ovaries.
9.   i.e. removal of adrenals.
10.   i.e. removal of liver.
11.   See infra, pp. 63-4.
12.   Nalbandov, A.V., Reproductive Physiology of Mammals and Birds, (3rd Ed.), New York, W.H. Freeman, 1976.
13.   i.e. ribonucleic acid.
14.   Eccles, J.C., The Understanding of the Brain, New York, McGraw-Hill, 1973.
15.   i.e. the onset of adult ovarian function.
16.   Johnson, M., and Everitt, B., Essential Reproduction, Oxford, Blackwell Scientific Publications, 1980.
17.   Leake, R.E., and Cowan, S.K., in Agarwal, M.K., (ed), Anti-Hormones, Holland, Elsevier, 1979.
18.   Sridaran, R., and Blake, C.A., 'Effects of long-term adrenalectomy on periovulatory increases in serum gonadotropins and ovulation in rats', J. Endocrinol., 84, 75, (1980); for review of endocrinectomized laboratory rodents, see Charles River Digest, XX, 1, Charles River, Wilmington, Mass., U.S.A.

19. see infra, pp. 59-61.
20. i.e. very high doses.
21. See Leake, R.E., and Cowan, S.K., loc.cit.
22. See infra pp. 63-4.
23. i.e. they are not molecules which can cause cancer.
24. Voller, A., Bidwell, D.E., Bartlett, A., 'Enzyme immunoassays in diagnostic medicine theory and practice', Bulletin World Health Organization, 53, 55, (1976).
25. See, infra p. 6.
26. Kanatsuka, A., et al., 'Effect of hypophysectomy and growth hormone administration on somatostatin content in the rat hypothalamus', Neuroendocrinology, 29, 186, (1979).
27. Fishman, P.H., Bailey, J.M., 'Active Transport of Glucose by Ehrlich Ascites Cells', Nature New Biology, 243, 59, (1973).
28. Smithers, S.R., Terry, R.J., 'Naturally acquired resistance to experimental infections of Schistosoma mansoni in the Rhesus monkey (macaca mulatta)', Parasitology, 55, 701, (1965).
29. id.
30. Smithers, S.R., Terry, R.J., 'Acquired resistance to experimental infections in Schistosoma mansoni in the albino rat', Parasitology, 55, 711, (1965).
31. Sher, A., Smithers, S.R., Mackenzie, P., 'Positive transfer of acquired resistance to Schistosoma mansoni in laboratory mice', Parasitology, 70, 347, (1975).
32. Graham, J.D.P., An Introduction to Human Pharmacology, O.U.P., 1979.
33. Krieger, et al., 'ACTH Beta Lipotropin and related peptides in brain, pituitary and blood', Recent Progress in Hormone Research, 36, 277, (1980).
34. Edwards, D.P., Chamness, G.C., McGuire, W.L., 'Estrogen and progesterone receptors in breast cancer', Biochim. Biophys. Acta, 560, 457, (1979).
35. Furr, B.J.A., et al., 'Tamoxifen', in Goldberg, M.E., (ed), Pharmacological and Biochemical Properties of Drug Substances, Vol. II, New York, A.P., 1980.
36. Jordan, V.C., Dowse, L.J., 'Tamoxifen as an anti tumour agent: effect on oestrogen binding', J. Endocrinol., 68, 297, (1975).
37. 'An association between Vitamin A and cancer', Editorial, Brit. Med. J., 2, 957, (1980)
38. An unsaturated fatty acid essential in the diet and found as an integral part of cell membranes.
39. See infra, p. 61.
40. Cook, D.B., Gibb, I., 'Competitive inhibition by Danazol of ocotradiol binding to rabbit and ovine uterine oestradiol receptor', J. Steroid Biochem., 13, 1325, (1980).
41. Short, R.V., Austin, C.R., (eds), Artificial Control of Reproduction: Book 5 of Reproduction in Animals, Cambridge University Press, 1976.
42. See infra, p. 61.
43. Newsholme, E.A., Start, C., Regulation in metabolism, London, John Wiley, 1973.
44. For further discussion, see infra ch. 11.
45. See infra, p. 60.
46. Leake, R.E., Laing, L., Smith, D.C., in King, R.J.B., (ed), Steroid Receptor Assays in Human Breast Tumours:

        Methodological and Clinical Aspects, Cardiff, Alpha Omega
        Publishing, 1979.
47.   Walpole, A.L., in Hormonal Control of Breast Cancer, I.C.I.
        Pharmaceutical Publication, 1978.
48.   For further discussion, see infra ch. 11.
49.   For further discussion, see infra ch. 11.
50.   IARC Monographs on the evaluation of the carcinogenic risk of
        chemicals to humans, Supplement 2, Long- and short-term
        screening assays for carcinogens: a crtical appraisal, Lyon,
        International Agency for Reasearch on Cancer, 1980.
51.   Walker, E.A., Griciute, L., Castegnaro, M., Borzsonyi, M.,
        N-nitroso compounds: analysis, formation and occurrence,
        Lyon, IARC Scientific Publications, No 31, 1980.
52.   id.
53.   Walpole, op.cit.
54.   For a general discussion of the financial motivation in the
        drug industry, see Klass, A., There's Gold in Them Thar
        Pills, Penguin Books, 1975.
55.   For example, the Committee on Safety of Medicines requires
        animal experimentation to be carried out before granting a
        clinical trial licence. For further discussion, see infra
        chs. 9 and 11.
56.   See generally, Smyth, D.H., Alternatives to Animal
        Experiments, London, Scolar Press, 1978.
57.   Hall, D., Hawkins, S., Laboratory Manual of Cell Biology,
        London, Unibooks, EUP, 1975.
58.   Paul, J. Cell and Tissue Culture, London, Livingstone, 1970.
59.   IARC Monograph, op.cit.

6 Medical Products Liability
A. D. M. Forte

INTRODUCTION

This chapter discusses some aspects of medical product liability, a term which in itself suggests that it is merely a facet or branch of product liability generally. It is important to realise at the outset, however, that the expression 'product liability' does not refer to a discreet branch of law in the United Kingdom.[1]   In Britain the term is used to denote the 'civil liability of manufacturers and others where damage or loss is caused by products which fail to meet the standards claimed expressly or impliedly for them or which are defective or otherwise dangerous'.[2]   The sources of this liability are, however, diffuse, being found in the law of contract, the law of reparation and under statute.   Our law knows nothing of a general product liability code.   Yet there is presently being conducted in this country and in the macro context of Europe, a debate on reforming the present rather piecemeal approach and, indeed, wholesale reform appears to be inevitable.   What this chapter aims to do is to introduce the reader to this debate by looking, in the first instance, at the current state of the law on product liability in general and then examining, in some detail, that law as it applies to defective medical products.   Thereafter some comment will be possible on the general shape of reform of the law of product liability.

One point should, however, be borne in mind.   In the United Kingdom two separate legal systems co-exist.   On occasion the law of Scotland and that of England may overlap to a considerable extent, especially where a statute is the common source of a legal rule.[3] Sometimes, however, the systems differ, perhaps only in terminology but occasionally, more fundamentally, in effect.   It is the common approach which will be discussed here, and by and large the language of broad legal concepts rather than the precise vocabulary of either legal system will be used,[4] although, on occasion, conflation of terms has proved possible.[5]

PRODUCT LIABILITY - THE CURRENT LAW

Liability for injury caused to persons by reason of some defect[6] in a product may occur either in contract, tort/delict, or under statute, and in some cases a combination of any two or more of these may be present.[7]   Each of these will be examined, but it may be useful first to set out a case in which product liability is an issue.

In Donoghue v. Stevenson,[8] Mrs. Donoghue and a friend went into a cafe where the friend purchased for her a bottle of ginger-beer. The drink came in a sealed, opaque bottle.   The cafe proprietor poured half the contents into a glass and Mrs. Donoghue drank this. When her friend poured the remainder into a glass there floated out the decomposed remains of a snail.   As a result Mrs. Donoghue suffered severe gastro-enteritis and the question of liability, which will be discussed at a later stage, then arose.

Contractual Liability.

Contracts are agreements and the rights and liabilities of the parties thereto are expressed in the terms of the particular agreement. In contracts for the sale of goods, however, the law implies certain terms regardless of what the parties actually agree. Thus, for example, the Sale of Goods Act 1979 provides that goods must be of merchantable quality and be reasonably fit for their purpose.[9] If it is proved that they are not then the seller automatically becomes liable to compensate the buyer.

This automatic liability of the seller to make compensation is referred to as 'strict liability'. That is, the seller cannot argue as a defence that he has not been negligent in any way. In other words no fault, no failure to exercise reasonable care on the part of the seller, need be shown. It is enough that he has sold a product which fails to reach the standard required by the law. In Frost v. Aylesbury Dairy Co.,[10] milk contaminated by typhoid germs was sold and it was argued for the sellers that they should not be liable where no amount of care taken by them could have prevented or resulted in the discovery of the defect. This argument was, however, rejected.

However, if a party other than the buyer is injured by the product sold, he may not sue the seller for breach of an implied term of the contract of sale because there is no contractual nexus between seller and third party. The strict liability of the seller is contractual in nature and extends only to the buyer. This is called privity of contract.[11] Put simply, the doctrine of privity means that only the parties to a contract may acquire rights and incur liabilities under it. Accordingly, Mrs. Donoghue could not sue the manufacturer of the lemonade for breach of any contractual duty because no contract existed between them; nor could she sue the cafe proprietor who sold the drink since he sold it to her friend and not to her.

Tortious or Delictual Liability

Mrs. Donoghue did in fact sue the manufacturer for breach of a duty imposed by law, and independently of the parties' agreement, to take reasonable care that his product was free from defects. This is called tortious or delictual liability and depends on proof that the manufacturer failed to take reasonable care for the safety of the ultimate consumer. In other words, it must be shown that the manufacturer was negligent. It was in this type of action that Mrs. Donoghue was successful. Lord Atkin put the matter thus:

.... a manufacturer of products, which he sells in such a form as to show that he intends them to reach the ultimate consumer in the form in which they left him with no reasonable possibility of intermediate examination, and with the knowledge that the absence of reasonable care in the preparation...of the products will result in injury to the consumer's life or property, owes a duty to the consumer to take that reasonable care.[12]

It can be seen that in this judgement there is considerable stress on the word 'reasonable'. The manufacturer's duty is to take 'reasonable care': he must not be negligent. This duty of reasonable care raises several broad questions, viz.,

    (a) To whom is this duty owed?
    (b) What conduct does this duty cover?
    (c) How does one establish liability?

(a) Persons covered by the manufacturer's duty. The duty to take reasonable care extends beyond those who merely purchase goods and includes all persons reasonably foreseeable as being likely to be injured by the product; people who are within the reasonable contemplation of the manufacturer. In Lambert v. Lewis,[13] for example, the occupants of a car were either killed or injured when a defective coupling broke, causing a trailer towed by another vehicle to career across the road and collide with their vehicle. The injured parties and relatives of the deceased were held to have a good claim against the manufacturer of the coupling.

(b) Extent of the duty.[14] This covers defects in design,[15] and in the manufacturing process.[16] It also extends to marketing products whose containers are inadequate,[17] or which fail to give adequate warnings or instructions for use.[18]

(c) Proof of breach of duty. The victim has in theory to show: first, that the product was defective; second, that the defect was due to the manufacturer's negligence; and third, that the defect caused him loss. If he fails to establish any one of these points he has no case. It should be borne in mind, however, that the trend of modern case law indicates a fairly high degree of willingness on the part of the courts to hold that negligence has been established.[19] In Grant v. Australian Knitting Mills,[20] for example, the manufacturer of woollen undergarments was held liable for dermatitis caused by an excess of sulphite in a pair of underpants. It was said that:

> According to the evidence, the method of manufacture was correct: the danger of excess sulphites being left was recognised and was guarded against: the process was intended to be fool proof. If excess sulphites were left in the garment, that could only be because someone was at fault.[21]

Accordingly, the manufacturer may now find himself in something of a dilemma, since the more evidence he can produce to show that his system was adequate or fool proof the more the court is driven to conclude that, if harm results, then one of his employees must have been careless in operating the system.[22] Nor is it necessary for the victim to identify the exact person responsible and specify where he went wrong. Negligence may now be more a matter of inference from the fact that the product is defective when taken in connection with all the known circumstances.[23]. In Donoghue v. Concrete Products (Kirkcaldy)Ltd.,[24] a workman was injured when a concrete slab broke because it was 'green' inside. It was said that there was no need to aver the precise cause of the defect. Negligence was inferred from the fact that such a slab did actually get into circulation, and this was the sort of accident that would not have occurred had the system been working properly. It was therefore no excuse to say that it must have been attributable to an isolated negligent act by an employee. Cases such as these when coupled to the objectivity of the standard of the duty of care and, perhaps, the use of the res ipsa loquitur maxim,[25] have led some writers to comment that there is a 'trend towards something that might also be called "strict liability" within the concept of negligence'.[26]

Statutory Liability.

An example of this is provided by the Consumer Safety Act 1978,[27]

which provides a limited measure of strict liability.[28]   It
authorises the government to make safety regulations in respect of
certain designated products.[29] These regulations may relate to
composition, construction, finish, design, or packing of products[30]
and can require conformity with approved standards.[31]   Moreover,
they can also require that warnings, instructions or other information
be given.[32]   Section 2 provides that it is an offence to supply
goods other than in accordance with any relevant regulations and the
government may also issue 'prohibition notices' and 'warning notices'
concerning goods which are considered to be unsafe,[33] contravention
of these being a criminal offence.[34]

     It can be seen then, that the current pattern of compensation for
those who suffer harm as a consequence of using a defective product is
somewhat fragmented.   In some cases a remedy exists both in contract
and in tort/delict.   In others it exists in either contract or
tort/delict.   The basis of liability is, however, different in each
case.   In contract, it is strict; whereas in tort/delict it is based
on negligence.[35]   This can lead to a situation where victims
suffering identical injuries do not have equal access to
compensation.   The doctrine of privity in particular adds to the
imbalance present in the law as it now stands, and it is generally
considered that reform is needed.

MEDICAL PRODUCT LIABILITY

The purpose of this section is to present some of the problems which
may be posed by medical products and to give a brief account of the
law's response.

Blood and Organs

It has been shown that contractual liability is strict in the sense
that if the product is defective then all that need be proved is that
it caused harm to the purchaser for the seller to be liable.   It does
not matter that the seller was not negligent.   What then would be the
position as regards blood supplied to a patient by transfusion or an
organ transplant, should it turn out that the blood was affected by a
jaundice-producing agent, for example, or that the organ was
diseased?   Could the patient (or his next-of-kin) argue that
liability is strict, or would he have to show negligence?   There is
no British authority on this point, but in the United States the New
York Court of Appeals was faced with just such a problem in Perlmutter
v. Beth David Hospital,[36] where a private patient was given a
transfusion of tainted blood and contracted hepatitis.   The blood was
charged separately to the patient's account.   The court refused to
find that the blood had been sold but said that this was a contract
for the supply of services and contained no implied warranty of
fitness.

     It is difficult to appreciate just why contaminated blood cannot
be described as defective and just as difficult to see why, in a
contract for the supply of medical services, there is not an implied
warranty imposing strict liability.   Such arguments, in fact, serve
only to deflect attention from the real reason for the decision in
Perlmutter's case which was one of policy.
The court made the point that:
     There is today neither a means of detecting the presence of

the jaundice-producing agent in the donor's blood nor a practical method of treating the blood....so that the danger may be eliminated.[37]

In the United Kingdom it is unlikely that the relationship between those who are responsible for the administration and provision of services under the National Health Service, and patients, can be described as being contractual in nature,[38] but in the context of private medicine, there seems to be no reason to regard this as anything but a contract and certainly the relationship between private patient and private clinic or nursing home must be contractual.[39] Here, however, the difficulty lies in the type of contract involved. Is it sale; or is it a contract for services when blood or drugs are supplied to a patient? Ordinarily the distinction between sale, services, and the supply of work and materials does not matter, since in the United Kingdom the courts are generally prepared to imply terms as to quality and fitness in all these cases.[40] It may, however, be the case that the courts would be unlikely to treat the supply of blood as a sale and it would seem that in contracts for medical services they would appear to be reluctant to impose strict liability.[41] The result of this is, that although it is much easier to recover damages where strict liability can be shown, in the case of contaminated blood the victim will probably have to show negligence on the part of his supplier.

Drugs

One usually expects the product liability debate to occur in the context of a qualitative dispute; for example, that the car bought from a garage has a persistent leak,[42] or that one's beer, in addition to its normal ingredients, also contained arsenic.[43] It is, however, possible that a product may be properly produced and yet be intrinsically harmful to the user. Nowhere is this problem more acute than in the case of drugs. In some cases the defect may consist simply in failing to market a drug correctly as, for example, by not providing adequate instructions for use or proper warnings.[44] The real difficulties, however, centre on issues such as the subsequent discovery of harmful side effects, vaccine damage and pre-natal injury.

(a) Harmful effects. It is not entirely unusual to hear periodically that the X Motor Company has recalled all its models for a particular year because a fault in the steering has been discovered. Thus, if a drug is, after marketing, subsequently discovered to have, for example, a teratogenic effect, it might be expected that it too would be withdrawn or that warnings might be given of possible harmful side effects.[45] The question is whether a manufacturer is under any duty to warn the public, and if failure to do so would be accounted negligence on his part for which he would be liable.[46] This may be a very important issue since it will generally be difficult to establish negligence in production,[47] but much easier to demonstrate that he continued to market a drug known to be harmful. The difficulty, however, lies in the fact that at present the existence of such a duty and its extent are debatable issues.[48] Is there, for example, a duty to warn people who have already used the drug, or only potential users?[49] Do individual warnings have to be given or is it enough to give a public warning, and what form should the warning take? Presumably, a drug possessing carcinogenic properties would require a warning to the effect that it should not be used[50];

whereas in the case of more simple side effects it might be enough to warn of that possibility and give recommendations for use.

One further point merits consideration in this context, concerning the giving of instructions or warnings as to the possibility of side effects or, indeed, subsequent warning that a drug has been discovered to be harmful. This would seem especially pertinent in the case of drugs available only on prescription. For example, Eraldin continued to be prescribed after its withdrawal by the manufacturer. The question here must be whether or not it is sufficient to discharge his duty of care for the manufacturer to warn an intermediary between himself and the patient, for example, a doctor. There is no simple answer,[51] although it is _probable_ that, by warning a doctor of the dangers associated with use of a particular drug and providing him with instructions for its use, the manufacturer will have discharged his duty in the case of new or existing (and beneficial) drugs.[52] So far as subseqently discovered side effects are concerned much would depend on their seriousness.

(b) Vaccine Damage[53]   The recent debate in the United Kingdom as to the desirability of vaccination was provoked by allegations that whooping cough vaccine was responsible for causing brain damage in a number of young children.   In 1973 the Association of Parents of Vaccine Damaged Children was formed and pressed for compensation in respect of their children and others who were allegedly damaged in this way.   The question was considered by the Joint Committee on Vaccination and Immunisation,[54] and Jack Ashley M.P. referred the matter to the Ombudsman.[55]   As a result of the increasing debate on this subject, the Vaccine Damage Payments Act was passed in 1979..

In many ways the whooping cough vaccine issue highlights the dilemmas facing the drug industry, the medical profession and the public affected by immunisation.   The vaccine may be properly prepared, the Health Authorities may offer adequate advice to doctors on precautions and contra-indications, and the statistics may demonstrate the overall beneficial effects of vaccination.   Yet in some cases the consequences for an individual child may be terrible.

At common law the likelihood of obtaining compensation would probably be slight and would depend on proof of negligence either against doctors, manufacturers or government agencies.   It would be difficult to establish that a doctor administering a vaccine in accordance with official guidance and observing usual medical practice should be regarded as negligent[56] and manufacturers could probably escape liability by showing that the state of scientific knowledge did not indicate that the vaccine should not have been made or that it had hidden defects.[57]   Compensation, therefore, remains a problem since there is in the United Kingdom no strict liability regime for drugs comparable to that found in some parts of the United States.[58]

The Pearson Commission considered the question of vaccine damage and their main recommendations may be summarised as follows:

(1) that since vaccination is recommended by the state, the public authorities should be strictly liable in tort/delict[59]; and,

(2) that children suffering apparent vaccine damage should be entitled to a weekly benefit paid as a supplement to child benefit.[60]

The Vaccine Damage Payments Act 1979[61] now governs cases of death or severe disablement which on a balance of probabilities were caused by vaccination against certain prescribed diseases, including whooping cough, poliomyelitis and diphtheria.[62]   Assuming that a causal link can be shown and that disablement is at least eighty per

cent, a lump sum of £10,000 is payable by way of compensation.[63]
It may be observed that, by current levels of compensation, £10,000 is
not an over-generous sum, which is tacitly acknowledged by the fact
that the Act expressly permits a civil action for damages to be
raised.[64]   As has been pointed out, however, such an action being
dependent upon proof of negligence will have little hope of
success.[65]

(c) Ante-natal injuries[66]   Ante-natal injuries were defined by the
Pearson Commission as 'an acquired change or event, before or after
conception, which leads to any derangement in the developing tissues
or organs of the embryo or foetus, or any other event which may harm
the fully developed foetus before birth'.[67]   They added that they
would extend this to include perinatal injury.[68]
     Concern about drug related causes of such injuries came into
prominence over the use of Thalidomide by pregnant women to control
hyperemesis gravidarum,[69] although in this case the general question
as to the nature and extent of liability for ante-natal injury was
never answered.[70]   Both the Law Commission and the Scottish Law
Commission prepared reports on the topic.[71]   Of the two the
Scottish Law Commission was the more positive, stating that:
       although there is no express Scottish decision on the point,
       a right to reparation would, on existing principles, be
       accorded by Scots Law to a child for harm wrongfully
       occasioned to it while in its mother's womb, provided that it
       was born alive.[72]
On the matter of pre-conception injury they again thought that Scots
Law would provide a remedy based on existing principles.[73]   The Law
Commission were less sanguine and thought it highly probable that the
common law of England would provide a remedy[74] and recommended,
therefore, that legislation was needed for the avoidance of doubt.
Certainly decisions such as that of the Supreme Court of Victoria in
Watt v. Rama,[75] or of an Ontario court in Duval v. Seguin,[76]
indicated that a right to compensation would exist, at least under
these legal systems.
     The Congenital Disabilities (Civil Liability) Act 1976 now governs
the position in England (but not in Scotland) and what follows is a
short summary of the scope of liability under that Act and probably at
common law also.   In the first instance the child must be 'born
disabled'.[77]   This emphasis on being born alive contemplates what
the American courts would call 'wrongful life' claims.   In Gleitman
v. Cosgrove,[78] for example, a pregnant woman told her doctor that
she had suffered an attack of rubella and was told that the child
would not be endangered, the same assurance being repeated
subsequently.   In fact the child was born both physically and
mentally handicapped, and the Supreme Court of the State of New Jersey
held that the infant plaintiff had no ground of action, since:
       The infant plaintiff is ....required to say not that he
       should have been born without defects but that he should not
       have been born at all.....This court cannot weigh the value
       of life with impairments against the non-existence of life
       itself.   By asserting that he should not have been born, the
       infant plaintiff makes it logically impossible for a court to
       measure his alleged damages because of the impossibility of
       making the comparison required by compensatory remedies.[79]
It may confidently be supposed that at common law such a claim would
also fail in both England and Scotland.

73

Secondly, there can be liability for harm caused prior to conception,[80] but the child's claim will fail if, at that time, the parents knew of and accepted the risk that the child might be born damaged.[81]

Thirdly, the Act stipulates that the child must not simply be born alive, but enjoy 'a life separate from its mother'.[82] Thus a child which is still-born has no claim, although its parents may well have.   In White v. Yupp,[83] such a claim was permitted but it seems most unlikely that liability would exist under the common law of either England or Scotland.

It should be noted that a manufacturer may be able to escape liability completely by demonstrating that the injured party voluntarily accepted the risk of injury.   This defence is expressed in the maxim volenti non fit injuria[84] which does not depend solely on a mere knowledge of the risk of injury.[85]   It must be shown that the victim either expressly or impliedly consented 'to waive any claim for injury that might befall him due to the lack of reasonable care by the defendant'.[86]   The victim must also be volens and sciens.   It has already been seen that under the Congenital Disabilities (Civil Liability) Act 1976 voluntary assumption of risk by the mother is a defence.   There is, in general, a risk with most drugs that side-effects will result which may be simply unpleasant in some cases, and highly dangerous in others,[87] and if the patient is warned of the risk inherent in a particular drug, it may be argued that by proceeding with the treatment he has shown that he is willing to take the risk of injury.

Voluntary assumption of risk of injury is a complete defence. Contributory negligence, on the other hand, is not; rather it is an argument which shows that both parties were, in some degree, at fault.   The effect of such a partial defence is to justify a reduction in the amount of damages awarded, 'to such an extent as the court thinks just and equitable having regard to the claimant's share in the responsibility for the damage'.[88]   Thus, failure to follow instructions on how to use a product and, indeed, failure generally to take reasonable care for his own safety, may mean that the amount of damages awarded will be reduced.[89]

REFORMS

Product Liability Generally

There are a number of recent proposals for reform of the law relating to product liability in Europe generally.   In Britain reforms have been proposed by both Law Commissions[90] and also by the Pearson Commission.[91]   There are also European proposals which, if implemented, would affect the United Kingdom, for example, the Strasbourg Convention,[92] which is a Council of Europe proposal, and an E.E.C. proposed Directive on liability for defective products.[93]   These proposals do not by any means adopt a uniform approach although it is possible to identify some common threads running through all of them.   In the first place, so far as death and personal injury are concerned, they all contemplate strict liability in respect of commercial products.   This would mean that a victim would have to prove (1) that he was injured; (2) that the product was defective; (3) that his injury was caused by the defective product; and (4) that the defender had either produced the product or was a party under the same liability as the actual producer.

Secondly, all the schemes contemplate not only liability on the part of the producer of the finished product but also, in some circumstances, on component producers, distributors or importers.[94]

Thirdly, save for the European proposals, there seems to be broad support for a system which does not contemplate financial limitation of liability.

Medical Products

Because the Pearson Commission[95] made clear in some detail their proposals for reform in this area, and since these reflect the 'common threads' already referred to, it is possible to give a brief account of the ways in which reform in general may affect the issue of medical product liability.

In relation to the supply of blood and organs, the Pearson Commission have recommended that these be treated as products and that the authorities responsible for their distribution are to be regarded as producers.[96] Where such products are defective the producer, it is suggested, ought to be made strictly liable, without financial limit, for death or personal injury caused by them.[97]

On the matter of liability for drugs in general both the Pearson Commission and the Law Commissions acknowledged the special problems involved.[98] In particular, consideration was given to permitting a defence based on the 'state of the art', thereby taking notice of the existence of the risks necessarily inherent in the production of many, if not all, drugs.[99] This suggestion was ultimately rejected on an evaluation of policy considerations. It may be said, for example, that the producer of defective drugs creates the risk of harm; that he is best placed to exercise effective quality control and to insure against the possibility of having to meet claims.[100] It is interesting to note, however, that in this respect the Scottish Law Commission[101] has been a little less sanguine than its English counterpart, pointing to recent German legislation and suggesting that there should perhaps be strict liability only where the injury is caused either by the defective production of the drug or has its source in its development, thereby excluding minor side effects.[102]

On the issue of vaccine damage the recommendation favoured strict liability for severe damage suffered as a result of vaccination recommended in the interests of the community,[103] and this has in fact led to the passing of the Vaccine Damage Payments Act 1979.

In the area of ante-natal injury, the present law (in both its statutory and its common law form) is based on negligence.[104] The Pearson Commission expressed grave misgivings about this but nonetheless made their recommendations within the framework of liability for negligence; although, in view of the difficulties inherent in a negligence action in this field, this may be a little surprising.

CONCLUSION

It can be seen, therefore, that there are often considerable difficulties associated with the compensation of victims injured by defective medical products. At present there exists an imbalance between those remedies which are contractual and those which are tortious/delictual. The former, by removing the issue of negligence from the liability equation, make it easier to obtain compensation. The latter, however, being dependent on establishing fault, involve difficult problems of proving both fault and causation. In the field of medical product liability in particular, the tort/delict action may be more of an illusion than a real possibility.

Strict liability on the other hand represents a compensation regime of not inconsiderable attraction not only to victims or potential victims of defective products but also to law reformers[105] judges[106] and academics.[107] There are a number of reasons why this is so. In the first place there is the moral argument that loss should be borne by those who create the risk in putting the product on the market. Secondly, on grounds of economic equity, it might be argued that the mass producer of medical products is able to underwrite the loss or possibility of loss caused by having to pay compensation, by means of his own pricing policy. Furthermore, manufacturers are better placed to insure against the risk of loss than is the consumer and this would also doubtless be reflected in the price of the product.[108] Thirdly, at a practical level, it could be suggested convincingly that liability should be placed on the shoulders of those best in a position to influence the quality and safety of the product, i.e. the manufacturer. As a beneficial off-spin this system of liability would produce a greater consciousness of the issue of safety. Strict liability underlies all the proposals for reform in this area and, as has been observed, it seems to have the advantage of 'being in step with the spirit of the age which generally favours compensating the victims of misfortunes'.[109]

Some reform can, then, be anticipated in the future, although it is difficult to estimate the time-scale for such change. In regard to the E.E.C. proposed draft Directive, for example, a prolonged debate seems likely, especially in view of the British Government's rejection of the 'state of the art' defence. It may be observed that in view of the fact that the whole thrust of the Directive and, for that matter, of the other reform proposals, is towards the imposition of strict liability on manufacturers, to introduce a defence based on development risks would substantially erode that objective. For the present, however, the current mixed, and perhaps unsatisfactory, system of compensation will continue.

A.D.M. Forte

NOTES

1. The term 'product liability' is of American provenance. See, generally, Miller and Lovell, Product Liability London, Butterworths, 1977, cap. 1.
2. Miller and Lovell, op.cit., 1. Donoghue v. Concrete Products (Kirkcaldy) Ltd. 1976 S.L.T. 58.
3. See, e.g. the Sale of Goods Act 1979. Even here there can be problems: see Millars of Falkirk Ltd. v. Turpie, 1976 S.L.T.(Notes) 66.
4. e.g. 'negligence' in preference to delict (Scottish) or tort (English). For an account of the distinction between the English law of torts and the Scottish Law of delict see Walker, The Law of Delict in Scotland, Edinburgh, W.Green

& Son, 1966, Vol, 1, at p. 30.

5. e.g. 'tort/delict' to denote the English tort of negligence and the Scottish delict.

6. Not an easy term to define: see Liability for Defective Products (1977) Law Com. No. 82; Scot. Law Com. No. 45, Cmnd. 6831, paras. 45-49; Royal Commission on Civil Liability and Compensation for Personal Injury Cmnd. 7054-1/1978 para. 137. This Report is hereinafter referred to as the Pearson Commission.

7. Thus the passenger injured in an accident while travelling by bus may claim reparation against the bus company either ex contractu, for breach of an implied contract term to carry him safely, or ex delicto for breach of a duty imposed by the general law not to injure him.

8. 1932. S.C.(H.L.) 31; [1932] A.C. 562.

9. S.14(2), (3). See also s.12 (title); s.13(description); and s. 15 (sample). In 'consumer contracts' these terms cannot be excluded by agreement: see the Unfair Contract Terms Act 1977, ss. 6 and 20.

10. [1905] 1 K.B. 608. See also Grant v. Australian Knitting Mills Ltd. [1936] A.C. 85; Ashington Piggeries Ltd. v. Christopher Hill Ltd. [1972] A.C. 441.

11. Scots Law acknowledges a jus quaesitum tertio which may in certain circumstances permit a third party to sue where it can be shown that the contract was made for his benefit: see Walker, The Law of Contracts and Related Obligations in Scotland, London, Butterworths, 1979 paras. 29.11-17. There is no such general principle in English Law as was pointed out by the House of Lords in Woodar Investment Development Ltd. v. Wimpey Constructions U.K. Ltd. [1980] 1 All E.R. 571. See also Forte, 'Does Unjustified Rescission Amount to Repudiation?' (1981) 26 J. Law Soc. Scot. 32. In the United States the privity doctrine is relaxed by art. 2-318 of the Uniform Commercial Code and s.402A of the Restatement of Torts (2nd ed.).

12. 1932 S.C. (H.L.) 31 at p. 57; 1932 A.C. 562 at p. 599.

13. [1980] 1 All E.R. 978. See also Donoghue v. Stevenson supra, per Lord Atkin at p. 44 and at p. 580.

14. See, generally Miller and Lovell, op.cit., caps 10-12; Miller, Product Liability and Safety Encyclopaedia, London, Butterworths, Part III, paras. 21-34.

15. Lambert v. Lewis , supra; Wyngrave's Exrx v. Scottish Omnibuses Ltd 1966 S.C.(H.L.) 47. As to the criminal law aspects of this, see the Consumer Protection Act 1961, s. 3(2). As one might expect in the area of design, American law appears to be more developed than our own.

16. e.g. Donoghue v. Stevenson, supra. (Snail in bottle of ginger beer): Grant v. Australian Knitting Mills Ltd. supra. (excess sulphite in underpants).

17. e.g. Hill v. James Crowe(Cases)Ltd. [1978] 1 All E.R. 812 (packing case).

18. e.g. Vacwell Engineering Co., Ltd. v. B.D.H. Chemicals Ltd. [1971] 1 Q.B. 88; Fisher v. Harrods Ltd. [1966] 1 Lloyd's Rep. 500.

19. See, generally, Millner, Negligence in Modern Law, London, Butterworths, 1966); Williams and Hepple, Foundations of

the Law of Tort, London, Butterworths, 1976; Atiyah, Accidents, Compensation and the Law, (3rd ed.), London, Weidenfeld and Nicolson, 1980.

20. supra.
21. Lord Wright at p. 101.
22. Grant v. Australian Knitting Mills Ltd., supra.
23. Grant v. Australian Knitting Mills Ltd., supra; Donoghue v. Concrete Products(Kirkcaldy)Ltd., supra.
24. supra.
25. Broadly this means that the facts speak for themselves, i.e. that liability is in no doubt.
26. Williams and Hepple, op.cit., 96.
27. Which will gradually replace the Consumer Protection Act 1961. The 1978 Act has been in force since Nov.1, 1978.
28. S.6(1).
29. ss. 1, 9(4). Excluded from the purview of the Act are 'medicinal products' as defined by the Medicines Act 1968, s.130 and 'controlled drugs' as defined by the Misuse of Drugs Act 1971, s. 2(1)(a).
30. S.1(2)(a).
31. S.1(2)(b).
32. S.1(2)(g).
33. S.3(1)(a)-(c).
34. S.3(3).
35. That is not to say that strict liability is not found in the tort/delict field. English law can speak of torts of strict liability and the concept of strict liability is equally well-known to Scots Law, e.g. nuisance, or liability with regard to animals ferae naturae. However, in the field of product liability, strict or no-fault liability has, at present, no place in the tort/delict remedy. See, generally, Atiyah, op.cit., at pp. 170-172.
36. 123 N.E. 2nd 792 (N.Y. 1954).
37. ibid., at p. 795.
38. Pearson Commission, para. 1313.
39. id.
40. This does not mean that in contracts for work and materials or for services that the Sale of Goods Act 1979 s.14(2)(3) applies, but rather that in these contracts 'the larger the element of supply of particular goods in the contract, the closer should be the similarity of warranties to be implied with those arising on a sale'. see Young and Marten Ltd. v. McManus Childs Ltd. [1969] A.C. 454 at pp. 476-477 per Lord Wilberforce. In Lockett v. A. & M. Charles Ltd. [1938] 4 All E.R. 170 the provision of food in a restaurant was treated as sale. In Watson v. Buckley, Osborne, Garrett & Co., Ltd. [1940] 1 All E.R. 174 (use of a dye by hairdresser) it was said (at p. 180, per Stable J.) that an implied term as to merchantability was 'no less than it would be in the case of the sale of goods simply'. This was a contract for the supply of services. The law on implied terms in contracts other than for sale of goods and hire purchase may be changed in the near future so as to extend these statutorily implied terms to other similar contracts: see Implied Terms in Contracts for the Supply of Goods (1979) Law Com. No. 95.
41. See Perlmutter v. Beth David Hospital, supra.: Magrine

v. <u>Krasnica</u>, 241A. 2d 637 (N.J. 1968) - dealing with a
hypodermic needle which broke in the patient's mouth. cf.
Dodd v. <u>Wilson</u> [1946] 1 All E.R. 691.

42. <u>Millars of Falkirk Ltd.</u>, supra.

43. <u>Wren</u> v. <u>Holt</u> [1903] 1 K.B. 610.

44. See, for example, <u>Fisher</u> v. <u>Harrods Ltd.</u>, supra.
(cleaning fluid); <u>Kershaw</u> v. <u>Sterling Drug Inc.</u> 415F 2d
1009 (5th Cir., 1969), (harmful effect of chloroquine
phosphate on vision); <u>Stevens</u> v. <u>Parke, Davis and Co.</u>
107 Cal. Rptr. 45 (Cal.Sup.Ct.1973), (danger of plastic
anaemia inherent in chloromycetin).

45. Eraldin, for example, was withdrawn by the manufacturer
because of its harmful side effects. See Pearson Commission,
para. 1253.

46. See <u>Wright</u> v. <u>Dunlop Rubber Co., Ltd.</u> [1972] 13 K.I.R. 255.
The extent of the duty to warn laid down in this case is
unclear: see Miller and Lovell, op.cit., at p. 248.   The
American cases, e.g. <u>Comstock</u> v. <u>General Motors Corprn.</u>
99 N.W. 2d. 627, 78 A.L.R. 2d 449 (Mich. 1961), recognise a
duty to warn <u>past</u> as well as potential users.

47. In the case of Thalidomide, for example, the Distillers
Company always denied negligence and the Pearson Commission
accepted that 'it is only in the rarest of cases that even
the physical cause of congenital deformity can be ascertained,
and even if that is ascertainable the plaintiff in an action
of tort would still have to prove that the deformity was
caused by fault, usually negligence, on the part of the
defendent'. See para. 1432. See also Tizard, 'Birth
Injury', Pearson Commission Report, Annex 12; Renwick, 'The
Biology of Human Prenatally Determined Injury', ibid.,
Annex 13.

48. Note the power to issue warning notices under the Consumer
Safety Act 1978; but that Act does not cover medicines and
drugs and non-compliance with such notice does not give rise
to civil liability.   See notes 29-34 supra.

49. See note 46 supra.

50. <u>Wright</u> v. <u>Dunlop Rubber Co., Ltd.</u>, supra.

51. The difficulty started with <u>Donoghue</u> v. <u>Stevenson</u>, supra,
where Lord Atkin talked about the reasonable
possibility of intermediate examination interrupting the
chain of causation.   This is well explained in Miller and
Lovell, op.cit., at pp. 284-290.   In <u>Waltons</u> v. <u>British
Leyland U.K. and Others</u> (1978, unreported), B.L. were found
to be negligent in failing to recall cars once a fault had
been discovered.   They had warned their own dealers, but not
the general public.

52. <u>Toole</u> v. <u>Richardson-Merrell</u>, 60 Cal. Rptr. 398 (Cal.1967)
<u>Holmes</u> v. <u>Ashford</u> [1950] 2 All E.R. 76.

53. See the Pearson Commission, cap. 25.   See also, infra pp.
35-7.

54. Review of the Evidence on Whooping Cough Vaccination (1977)
H.M.S.O.

55. Whooping Cough Vaccination (H.C. 571).

56. <u>Hunter</u> v. <u>Hanley</u>, 1955 S.C. 200.

57. This is known as the 'state of the art' defence and is
closely linked to the issue of development risks: see
<u>Roe</u> v. <u>Ministry of Health</u> [1954] 2 Q.B. 66.

58.   Pearson Commission, para. 1405.
59.   ibid., para. 1413.
60.   ibid., para. 1531.
61.   For an account of this Act and its background see Gamble,
        A.J., 'Vaccine Damage Payments Act' (1979) 36 Scolag Bull.
        136.   See also, Teff, 'Compensating Vaccine Damaged Children'
        (1977) 127 N.L.J. 904.   For a highly critical view of the
        approach to compensating vaccine-damaged children see Atiyah,
        op.cit., at pp. 173-174.
62.   1979 Act s.1.
63.   ibid., s. 1(2).
64.   ibid., s.6(4).
65.   See Gamble, loc. cit., at p. 137.
66.   See infra, ch. 11.
67.   See the Pearson Commission, cap. 26. See Also Lovell and
        Griffith-Jones, 'The Sins of the Fathers: tort liability for
        pre-natal injuries', (1974) 90 L.Q.R. 531.
68.   ibid. para. 1453.
69.   ibid.
70.   S. v. Distillers Co.(Biochemicals) Ltd.. [1969] 1 All E.R.
        1412 (question of settlement); Distillers Co.(Biochemicals)
        Ltd. v. Thompson [1971] 1 All E.R. 694(jurisdiction).
71.   Report on Injuries to Unborn Children, Law Com. No. 60,
        Cmnd. 5709/1974; Liability for Ante-Natal Injury, Scot. Law
        Com. No. 30, Cmnd. 5371/1973.   See also Fletcher,
        'Litigation by Disabled Children' (1975) 125 N.L.J. 476.
72.   Scot. Law Com. No. 30, para. 19.
73.   ibid., para. 21.
74.   Law Com. No. 60, para. 8.
75.   [1972] V.R. 353.
76.   [1972] 26 D.L.R. (3d) 418.
77.   1976 Act, s.1 (1).
78.   49 N.J. 22, 227 A.2d. 689 (1967).
79.   per Proctor J., at p. 692.
80.   1976 Act, s. 1(4). See, for example, Jorgensen v. Meade
        Johnson Laboratories Inc. 483F 2d 237 (10th Cir., 1973).
        This case dealt with the liability of the manufacturer of
        birth control pills alleged to have had a teratogenic effect
        on the child a woman had conceived after she had ceased taking
        the pills.
81.   This is certainly not the common law of Scotland. If the
        parents voluntarily accept the risk of injury the law could
        apply the maxim volenti non fit injuria and deny them a
        claim.   The manufacturer, however, could not plead the
        parents' acceptance of the risk against the injured child
        who had not himself done anything of the sort.   The Pearson
        Commission (para. 1483) recommended bringing Scots Law into
        line with the rest of the United Kingdom on this matter.   It
        is a matter of opinion whether this would be a wise decision.
82.   1976 Act, s.4(2).
83.   458 P. 2d 617 (Nev. 1969).
84.   For further discussion of the application of this defence, see
        infra, ch. 8.
85.   See, for example, Nettleship v. Weston [1971] 3 All E.R. 581.
86.   ibid., at p. 587 per Lord Denning M.R.   See also McCaig v.
        Langan 1964 S.L.T. 121
87.   e.g. the drug M.E.R./29, though it reduced cholesterol in the

blood, was found to produce cataracts on the user's eyes. See Prosser, Torts, (4th. Ed.), St. Paul, Minn., West Publishing Co., 1971, at pp.658-662.

88. Law Reform (Contributory Negligence) Act 1945, s.1(1).
89. See generally Vacwell Engineering v. B.D.H. Chemicals, supra. Dallison v. Sears, Roebuck & Co. 313 F 2d. 343 (10th. Cir., 1962).
90. See note 6, supra.
91. ibid.
92. The European Convention on Products Liability in regard to personal injury and death. See Miller, op.cit. V, 173-194.
93. Proposal for a Council Directive relating to the approximation of the laws, regulations and administrative provisions of the Member States concerning liability for defective products. See Miller, op.cit. V, 208-250.
94. So-called 'channelling of liability'. See, for example, Pearson Commission, paras. 1238-1250; Strasbourg Convention Arts. 2,3; proposed E.E.C. Directive, arts. 2.
95. Caps. 22, 25, 26.
96. Para. 1276.
97. Paras. 1236, 1264. The Pearson Commission would not allow a defence of official certification. So compliance with standards laid down by screening bodies such as the Committee on Safety of Medicines would not be a good argument. See the Medicines Act 1968, ss. 2,4.
98. Pearson Commission, paras. 1258-1259; 1273-75; Law Com. No. 82, Scot. Law Com. No. 45, paras. 55-65.
99. For further discussion, see infra, ch. 9.
100. Law Com. No. 82, Scot. Law Com. No. 45, para. 61.
101. ibid., paras. 62-65.
102. Gesetz zur Neordnung des Arzneimittelrechts, 1976 Bundesgesetzblatt 1976, 2445.
103. Pearson Commission, para. 1413.
104. It would be a mistake to think, as the Pearson Commission thought many people might (para. 1438), that the Congenital Disabilities (Civil Liability) Act 1976 gives an automatic right to compensation. Proof of negligence underpins the legislation.
105. See, for example, Law Comm. No. 82; Scott. Law Comm. No. 45, paras. 38-42. See also Pearson Commission, passim.
106. MacKenna, J., 'No Fault Liability', (1974) 25 N.I.L.Q. 373
107. Atiyah, op.cit.; Atiyah, 'No Fault Compensation: A Question That Will Not Go Away' (1980) 54 Tul.L.Rev. 271; Ison, 'The Politics of Reform in Personal Injury Compensation' (1977) 27 U.T.L.J. 385.
108. See generally, Atiyah, op.cit., passim.
109. Miller and Lovell, op.cit., at p. 357.

7 Professional Liability
A. J. Gamble

The purpose of this chapter is to outline and discuss the enforcement of legal responsibility, especially for negligence, in respect of members of the medical and legal professions, by civil action in the ordinary courts.

THE CONCEPT OF NEGLIGENCE.

Before turning to a detailed statment of the law in regard to professional negligence, it is useful to outline briefly the main constituents of the legal concept of negligence.[1]   It is important to note that it forms part of the body of law known as delict in Scotland and tort in England and other English-based legal systems, and deals with an obligation imposed by law to compensate for loss or injury unlawfully caused.

Negligence as it is understood in modern English and Scots law essentially consists of the following elements:-

(a)   that a duty of care exists between A and B.   Whether this is so or not depends on the question of 'proximity', i.e., is B one whom A would reasonably foresee as being injured by the effect of his actions?[2]

(b)   that the duty of care has been broken by A's conduct. Normally the standard imposed is that of reasonable care.   This is designed to be 'objective' in that it eliminates the personal factor.[3]   Thus, although this system of compensation for injury is often called a 'fault system', it is hardly based, nowadays at least, on actual moral blame.[4]

(c)   that this breach has caused the injury or loss sustained by B.   To use the legal expressions, there must be a conjunction of damnum (i.e. loss) and injuria (i.e. a legally recognised wrong).[5] Difficult questions of causation can arise at this point.[6]

In the case of professional negligence, there is rarely any question as to a) supra.   Issues relating to b) and c) are the ones causing controversy and dispute.   It has increasingly been recognised by the courts that in applying these criteria, especially in new areas where negligence liability has not before been imposed, essentially what is involved is a matter of legal policy.[7]   Thus the application of negligence by means of formulae like 'reasonable care', 'reasonable foreseeability' and so on indicate that what is at issue is a legal standard.   However 'objective' it may be said to be vis-a-vis the parties involved and especially vis-a-vis the alleged perpetrator of the negligent act, it is highly 'subjective' in that ultimately these questions of 'reasonableness' are decided as policy questions by the judges.

Increasingly, despite the use of the formula of 'fault' - or to use the older Scots expression, culpa - it is being recognised that in extending the categories of negligence, the court is really deciding who should bear the risk of a particular loss.[8]   As has sometimes been said, the courts are essentially involved in working out 'the calculus of risk',[9] and the growth of insurance cover has obviously played a part here.

In recent years there has been a general tendency to extend the categories of negligence liability to situations previously thought to be excluded from its ambit, e.g. liability for mis-statement,[10] liability for architects certifying building work,[11] liability of housing inspectors,[12] and of accountants valuing shares.[13] This has had important consequences for the negligence liability of the legal profession, as will be noted, and is a vitally important background to the law of professional negligence in general.

The one respect in which the courts appear to be resisting extensions of negligence liability is in the area of pure economic loss unconnected with physical damage, at least in cases where such damage is also caused.[14] It seems, however, that this cannot apply in situations where economic loss is the very species of loss or damage sustained by the person alleging negligence.[15]

Concurrent with the expansion of negligence liability there has been a trend of opinion calling attention to the inequities and uncertainties which the negligence action can produce in regard to compensation for personal injuries.[16] This aspect is particularly relevant to actions raised in respect of medical negligence. The suggestion has been made that if negligence liability were replaced by some form of comprehensive state insurance scheme, this would be both a more efficient and a more equitable social policy towards disabled people, as for example in the scheme introduced in New Zealand in 1974. Dissatisfaction with the negligence oriented system of compensation in general, and especially as it operated in the case of the victims of the drug Thalidomide,[17] led to the appointment of the Royal Commission on Civil Liability and Compensation for Personal Injury (the Pearson Commission) reporting in 1978.[18] The Pearson Report is felt by many to be a timid and conservative document since it offered no radical change in the system[19] and in any event its proposals have largely been shelved.[20]

CONTRACTUAL LIABILITY.

In addition to liability imposed by the general law, obligations can arise by means of contracts, i.e., legally recognised and enforced agreements.[21] Professional persons are usually engaged on a contract of services and such contracts also impose duties of care and skill by means of implied terms. The content of the duty imposed is now seen as being almost identical to that imposed ex lege, i.e., reasonable care, but the relationship of the contractual to the tortious/delictual duties has been an important factor in the development of the law of professional negligence especially in respect of the legal profession. Due to the introduction of the National Health Service in the U.K. this issue has not arisen so sharply in regard to medical negligence. Indeed, as long ago as 1914 some of the potential problems were solved in this area by Scots Law, following earlier English authority.[22] The position now seems to be that delictual or tortious liability is independent of, but can in some cases exist concurrently with, contractual liability and in the latter situation it seems the party suing can elect on which ground to proceed. This situation also exists in other areas of the law, e.g., carriers of goods or passenger and also in respect of defective products.[23]

LIABILITY FOR THE NEGLIGENCE OF LAWYERS

It is essential to the understanding of this branch of law to note
that there is a clear distinction in professional status between
members of the Bar (barristers in England and advocates in Scotland)
often referred to as counsel, and solicitors (formerly known in
Scotland as law Agents).[24]   Members of the Bar have exclusive right
of audience in the superior civil and criminal courts and are a
distinct profession from solicitors.   In addition to court
appearances, they are often consulted on legal issues with a view to
their rendering written 'opinions' whether or not litigation is in
prospect.   It is important to stress that barristers or advocates
cannot be directly approached or instructed on professional matters by
members of the public or corporate clients.   They are instructed by
solicitors as necessary intermediaries for clients.   Thus although no
contractual relationship exists between counsel and solicitor or
counsel and client (with the consequence that counsel cannot sue for
their fees which are thus strictly honoraria), by contrast solicitors
were, and are, seen as being bound to clients by a contract of agency.

This dichotomy appears clearly to be behind the decision in
Swinfen v. Lord Chelmsford in 1860,[25] where an attempt was made to
argue that counsel was liable for an alleged wrongful settling of an
action.   It was held that such a claim could not be pursued in the
absence of malice or fraud and that counsel were not liable for errors
of fact or law, thus effectively creating an immunity from negligence
liability for them.   This immunity was said to rest on several
grounds, for example, the duties owed by counsel to court and public
as well as to his client, the discretion necessarily entrusted to
counsel in the conduct of litigation and especially the absence of a
contractual relationship with the client.   This justification applied
to all of counsel's work, not merely litigation, and was the leading
support for the lack of negligence liability in their respect.   In
the Scottish case of Batchelor v. Pattison and Mackersky in 1876,[26]
the rule of immunity was also accepted with the absence of a
contractual tie figuring prominently in its justification.

The traditional legal response then, was that the absence of
contract led to a complete immunity from negligence liability for
counsel.   This preceded and antedated the development of negligence
generally which has been outlined supra.   It is difficult to justify
this response logically and it can only be explained by the very
rudimentary concepts of negligence then existing.   Paradoxically the
law also formerly held to the position that a contractual liability to
A excluded delictual liability to B and probably also to A,[27] while
simultaneously proclaiming that the absence of contractual liability
excluded any liability at all.

The situation comes into sharper focus when one considers that
solicitors or law agents were held liable for breaches of duties of
care.   This rested however on the contract of agency and thus, for
example, in the case of Hart v. Frame & Co.[28] law agents were held
liable on this basis for lack of the usual care and diligence of
members of that profession.[29]   It was the existence of the agency
relationship by contract which was seen to make the crucial
difference, in that in these terms a solicitor could be liable even in
respect of advocacy in those courts where he has rights of
audience.[30]

The present law, which has arisen largely from two important
decisions of the House of Lords in English appeals, must be seen in

context as being the necessary consequence and application of the important general development of negligence already discussed. The former law rested on foundations no longer tenable. The present law is really a compromise between the traditional view and the logical implications of the vast increase in negligence liability. This compromise rests ultimately on a view of public policy explicitly articulated in these cases and considered by the judges to prevail over a complete application of full negligence liability. As will be observed, contrary to prevailing trends, there remains a measure of immunity for certain acts of the legal profession, which does not apparently exist for the medical profession. Nevertheless, there are certain parallels at a very broad level between medical and legal negligence, so that, although no formal immunity exists in medical cases, considerations of policy have repeatedly been invoked not to extend but rather to limit the ambit of their negligence liability.

The two important cases referred to supra as shaping the development of the law of lawyers negligence are Rondel v. Worsley,[31] and Saif Ali v. Sydney Mitchell & Co.[32] In a sense, however, just as important is the decision in respect of negligent mis-statement in Hedley Byrne Ltd. v. Heller and Partners.[33] It seems that it was in fact after that decision that counsel commenced carrying professional indemnity insurance cover. Its effect was to destroy any basis for immunity in the absence of contract, as it established that liability for negligent advice could arise by force of law, and this remains the situation despite the later attempt of the Judicial Committee of the Privy Council to limit Hedley Byrne to professional advisers.[34] Indeed, it has been stated judicially by Lord Salmon that the theory basing immunity on the lack of contract 'vanished with Hedley Byrne'.[35]

The possible impact of this case was first tested in Rondel v. Worsley, supra, where a convicted criminal sought to sue his counsel for alleged negligence in the conduct of his defence. It was held that he could not make such a claim, i.e., that immunity remained, although the justification given was based in this case on public policy, rather than on the absence of contract. Three reasons for the immunity were suggested :- the undesirability of essentially re-trying court cases; the 'cab rank' rule by which counsel are obliged to accept any willing client, and the existence of duties to the court on the part of counsel.[35] Equally significant in this case was the assertion obiter that solicitors probably enjoyed the same immunity when acting as advocates in the lower courts,[37] and that counsel were potentially liable in respect of negligence in the preparation of opinions or advice unconnected with litigation.[38]

The implications of this case are that the question of immunity turns on the nature of the professional function when the act in question was done, rather than on formal professional status. However, it is fair to say that the case still leaves the general impression that, in respect of counsel, the rule is still immunity subject to certain exceptions, rather than a denial that immunity exists.

The importance of Saif Ali v. Sydney Mitchell & Co., supra, is that it seems to emphasise that potential liability is now the generally accepted rule and that this applies to counsel and solicitors subject to a fairly well defined exception. Although the result in any given case might not be affected by this decision, nonetheless it represents an important change in atmosphere. Indeed there is a hint in at least one of the speeches in the Lords that some attention would have been given to the argument that there should be no immunity and that Rondel v. Worsley, supra, should have been overruled.[39]   However, this was not argued, and the case proceeded on a debate as to the precise limits of the immunity established in Rondel v. Worsley, supra, which, it must be stressed, could be overruled in the future.   As it is, the immunity has been more precisely and narrowly delimited, and it would seem that all of this stems from the application to counsel of 'the negligence explosion' referred to earlier.[40]

In Saif Ali, supra, an accident victim was deprived of a claim against the alleged wrongdoer in the accident because of the operation of the three year time bar for personal injuries litigation.   He then sued his solicitors for negligence.   By third party notice they brought into the case the barrister whom they had instructed alleging negligent advice by him as to the proper defendant and negligence in the written pleadings.   His defence was that his immunity from liability applied and that there was no reasonable cause of action against him.   The eventual decision of the House of Lords was based on the issue of whether immunity applied, and there is therefore no actual decision on whether or not there was negligence in the case. The Lords decided by a majority of three to two that immunity from liability for negligence only extended to court appearances and work intimately connected with these and that the work under attack did not come into that category.   The decision was stated to apply to solicitors when acting as advocates as well as to counsel.[41]   This additional exception will certainly be fairly strictly limited.   The three majority speeches stress that general public policy would be in favour of every wrong having a remedy and thus imposing negligence liability on givers of advice who allegedly possess some special skill.   These considerations are, however, overcome by the public interest in the administration of justice, especially in regard to the undesirability of retrying cases which is generally frowned on by legal systems under the heading of res judicata, and to a lesser extent in regard to counsel's duties to the court.

Thus, both counsel and solicitors are granted the privilege of immunity in a fairly restricted class of case.   Not even written pleadings will per se be exempt or immune from attack for alleged negligence.   Only court appearances and work intimately linked with them, as for example (probably) decisions on which witnesses to call or which documents to produce, are covered by the immunity.

Before dealing with what actually constitutes negligence in respect of lawyers, it is probably also necessary to comment briefly on another aspect of the dichotomy between contract and tort/delict. Whereas it is clear that any liability of counsel rests on delict or tort grounds alone, questions have arisen in respect of the basis of solicitor's liability.   Despite some conflicting authority it now seems to be the law that a solicitor owes duties to his client not only in contract but also in delict or tort.   This is now fairly clear in Scotland,[42] and England,[43] and it seems to be for the client to choose on which basis to sue, or whether to use each as alternatives.   Although it will rarely make much practical difference, in some cases questions of time bar or measure of damages may be highly relevant.[44]   Recent developments in the law of contract, in the so-called holiday cases,[45] have been applied in a case of breach of contract against a solicitor to allow some measure of recovery for emotional loss as well as purely financial,[46] thus apparently seeming to remove any advantage in that regard which may seem to be possessed by a tortious/delictual claim.

The key point is that generally speaking the law is taken to apply the same standard of care, i.e. that of a reasonably competent solicitor, both in cases based on contract and those based on delict.[47]   The standard applies as an implied contractual term in the first case and ex lege in the second.   This general view may require some modification in the light of some comments by Megarry, J., in Duchess of Argyle v. Beuselink.[48]   This case raises the highly significant question, very relevant in regard to medical negligence also, as to whether the employment of a specialist does not necessarily imply the imposition of a higher standard on him than the usual one, i.e., not the care and skill of the reasonably competent solicitor but rather the care and skill of that particular especially expert individual.   It must be stressed that the case does not decide the question, but an obiter suggestion by the judge, based very much on the idea of the contractual relationship, seems to demand quotation:

But to say that in tort the standard of care is uniform does not necessarily carry the point in circumstances where the action is for a breach of an implied duty of care in a contract whereby a client retains a solicitor.   No doubt the inexperienced solicitor is liable if he fails to attain the standard of a reasonably competent solicitor.   But if the client employs a solicitor of high standing and great experience, will an action for negligence fail if it appears that the solicitor did not exercise the care and skill to be expected of him, though he did not fall below the standard of a reasonably competent solicitor?   If the client engages an expert, and doubtless expects to pay commensurate fees, is he not entitled to expect something more than the standard of the reasonably competent?   I am speaking not merely of those expert in a particular branch of the law, as contrasted with a general practitioner but also of those of long experience and great skill as contrasted with those practising in the same field of the law but being of a more ordinary calibre and having less experience.   The essence of the contract of retainer, it may be said, is that the client is retaining the particular solicitor or firm in question, and he is therefore entitled to expect from that solicitor or firm a standard of care and skill commensurate with the skill and experience which that solicitor or firm has.   The uniform standard of care postulated for the world at large in tort hardly seems appropriate when the duty is not one imposed by the law of tort but arises from a contractual obligation existing between the client and the particular solicitor or firm in question.[49]

These remarks seem highly germane, not just to questions relating to the use of legal advice, but also to cases of private medical treatment by a particular specialist.

Another issue relating to the problem caused by the contract or tort/delict dichotomy also came before the same judge, in the recent case of Ross v. Caunters,[50] where it was held that in circumstances where the usual tests of proximity are met, a solicitor can be liable to third parties as well as to clients.   In reaching that conclusion His Lordship reiterated the view that the existence of a contractual duty to A did not preclude the existence of a tortious/delictual duty to B, and that to argue otherwise on the ground of so called privity is to put forward an exploded legal heresy.   This result was almost inevitable in current conditions. The third party in that case was one who was certainly immediately affected by the solicitor's omissions in that she lost her rights since a relative's will was rendered void as a result of their negligent advice in respect of witnessing formalities. Due to the tests of proximity this decision may not be so drastic as it seems. Indeed, it has been suggested[51] that the plaintiff in Ross v. Caunters, supra, was in fact more directly affected than the client, the testator. Although for technical reasons of precedent it might be argued that this case may not be good law in Scotland, it is a highly persuasive decision which probably corresponds with current Scots law. Closely affected third parties have now, despite the absence of contract, claims for professional negligence against solicitors.

The relevance of this case to the medical profession should also be noted. For example a doctor engaged to advise a company on matters of safety and employee health who carries out his remit with lack of due care may be liable to injured employees. This seems to be so if he is a full-time 'in house' employee of the company,[52] and it may be that, in view of the decision in Ross v. Caunters, supra, the outside medical adviser may also be liable in these circumstances, for example the doctor who fails timeously fails to fill in a report on a patient who is seeking life insurance, may well be liable in negligence for this omission.

To conclude the discussion of lawyer's negligence, it should briefly be mentioned that this is generally to be judged by the standards of the reasonably competent practitioner, either counsel or solicitor.[53] Liability therefore may cover errors of law,[54] mistakes in raising court actions,[55] allowing time-bars to run,[56] or failure properly to check documents.[57] Failure to take all steps necessary to secure the result desired by the client and for which he instructed the lawyer, will be negligence subject to the application of the test of the average practitioner.[58]

In contrast to medical negligence cases, expert evidence is not regarded as useful in cases of legal negligence since the general practice of the Bar, and probably of solicitors, is deemed to be within judicial knowledge.[59] The relevance of the average practitioner test is that it is used to stress that not every mistake, even where it leads to a client's loss, is necessarily negligence. Errors of judgment will rarely be such,[60] although it seems that the correct view is to accept that they can be if judged by this test.[61] The value of this test for negligence in the case of the legal profession may be questioned due to increasing specialisation, but presumably it is flexible enough to take account of this factor. What is probably the most important feature in this area is the general trend towards stressing that negligence applies to lawyers as well as to other professions.

MEDICAL NEGLIGENCE

Unlike the situation in respect of legal negligence, the law concerning medical negligence has not been bedevilled by the existence of an immunity, nor to any great extent by the distinctions between contract and delict/tort. However, one problem relating exclusively to medical cases was the extent of the vicarious liability of hospital boards for the actions of medical personnel. As a result of decisions in the early 1950s it is now well accepted that vicarious liability exists in respects of all medical staff who are employees.[62]   Former authorities to the contrary no longer represent the law,[63] and even if there is doubt as to the strict application of vicarious liability for employees in any particular case, the hospital authorities can often be found liable on the alternative ground of a failure to carry out their statutory duties.[64]

The law on medical liability can be simply stated.   The standard of care to be expected is that of an ordinary skilled practitioner in the relevant situation.   Perhaps the best fairly early example of the rule being stated is in R v. Bateman,[65] where in the course of a discussion of criminal liability for manslaughter due to negligence the civil position was also discussed.   A medical practitioner was stated to be under a duty to his patient to use diligence, care, knowledge, skill and caution in his administration of treatment.   The standard was stated to be a fair and reasonable one of care and competence, not a very high standard, certainly not the highest standard, but neither is it a particularly low standard.[66]   In later cases both in Scotland[67] and England[68], it was defined more closely by reference to usual professional practice and by borrowing the reasonably careful practitioner notion from the test applied to solicitors.   This test has received the imprimatur both of the Judicial Committee of the Privy Council[69] and recently of the House of Lords.[70]   It should also be mentioned that in articulating this test in respect of the medical profession, greater stress is placed on the professional position and speciality of the doctor involved, than is the case in cases of legal professional negligence.[71]   Further, it should be noted that some cases emphasise the importance of the state of medical and/or scientific knowledge at the time of the episode in question and deprecate any tendency to apply hindsight and judge by later developments.[72]

In the recent cases on professional negligence of doctors two features stand out as worthy of comment.   Both have broadly the effect of restricting the ambit of liability and both also stand as exceptions to general trends in the law of negligence.   Despite the fact that medical practice is an application of skill and can also be an inherently dangerous task, and that each of these factors is often used to emphasise and stress the general ambit of negligence,[73] other policy factors have been explicitly articulated to counter their effect in medical cases, especially by Lord Denning.[74]   Secondly, the emphasis and importance given to the notion of 'usual practice' in medical cases is much greater than in other aspects of modern negligence case law.

There has been a surprisingly strong emphasis on policy, not so much to expand, but rather to limit, the application of negligence to doctors.   For example in Roe v. Minister of Health,[75] the risk factor in surgery was used to counter the application of negligence because there would be, it was stated, no advance medical science without risks.[76]   However, it is clear that in general the very existence of higher risks is usually thought to justify imposition of a higher degree of care.   The policy argument is clearly that there is a need to encourage medical advancement, or at least not to impede it by imposing a high level of legal liability on doctors.   To that end the usual rights of patients would seem to be sacrificed so that doctors can 'learn by experience - [which] often teaches in a hard way'.   Stress is also laid on the argument that 'Doctors would be led to think more of their own safety than of the good of their patients.   Initiative would be stifled and confidence shaken',[77] were liability to be imposed in these circumstances.

This attitude reflects the view that, were doctors to be held liable, then they might choose to practice what has been called 'defensive medicine', and the use of certain therapies, perhaps experimental, would be inhibited, even although they may offer the best chance for the patient.   In the case of Lim Poh Choo v. Camden and Islington Area Health Authority,[78] a case where the important issue was the measure and calculation of damages, Lord Denning M.R. in the Court of Appeal mused on the dangers of allowing medical malpractice suits to lead to too great a strain on the resources of the National Health Service 'which have to be carefully husbanded and spent on essential services'.[79]   Although directed primarily at the amount of damages awarded, this argument seems to apply, in His Lordship's thinking, to the prior decision on the merits.   This is an argument which is not generally accepted in other cases of negligence and it is very important to note that these statements were disapproved of in the House of Lords where Lord Scarman rejected judicial reliance on questions of burden to the public or on consideration of the consequences of a high award on a wrongdoer or those financing him.[80]

There are in this case certain parallels with the recent case of Whitehouse v. Jordan,[81] where Lord Denning re-emphasised policy arguments with the same general effect and with even more extreme results, by referring to the dangers to the profession, and to society itself, in medical negligence claims, especially if the damages awarded are very high.   Basically by analogy with the U.S.A., he warned in fairly strong terms of the dangers of defensive medicine which might even lead to a refusal to treat patients, or to people being deterred from entering the profession.   These considerations led him to the conclusion that 'in a professional man, error of judgment is not negligence'.[82]   Even more astonishing perhaps was Lawton L.J.'s view in the same case that allegations of professional negligence against medical practitioners should, for purposes of the standard of proof, be equated with allegations of crime in a civil case as 'serious allegations'.[83]   This, however, does not seem to apply in other cases of negligence, where those alleged to have been negligent might equally feel a claim against them to be 'serious'. The basis of this assertion would seem to be first, the serious repercussions of a finding of negligence on a doctor's career and secondly, the public interest in avoiding the practice of defensive medicine.[84]

When Whitehouse v. Jordan, supra, reached the House of Lords, the issue most discussed in the speeches concerned the type of situation in which it would be appropriate to interfere with first instance decisions on fact (which was the basis for the appeal) and consequently discussion centred on the detailed facts at issue.[85] There was no discussion whatever of the policy arguments so favoured by Lord Denning.   However, three of the judges went out of their way to stress that errors of judgment can in certain cases be negligence - for example where the error of judgment would not have been made by a reasonably competent professional person acting with the appropriate standard of care to the degree of skill which the defendant held himself out as possessing.[86]   The Lords also re-affirmed the rule of the reasonably competent practitioner, although it is interesting to note that they did not expressly dissociate themselves from Lawton, L.J.'s dictum on proof.[87]

While it is important to stress that an extreme view on errors of judgment was rejected and that none of the policy arguments were articulated by the Lords in this case, these views on policy have in previous cases had considerable influence and have had the effect of insulating medical practice from general developments in the field of negligence which have affected the legal profession.

The application of the test of the reasonably competent practitioner has led to a great emphasis being placed on the concept of usual professional practice. The rule developed in the case of Hunter v. Hanley,[88] stressed that deviation from a usual practice is not negligence per se, but it will become negligence if the deviation was one which no professional man of ordinary skill would have made if he had acted with ordinary care.[89] In the English case of Bolam v. Friern Hospital Management Committee,[90] McNair J., purporting to apply Hunter v. Hanley, supra, stated that: 'A doctor is not guilty of negligence if he has acted in accordance with a practice accepted as proper by a responsible body of medical men skilled in that particular art'.[91]

This may represent an unduly high emphasis on usual practice which is anomalous once the law of negligence in general is considered. For example, in the field of employer's liability at common law, whereas the notion of general practice traditionally was regarded as almost the conclusive factor in allegations of negligence,[92] this is no longer the case and it has now only a subsidiary role. There are now cases where normal practice has been followed but negligence has nonetheless been held to have been established,[93] and vice versa.[94] Admittedly, this concept is important in areas other than medicine,[95] but its role in medical cases is perhaps stressed much more. Combined with the use of policy arguments, medical negligence (and perhaps also legal negligence) would seem to be out of step with the apparent trend of development in negligence generally. Further, it is submitted that too much stress on standard practice as a means of limiting liability, effectively takes the role of judging professional behaviour away from the courts and allows that it may effectively be carried out by the fellow professionals of the defendant, thereby removing the opportunity for independent control, in the public interest, over professional conduct.

The law of negligence has been one of the growth areas in the legal system in the 1960s and 1970s. During that period it has also been increasingly recognised that policy plays a vital role in the developments in this area. These factors have led to a considerable explosion of the negligence liability of lawyers, whereas in contrast, policy has been invoked to restrict what could otherwise have been negligence in respect of doctors. Admittedly, such factors can be validly invoked to limit the ambit of negligence,[96] but it would appear that undue stress has been placed on countervailing arguments to an extension of negligence in the medical area, and it is to be hoped that the parallel developments in the law of negligence in the field of legal professional negligence and the 'negligence explosion' generally, will serve to ensure that doctors are no longer treated in such a special way as they seem to be at present.

A.J. Gamble

NOTES

1. For fuller information see 'The Analysis of Negligence', in
   Wilson, W.A., Introductory Essays on Scots Law, Edinburgh,
   W.Green & Son, 1978, at pp.121-144. For a detailed
   exposition of the law of Scotland see Walker, D.M. The Law of
   Delict in Scotland, Edinburgh, W.Green & Son, 1966, Volume
   I, at pp. 176-288. The leading English textbook is
   Charlesworth on Negligence, (6th Ed.), London, Sweet &
   Maxwell, 1977. Much helpful material can also be found in
   Winfield and Jolowicz on Tort, (11th Ed.), London, Sweet
   & Maxwell, 1979, at pp. 66-106.
2. Donoghue v. Stevenson 1932 S.C. (H.L.) 31.
3. See e.g. Lord MacMillan in Glasgow Corporation v. Muir 1943
   S.C.(H.L.) 3 at p.10; and Lord Denning, M.R. in Nettleship
   v. Weston [1971] 3 All E.R. 581 at p.586.
4. This is especially apparent from the dictum of Lord Denning
   cited from Nettleship v. Weston, supra.
5. See Charlesworth, op.cit. at p.220, and Wakelin v. London
   and S.W. Rly. Co. (1886) 12 App. Cases 41.
6. See e.g. Walker, op.cit., at pp. 213-238.
   In some cases having materially increased the risk of harm
   is taken as equivalent to having caused the harm. c.f.
   McGhee v. N.C.B. 1973 S.L.T. 14.
7. Home Office v. Dorset Yacht Co. Ltd. [1970] 2 All E.R. 294,
   per Lord Reid at p.302, Lord Morris of Borth-y-Gest at p.309,
   Lord Pearson at pp.322-23, in the context of economic loss
   see Lord Denning, M.R., in Spartan Steels Ltd. v. Martin
   [1972] 3 All E.R. 557, at pp.561-64. As will be noted, policy
   questions have been extensively canvassed in professional
   negligence cases, probably more so than in other areas of
   negligence.
8. See the dictum of Lord Denning, M.R., in Nettleship v. Weston,
   note 4, supra.
9. See Wilson, op.cit. at p.128.
10. Hedley Byrne & Co., Ltd. v. Heller and Partners [1963] 2 All
    E.R. 575. The Scottish position on this matter is a little
    confused. Consider the conflicting decisions in John Kennedy
    Ltd. v. Orcantic Ltd. 1980 S.L.T. 46 and Foster v. Craigmillar
    Laundry Ltd. 1980 S.L.T.(Sh.Ct.) 100.
11. Sutcliffe v. Thackrah [1974] 1 All E.R. 462.
12. Dutton v. Bognor Regis U.D.C. [1972] 1 All E.R. 462.
    Anns v. London Borough of Merton [1977] 2 All E.R. 492.
13. Arenson v. Casson, Beckman, Rutley & Co. [1975] 3 All E.R.
    901.
14. c.f. Spartan Steels Ltd. v. Martin, supra, and Dynamco v.
    Holland and Hanner and Cubitts (Scotland) Ltd. 1972
    S.L.T. 38.
15. Ministry of Housing and Local Government v. Sharp [1970]
    1 All E.R. 1009; Ross v. Caunters [1979] 3 All E.R. 580.
16. For an excellent discussion see Atiyah, P.S., Accidents,
    Compensation and The Law, (3rd Ed.), London, Weidenfeld
    & Nicolson, 1980. For a judicial recognition of the
    relevance of these issues in the medical negligence context,
    see Lawton, L.J. in Whitehouse v. Jordan [1980] 1 All E.R.
    650 at p. 662 where he states that: 'The victims of medical
    mishaps...should, in my opinion, be cared for by the

       community not by the hazards of litigation'.

17.   For further discussion, see infra, ch. 11.
18.   Cmnd. 7054/1978
19.   For an outline of the Report's proposals see, Gamble, A.J.,
       and Forte, A.D.M., 'The Pearson Report' (1978) Scolag
       Bulletin 101. For a fairly trenchant criticism, see Ogus,
       A.I., Corfield, P., and Harris, D.R., 'Pearson: Principled
       Reform or Political Compromise?' (1978) 7 I.L.J. 143.
20.   No definite legislative proposals had been brought forward by
       March, 1981.
21.   For further discussion see infra ch. 6.
22.   Edgar v. Lamont 1914 S.C. 277, especially at p.279. In that
       case a doctor was held liable in negligence directly to a
       patient although employed by the patient's husband. Her
       title to sue was based on the breach of tortious/delictual
       duty.
23.   These cases are not entirely parallel in that duties placed
       on common carriers and sellers of goods can be strict, i.e.,
       no proof of fault is required. It must also be stressed that
       an injured person with a contractual claim can sue on either
       ground but someone without any contractual nexus is restricted
       to a delictual claim.
24.   For a general discussion, see e.g., Zander M., Legal Services
       for the Community, London, Temple Smith, 1978; Walker and
       Walker, The English Legal System, (4th Ed.), London,
       Butterworths, 1976, Chapter 12; Walker, D.M., The Scottish
       Legal System (4th Ed.), Edinburgh, W. Green & Son, 1976.
25.   (1860) 5 H. and N. 890.
26.   (1876) 3 R 914.
27.   This position applied in regard to defective goods before
       Donoughue v. Stevenson, supra, and was based on the doctrine
       of privity of contract.
28.   (1839) MacLand Rob. 595.
29.   (1839) MacLand Rob. 595 at P.614.
30.   See e.g. Murray v. Reilly 1963 S.L.T. (Notes) 99.
31.   [1967] 3 All E.R. 993.
32.   [1978] 3 All E.R. 1003.
33.   See note 10, supra.
34.   Mutual Life Assurance Co., Ltd. v. Evatt [1971] A.C. 793.
35.   See Saif Ali, supra, at p. 1051.
36.   See especially Lord Reid's speech at pp.998-1000.
37.   See Lord Reid's speech at p.1001 and Lord Pearce's speech at
       p.1024.
38.   See Lord Reid at p.1001, and Lord Upjohn at p.1036.
39.   Saif Ali, supra,. at p.1045 per Lord Diplock.
40.   This is especially clear in the speeches of Lord Wilberforce
       and Lord Diplock in Saif Ali, supra.
41.   See Lord Wilberforce at p.1039, Lord Diplock at p.1046 and
       Lord Salmon at p.1048.
42.   Robertson v. Bannigan 1965 S.C. 20, especially pp.30-31)
       See also the pleadings in Dunlop v. McGowans 1979 S.L.T. 34
       at p.35.
43.   Midland Bank Trust Co., Ltd. v. Hett, Stubbs & Kemp [1978]
       3 All E.R. 571.
44.   Time bar points were at issue in Midland Bank Trust Co. v.
       Hett, Stubbs & Kemp, supra. In Haberstick v. McCormick
       and Nicolson 1975 S.L.T. 181, a case pled in contract, measure

of damages was tested by the contractual rules.

45. *Jarvis* v. *Swan Tours Ltd.* [1973] 1 All E.R. 71, *Jackson* v. *Horizon Holidays Ltd.* [1975] 3 All E.R. 92.

46. *Heywood* v. *Wellers* [1976] 1 All E.R. 300.

47. see *Midland Bank Trust Co., Ltd.* v. *Hett, Stubbs & Kemp* supra.

48. [1972] 2 Lloyds Rep. 172.

49. op.cit. at p.183.

50. See note 15, supra.

51. Gamble, A.J., 'Solicitors and Claims by Third Parties' 1980 J.L.S.S. 236.

52. *Stokes* v. *G.K.N.(Balls and Nuts)Ltd.* [1968] 1. W.L.R. 1776.

53. *Hart* v. *Frame & Co.*, supra, and *Saif Ali* v. *Sydney Mitchell & Co.*, supra. Presumably the standard demanded of counsel will be more exacting.

54. Perhaps not all; see *Free Church of Scotland* v. *McKnight's Trs.* 1916 S.C. 349.

55. *Hart* v. *Frame & Co.*, supra; *Simpson* v. *Kidston & Co.* 1913 1 S.L.T. 74.

56. *Welsh* v. *Knarston* 1974 S.L.T. 66.

57. *Ross* v. *Caunters*, supra.

58. *Heywood* v. *Wellers*, supra.

59. See *Midland Bank Trust Co.* v. *Hett, Stubbs & Kemp*, supra, at p.582.

60. See Lord Wilberforce in *Saif Ali*, supra, at p.1039; Lord Diplock at p.1043, Lord Salmon at p.1051.

61. *Whitehouse* v. *Jordan* [1981] 1 All E.R. 267, per Lord Edmund-Davies at pp.276-77, Lord Fraser of Tullybelton at p.281 and Lord Russel of Killowen at p.284.

62. For example, see *Cassidy* v. *Ministry of Health* [1951] 2 K.B. 343. *Roe* v. *Ministry of Health* [1954] 2 Q.B. 66, *MacDonald* v. *Glasgow Western Hospitals* 1954 S.C. 453.

63. The leading example of such a case is *Hillyer* v. *St. Bartholomew's Hospital* [1909] 2 K.B. 820.

64. See the cases cited in note 62, supra.

65. (1925) 41 T.L.R. 557.

66. ibid. at p.559.

67. *Hunter* v. *Hanley* 1955 S.C. 200.

68. *Bolam* v. *Friern Hospital Management Committee* [1957] 2 All E.R. 118.

69. *Chin Keow* v. *Government of Malaysia* [1967] 1 W.L.R. 813.

70. *Whitehouse* v. *Jordan*, supra.

71. For example in *Whitehouse* v. *Jordan*, supra, see the reference in the speech of Lord Fraser of Tullybelton to 'the standard and type of skill that the defendant held himself out as having', at p.281.

72. *Roe* v. *Ministry of Health*, supra, per Denning L.J. at p.84, where he states that 'We must not look at the 1947 accident with 1954 spectacles'.

73. For the former proposition the decisions cited in *Saif Ali*, supra, and that decision itself can be cited, for the latter see e.g. Lord MacMillan in *Glasgow Corporation* v. *Muir*, supra, at p.10 where he states that 'Those who engage in operations inherently dangerous must take precautions which are not required of persons engaged in the ordinary routine of life'.

74. Lord Denning's role here has been very significant. For a

concise account of it by himself, see Denning, <u>The Discipline of Law</u>, London, Butterworths, 1979, Chapter 2 of Part 6, entitled 'Doctors at Law'. For a trenchant criticism see McLean, S.A.M., 'Negligence - a Dagger at the Doctor's Back?' in Robson, P., and Watchman, P.,(eds), <u>Justice, Lord Denning and the Constitution</u>, Gower Publishing Company, 1981.

75. See note 62, supra.

76. For further discussion on the legal attitude to medical risks, see infra chs. 8 and 9.

77. Roe v. <u>Ministry of Health</u>, supra, at p.83 and p.86. These words were described as 'very wise' by McNair J. in <u>Bolam</u> v. <u>Friern Hospital Management Committee</u>, supra, at p.128.

78. [1979] 1 All E.R. 332.

79. ibid. at p.341.

80. [1979] 2 All E.R. 910 at pp.917-8.

81. In the Court of Appeal it is reported at [1980] 1 All E.R. 650. For the House of Lords citation see note 61, supra.

82. ibid. at p.658.

83. Lord Denning made a similar point in the case of <u>Hucks</u> v. <u>Cole</u> 'The Times' 9 May 1968.

84. ibid. at p.659.

85. Especially in the speech of Lord Wilberforce in [1981] 1 All E.R. 267, at pp.270-276.

86. The references are detailed in note 62, supra.

87. For further discussion, see infra, chs. 8 and 9.

88. See Footnote 66, supra.

89. See the judgment of Lord President Clyde, ibid., at p.206.

90. See note 68, supra.

91. at p.122. Perhaps an extreme statement of this view is that of Denning L.J. in <u>Hatcher</u> v. <u>Black</u>, 'The Times' 2 July, 1954 where His Lordship in charging a civil jury referred to the expert medical evidence and said, 'They did not condemn him [the defendant] nor should we.'

92. <u>Morton</u> v. <u>Dixon</u> 1909 S.C. 807.

93. <u>Cavanagh</u> v. <u>Ulster Weaving Co.</u> [1960] A.C. 145.

94. <u>Brown</u> v. <u>Rolls Royce</u> 1960 S.C. (H.L.) 22.

95. <u>McLaughlan</u> v. <u>Craig</u> 1948 S.C. 599.

96. See Lord Wilberforce in <u>Anns</u> v. <u>London Borough of Merton</u>, supra, at p. 498.

8 Consent in Medical Practice
S. A. M. McLean and A. J. McKay

Consent generally becomes a legal issue when attempts are made to raise it as a potential defence to allegations of a criminal or a civil nature. For example, a claim might be made that an alleged rape was not rape in fact since the complainer actually consented to the intercourse.[1]   The attitude of the criminal courts to consent as a defence has tended to be that it will only be a defence where an element of lack of consent is necessary to the charge, e.g. in the rape example, a reasonable belief that the victim consented would be an acceptable defence.[2]   This defence therefore is not applicable in the majority of criminal cases since:

> Subject to certain exceptions inherent in the nature of particular crimes, the criminal law has never permitted consent of the victim to be used as a defence.[3]

However, problems of consent in medical practice are dealt with by the civil and not the criminal law, where the defence is expressed in the maxim _volenti non fit injuria_.[4]   For this defence to be successful it must be shown that:

> the pursuer was both _sciens_ and _volens_, that he fully appreciated the dangerous character of the situation brought about and also exhibited a real consent to his own assumption of the risk in question without right to compensation from the defender.[5]

In other words, it must be shown that the party freely and with understanding consented to the procedure in question or to the particular agreement made, by accepting whatever the risk was in that situation and accepting that such an assumption of risk precluded him from claiming compensation in the event of that risk actually taking place.   However, this assumes that the nature of the risk is known or explicable.   As Walker has said:

> If the plea is to succeed it must be shown not that the pursuer consented to take the risk of _some_ harm befalling him, but that he consented to take the risk of _the particular kind_ of harm which in fact befell him.[6]

In medical practice, it is generally asserted that the consent of the patient is required before the doctor may intervene, the corollary of this being that: 'Where the patient gives informed consent, that consent is a complete defence to any action for damages based on assault.'[7]   The situation then is that '...the general principle of law is that a person cannot be medically treated without his consent'.[8]   The question of what amounts to real or informed consent will be discussed at a later stage, but attention must first be turned to the questions of how consent can be demonstrated, and who may competently give it.

As with other situations, the actual consent necessary in medical cases may be expressed in a number of ways.   It has been said, for example, that it may be '...taken as implied when the patient presents himself or herself for examination or treatment'.[9]   This might be taken to mean that by virtue of turning up at a consulting room, or calling a doctor for a home visit and no more than that, the patient could be deemed to have consented to whatever the doctor then does.

However, this would fall short of the nature of consent which is required in other areas of the civil law.

One way of highlighting this is to ask what it might be about the position of a doctor which would give rise to such an assumption. After all, A does not give carte blanche to a lawyer to take any steps that he considers necessary to secure A's interests simply by consulting him.   Nor is consent to a builder's renewing the roof of a house given merely by asking him to investigate the cause of a small leak.   It might, however, be claimed that a doctor is in a unique position which does somehow require that he can assume consent by implication.   But whatever arguments there might be for this, such a claim could be seen as emptying a doctrine of consent of any significant content.   In any event, there would be some difficulty in justifying the assertion that a doctor is necessarily in a substantially different position from other professionals or skilled workers.   The position would seem to be that: 'It is no longer good enough for the doctor to assume that he has the whole-hearted consent of his patient to treatment or to the undertaking of diagnostic procedures.'[10]

However, it is often stated that in medical practice: 'From a legal point of view, there is no need for the consent to be in writing.   It need not even be expressed in words...'.[11]   There is a parallel here with the notion of tacit consent as sometimes applied in political philosophy.   It is sometimes argued that a citizen of a state 'tacitly consents' to the authority of a government over him, or to actions it may take, in virtue of having voted (even if he does not vote for the particular party elected), or perhaps in virtue of continuing to live in the state, pay taxes, accept the benefits of the protection of the state, etc.[12]   But this parallel in no way favours the claim that a patient consents to treatment merely by consulting a doctor.

For whatever the merits of a doctrine of tacit consent may be as an ultimate justification of the authority that a government might claim over the members of a state, it is widely agreed, even by defenders of the doctrine as applied in political philosophy, that the claim that a citizen consents to the system of government by using its machinery in voting rests on the assumption that he understands something of the implications of the system and its processes.[13] Thus, to justify the claim that B has consented it has to be shown that B knows that in casting a vote he is participating in the democratic process.   Further, and more importantly in this context, it is also part of the 'consent' justification of democracy that the voter is offered a real choice between possible governments; political parties issue manifestos and announce their intentions; they justify their actions on the grounds that thay have a 'mandate' from the electorate, who could have chosen an alternative policy.   It is for this reason that states which do not offer their citizens a choice of policies for which to vote are criticised for not being 'truly democratic'.   Consent in this context thus requires that the individual is presented with alternatives, and that he knows the consequences, or likely consequences, of his actions.

Thus neither implied nor tacit consent would seem to be adequate definitions of consent in relation to medical practice, unless they are accompanied by an element of disclosure of alternatives by the doctor which allows the patient to make an understanding choice regarding whether or not to undergo the proposed treatment.   Medical treatment clearly involves the patient's personal integrity or right to self-determination in a very clear and direct way, and this may make the need for choices and acceptance of specific risk particularly important. Indeed it is generally stated to be fundamental to the notion of consent in medical practice that it is 'real' or 'informed', i.e. that the patient has access to certain information which permits him to understand the nature of the proposed intervention and to make informed choices on this basis.[14] Thus, in the case of _Devi_ v. West Midlands Regional Health Authority,[15] a woman who had consented to a minor operation on her womb, presumably with the implication that more major surgery might be necessary, was nonetheless not deemed to have consented to a sterilisation carried out under the terms of the original consent. This decision was based on the fact that

a) the operation was not of the type consented to in the original consent that was given, and

b) that the sterilisation was not necessary for the preservation of life.

It is clear then that '...the medical staff in a hospital must remain within the scope of the authority given to them by the patient to treat him',[16] and as Skegg has pointed out, '... merely because a patient has consulted him about a medical complaint...' a doctor cannot assume that '...the patient has impliedly consented to treatment for it'.[17]

There are further problems raised by the personal characteristics of the party purporting to offer real or valid consent. Obviously, this person must have the legal capacity to consent, and there are certain groups in the community concerning whose legal capacity to offer real consent there are doubts. For example, children and the mentally abnormal are generally not in a position to offer consent, since they are regarded as lacking the ability to make choices which would necessarily protect themselves and their interests. Thus, even although consent may be given on their behalf, the law generally requires that such consent is in the best interests of the incapax.[18] Equally, certain groups who are otherwise self-determining may not be able to offer valid consent in some situations, e.g. the prisoner may not be felt to be consenting freely in every situation.[19] These groups clearly present problems for any theory of consent, and the reasons for this bring out the extent to which consent must be real, and illustrate the major reasons for requiring a valid consent to be given. The particular difficulties with these groups relate to the fact that they are deemed not to be self-determining or capable of sufficient understanding, or that they are particularly vulnerable, and because of this they cannot give valid consent. Thus, the law protects their right not to be interfered with unless a validly authorised person, acting strictly in their interests, consents on their behalf.

Another vital factor in the use of the consent defence in the law is that the proposed actions are such that they are legally capable of being consented to. Thus, for example, one cannot legalise murder,[20] or euthanasia,[21] which remains a form of voluntary killing no matter its motivation, where it is knowingly carried out by a doctor or a layman. As Williams points out, killing even with the consent of the victim 'is still generally murder.'[22] One can however, render lawful the actions of a doctor which could otherwise constitute an assault.[23] However as Gordon has said:

In the case of surgical operations consent is a defence even
where the injuries are likely to cause danger to life. This
is probably because the injuries are inflicted in such cases

not for their own sake or in order to cause pain or gratify an intention to harm, but for the benefit of the patient.'[24]

The sane, adult patient then, can offer real consent to medical treatment which makes the intervention lawful, but such consent cannot be assumed to be a blanket consent.   It is also necessary that he consents to the particular type of intervention proposed, and this requires that he should be able to understand to what he is being asked to consent.   If it is true that: 'The understanding of consent, whether it be for medical treatment or to any other course of conduct, derives its meaning from the tacit assumption that the individual adult is self-determining...',[25] then it is clear that consent must involve choice.   This necessarily involves an element of disclosure by the doctor in respect of the proposed therapy, e.g. its benefits, risks, and likelihood of success.   The central point, then, in analysing the validity of consent is the nature and extent of the disclosure made.

Most philosophical or ethical discussions have seen special problems in reconciling the notion of meaningful consent with various attitudes often held by doctors.   It is, for example, sometimes suggested that the patient will only be needlessly distressed by a full explanation of risks.   The witholding of information from a patient on this basis may be seen as appropriate in line with what has been called the 'Prevention of Harm Argument'.   Indeed, Brazier has argued that in some situations the doctor might be negligent in disclosing too many of the risks, on the grounds that the patient's health may suffer.[26]

This 'Prevention of Harm Argument' can be, and has been, effectively challenged[27] by pointing out that for a doctor to be in a position to claim that he knows that the witholding of information is in the best interests of the patient, he, the doctor, needs to judge not only that giving the information will be harmful but also that witholding the information will not turn out to be more harmful.[28]   Such judgements require knowledge not only of the patient, but also perhaps of his family or associates, knowledge which extends well beyond any notion of what can be said to be purely medical matters, and which cannot plausibly be claimed to be possessed by most medical practitioners in such situations.   This latter point need not be in any way a criticism of doctors, though some might want to make it such.   It is merely a comment on their likely position in relation to many patients.

It is also the case that many judgements required by a policy of witholding information would appear to extend beyond any notion of what the average medical practitioner might feel to be his area of competence.   For example, the claim that access to certain types of information may make a patient suicidal might be validly asserted to be within the remit of the psychiatrist.   Equally, since a patient's interests may be bound up in part with issues to do with his family and business associates, his wishes for his dependents, etc., to insist that the best course for the patient will be ignorance of certain risks is to claim omniscience.   Merely to review the possibilities here is to see that such judgements will almost invariably involve elements which are certainly not medical.

Mention was previously made of the claim that there are special difficulties attached to groups such as children, and the insane,[29] who are unable to understand information which might be made available.   It would not be surprising if doctors were tempted to use the undoubted fact that some information is of a specialist and

technical sort to extend the range of such cases and use this as a
reason for non-disclosure, or to claim that the non-specialist patient
may not understand or be able to assess the risks involved in certain
forms of treatment. It is therefore sometimes argued that the
patient is unable to understand sufficient of an explanation for it to
be worthwhile, or that in any event the decision as to therapy is a
purely medical one requiring skills which the average patient does not
possess. Two points in particular need to be made about the position
of doctors in relation to the assessment and disclosure of risks.

First, as Buchanan points out,[30] a duty to disclose information
is not a duty to succeed in communicating information, and that one
cannot guarantee to succeed in communicating does not in itself
entitle one not to try. However, it has also been said that:

the doctrine of informed consent can only become meaningful
in terms of the patient's right to self-determination if he
actually comprehends the information which is given to
him.[31]

The combination of these two assertions would seem to indicate that
the doctor is under some duty to make such disclosure as the patient
might be deemed to be able to understand, but also that the doctor
cannot ultimately be held responsible for the patient's inability to
assimilate or completely comprehend the information.

Second, and this illustrates the point already made, what
constitutes an acceptable risk to a patient is not merely a matter of
degree of risk, which arguably is a medical matter. A man may be
willing to risk his job to save his life, but not to earn one thousand
pounds, even although in both cases the calculable degree of risk may
be the same. Similarly, whether it is rational for a patient to
accept some form of treatment which has a specifiable risk of failure
or causing harm is not just a matter of the likelihood of certain
medical consequences coming about, but is also a matter of how much
the outcome matters to the patient, and this of course may vary with
the individual. For instance, the risk of a speech impediment may be
acceptable to a radio technician but not to a radio announcer. Such
matters are not medical matters and cannot be considered other than by
the patient, who cannot take into account factors of which he is
ignorant.

In other words, for consent to be said to be protecting the right
of the patient to self-determination, it is essential that an element
of disclosure is made of risks and possibilities in order that the
patient may make an informed choice and that he may achieve some sort
of understanding. The necessity for a choice to be available has
been supported by case law in the United States, as for example in the
case of Canterbury v. Spence,[32] in which the court said that real
consent '...entails an opportunity to evaluate knowledgeably the
options available and the risks attendant on each'.[33] In line with
this judgement the doctor would be required to divulge sufficient
information for a choice to be available and consent to be a reality,
i.e. at least the salient points must be made known to the patient,
and the patient attempting to show that valid consent had not been
given would then have to establish that this 'reasonable disclosure'
had not been made.

Consent is not therefore simply an abstract power which all adults
are necessarily capable of possessing, but is a concept involving an
element of understanding as well as choice. It is precisely for this
reason that doctors and lawyers find it problematic. While it is
clear that understanding requires an element of explanation by the

doctor of the procedures and risks involved in a particular therapy, it is the nature and extent of this explanation or disclosure which is of prime importance and which may in turn be highly contentious.

If it is the case that for consent to treatment to be valid it must always follow information about the nature and consequences of that treatment, there are implications for the more mundane levels of medical care which are seldom pointed out. What of the run of the mill visit to a doctor which results in the fairly routine issuing of a prescription? In what proportion of such consultations is there any attempt to obtain informed consent to the treatment? It has already been argued that it will not do to say that the patient consents to treatment just by voluntarily visiting his doctor. Even explicit agreement to 'Take one of these after each meal and come back in a week's time' cannot constitute informed consent unless some criteria for the divulging of information about consequences, risks, possible side-effects, etc., are adhered to as would be necesssary if what were involved were a hospital operation. Although it has been suggested that: 'Generally consent will be implied by the patient's acceptance of the drug prescribed',[34] in any coherent definition of consent this implication cannot be drawn unless disclosure has been made to the appropriate extent. To implement such criteria fully would require far-reaching changes in the behaviour of many patients and doctors.

In the United States, the concept of 'informed consent' has been elevated to the standard of a legal doctrine by a series of cases which accept the need for disclosure, but seem uncertain as to the tests to be applied in order to ascertain whether or not the disclosure was adequate.[35] What is clear, however, is that the doctor cannot, in seeking real consent, simply rely on having answered all the questions which the patient has asked. In the first place, since the doctor may well depend on the fact that patients do not understand technical medical matters to explain his failure to communicate certain information, he cannot then rely on the patient's questions being 'informed'. In any event, there has to be some end to questioning and it would be unreasonable, to take an extreme case, if a doctor were obliged to answer every conceivable question a patient might ask before it could be claimed that the patient had enough information for consent to be informed. There would have, on this model, to be some way of distinguishing the relevant from the irrelevant, the important from the less important, and the medical from the non-medical.

In the second place, it may be that the patient asks the wrong questions; the right often claimed by doctors to decide what is medically important and relevant and should therefore be disclosed, goes with a duty to volunteer that kind of information whether or not it is requested. Simply responding to whatever questions the patient may have without informing him of the salient facts is further unsatisfactory since the doctor cannot assume that the only information which must be divulged is that which the patient is sufficiently informed, in advance, to seek. If consent is to have any meaning, it cannot be dependent on the type of question which the layman might ask, but must have a consistent element reflecting the duties of the doctor to his patient, and protecting the right of the patient to self-determination.

It has been said that, at least under Canadian law, the doctor's duty is '...simply to give a fair and reasonable explanation of the proposed treatment including the probable effect and any special or unusual risks.'[36]   Courts in Canada have considered in some detail the notion of what amounts to a 'special or unusual' risk, since the definition of this is clearly fundamental in deciding whether or not disclosure has been sufficient.[37]   In American courts, as in the case of Salvo v. Leland Stanford,etc.,Board of Trustees,[38] it has been said that:

> A physician violates his duty to his patient and subjects himself to liability if he witholds any facts which are necessary to form the basis of an intelligent consent by the patient to the proposed treatment.   Likewise the physician may not minimise the known dangers of a procedural operation in order to induce his patient's consent.[39]

In the United Kingdom a different approach has been adopted, which, while regarding disclosure (at least in theory) as being important, does not employ the notion of 'special risk'.   Rather, the British Courts have tended to rely on the notion of 'clinical judgement' or 'good medical practice' in assessing whether or not disclosure has been sufficient.   In Bolam v. Friern Hospital Management Committee,[40] it was suggested that a doctor need not disclose risks which he regards as being minimal.   This case is particularly interesting for the doctor since it was also indicated that disclosure of risks which the doctor regarded as minimal was not necessary even where the treatment involved was elective on the part of the doctor, i.e. it was a method favoured by the doctor, and the risk involved in this was peculiar to the particular form of treatment chosen.   There was no suggestion that the treatment (administering ECT without the use of a muscle relaxant) was in any way an inappropriate type of treatment, but rather that a muscle relaxant should have been given.   Evidence was led that some doctors always administered a relaxant (which has its own risks) whereas others do not.   The court stated that the doctor, being entitled to subscribe to the school of thought which preferred not to give a relaxant, was not negligent in not disclosing the relatively small risk of fracture.   Interestingly, the patient involved was severely depressive and may in any event not have been legally capax whatever information the doctor had divulged.   The court however expressed the view that:

> ...you may well think that when a doctor is dealing with a mentally sick man and has a strong belief that his only hope of cure is submission to electro-convulsive therapy, the doctor cannot be criticised if he does not stress the dangers, which he believes to be minimal, which are involved in that treatment.[41]

Implicit in this would seem to be the assumption that there exists a prima facie case that the doctor's choice of therapy is necessarily appropriate, and it may also seem to follow logically from this that the patient should undergo the treatment if the doctor believes it to be useful, unless there are powerful reasons for not doing so.

The case of Hatcher v. Black,[42] took this notion even further by indicating that not only can a doctor, in deciding that a particular form of treatment is appropriate, not be criticised for failing to disclose risks which are minimal, but that he is also justified in lying to a patient about the known, and in this case highly relevant, risks of treatment where he feels that disclosure of the risks would prevent the patient from undergoing the treatment or might cause the patient undue worry.   This case would seem to indicate that even if a risk is regarded as special in a non-technical sense, as opposed to merely minimal, the view of the doctor that therapy is needed, and that the therapy should be of a particular type, will be regarded in the United Kingdom as entitling him to fail to make full disclosure, in order to ensure that the patient accepts the proposed treatment.

In the United States, the assessment of what it is appropriate to disclose, for whatever reason, is referred to as the doctrine of 'therapeutic privilege', and is stated to obtain when '...risk-disclosure poses such a threat of detriment to the patient as to become unfeasible or contraindicated from a medical point of view', [43] and thus the 'Prevention of Harm Argument' would seem to have found acceptance. However, in contrast to the position adopted by the British Courts, American Courts following the case of Salvo, supra, would not regard it as sufficient justification for a failure to disclose necessary information, merely to claim that, in the doctor's opinion, the patient would have refused the treatment had he been made aware of the risks.

It may be easy, but it is also fallacious, to argue from the assertion that a doctor has the right to be the judge of what treatment is most likely to succeed, or to have certain specifiable consequences, to the claim that patients have no rights to choose. For, as can be seen, if factors such as stress, or the relative weight which might be given by a broadcaster to cure or losing her voice, are taken account of, there are frequently factors involved which are not purely medical and on which the doctor is not specially qualified to decide, and may indeed be the wrong person to be making a choice. Equally, a patient may legitimately choose to leave a diagnosed and treatable condition untreated, although in emergencies the doctor may lawfully proceed without consent where such is, for some reason, unobtainable.[44] Obtaining consent then would seem not simply to relate to the duties of a doctor to his patient, but also (and perhaps more importantly) to the right of the patient to make an understanding choice about what can be done to his body.

It would seem that consent must be real in order for it to be effective, and this may not be the case even when some disclosure has been made. In the case of Wells v. Surrey Area Health Authority,[45] a woman was awarded damages having been sterilised during a caesarean section, even although she had consented to the sterilisation. It was, however, deemed that the consent had been based on insufficient information. The recent case of Chatterton v. Gerson and Another[46] restated the nature of the consent necessary for medical procedures by concluding that: 'It is clear law that in any context in which consent of the injured party is a defence to what would otherwise be a crime or a civil wrong, that consent must be real',[47] and continued '...justice requires that in order to vitiate the reality of consent there must be a greater failure of communication between doctor and patient than that involved in a breach of duty if the claim is based on negligence.'[48] By implication, then, in any action against the doctor for assault, the patient will require to demonstrate a significant failure to communicate. If such a failure is demonstrated, then it becomes irrelevant whether or not the patient would or would not have consented had the information been disclosed. The proof required in this situation is simply that no real consent was given in the sense that the consent was not informed, and this would seem to require evidence that there was a substantial failure to disclose. It is likely that for there to be held to be a significant failure to disclose in such situations the doctor would have to have failed to notify the patient of obvious risks, which even in current practice is probably unusual. However, the assault based action does have the advantage of concentrating the issue squarely on the inviolability of the patient and his rights to self-determination.

It may well be, however, that there is a distasteful aspect to the use of concepts like assault in medical practice, particularly in view of the essentially therapeutic motivation of medicine and its practitioners. The use of this type of action is also problematic since generally assault is seen as connoting physical interference with another person,[49] which may be difficult to establish where the therapy in question is e.g. the prescription of drugs. Some legal discussions have, for obvious reasons, been concerned with the problems of establishing for the purposes of the assault action some kind of literal 'touching' of the patient.[50] Where this can be established there are few legal problems in the use of the assault action. The position is clear that any 'touching' by the doctor, which is not accompanied by the necessary 'real' or 'informed' consent, would technically amount to a battery or civil assault. Skegg defines battery (and for the purposes of this discussion, this will include assault in Scots Law) as '...the unlawful application of force to the person of another.'[51] Quest provides a more flexible definition by stating that: 'Any physical interference with another person without their consent amounts in law to an assault',[52] and this definition could more easily be taken to include those actions which alter the physical make-up of the person, e.g. the provision of drugs, but which do not specifically involve the doctor in 'touching' the patient. In any event, it is submitted that the arguments surrounding what amounts to touching have little contemporary relevance given the attitudes of courts, and that any definition of consent which is satisfactory must depend not on the nature of the intervention, but on the amount and type of information disclosed to the patient.

What is clear is that treatment must be pursuant to real consent if it is to say anything about the patient's right to self-determination. While the issues involved where there is a clear 'touching' are legally less complicated, any meaningful definition or theory of consent must also be able to take account of situations where the concept of 'touching' is less clear or relevant.

However it is now the case that:

> The modern trend in the courts is to view failure to provide adequate disclosure of alternatives and risks as a breach of the physician's duty to the patient and thus to require the patient to sue in negligence instead of battery.[53]

While this statement was expressly made in respect of the practice of courts in America, it would seem to be none the less true of the British attitude. In Chatterton, supra, Mr. Justice Bristow declared that 'it would be very much against the interests of justice if actions which were really based on a failure by the doctor to perform his duty adequately to inform were pleaded in trespass.'[54]

The move to the negligence rather than the assault action may seem to be logical in these terms, but as Robertson points out:

> To regard the obligation to disclose 'real' risks as part of the doctor's overall duty of care places too much emphasis on the doctor's duty to disclose, and insufficient emphasis on the patient's right to receive.[55]

Although the assault based action may require a high standard of proof of failure on the part of the doctor to disclose relevant information, and may require evidence of some form of 'touching', the negligence action poses its own special problems for the pursuer, even although it should, theoretically, reduce the burden of proof in respect of the extent of the doctor's failure to make disclosure   It is clearly established that there are considerable problems in raising a successful action in respect of medical negligence,[56] and, quite apart from these general problems, lack of consent requires proof beyond the normal.   As Skegg notes: '...there will be no question of the patient recovering damages in negligence unless he can establish that, had the required information been communicated, consent would not have been granted.' [57] This view was also made explicit by the court in the case of Bolam, supra.[58]

Clearly, this will be difficult for any patient to prove.   In the Canadian case of Jodouin v. Mitra et al.,[59] despite claims by the patient that consent would not have been given had full disclosure been made, the Court stated that knowledge of the potential damage in this case 'would not have deterred her or any other reasonable individual from undergoing the operation.'[60]   Here the courts would also seem to fall into the trap of assuming that the notion of what the 'reasonable patient' would choose can be decided solely on the basis of the medical information, and to ignore the argument already developed that this choice may well depend on non-medical considerations.   While it is clear that the doctor can only concern himself with medical matters, to restrict decision-making in this way is to minimise the argument that the patient has a right to self-determination.   Courts, however, may seem to work from the assumption that the 'reasonable patient' would require powerful medical reasons for refusing therapy, whereas the patient may prefer to make the kind of complete choice already outlined.

However, overlaid even on the difficulties of proving that the patient would not have undergone the treatment had certain information been disclosed (given that the simple declaration by the patient that he or she would not have agreed will be insufficient), there is also the paradox that, should a doctor feel that a particular intervention is necessary, he has been said to be entitled not to make full disclosure or even to lie to the patient, should he feel that a full disclosure might prevent the patient from agreeing to the proposed form of intervention.[61]   Thus the therapeutic model would seem to be regarded as of primary and fundamental importance in guiding the extent and nature of any disclosures made to a patient by a doctor. The patient cannot successfully simply appeal to his rights as an individual to make a choice in the light of what he would regard as sufficient information, but is dependent on showing that not only would he have declined the treatment had disclosure been made, but also that he was harmed by the failure to disclose (an essential component of any negligence action[62]).

Although it has already been argued[63] that consent must necessarily involve an element of real choice (and therefore by implication some element of disclosure, and perhaps even of understanding), nonetheless courts in the United Kingdom and to a lesser extent in the United States, have tended to interpret rules about consent with the discretion of the medical profession and the benefits of therapy very much in mind.   Indeed, it would seem that their interpretation goes a long way towards the theories of consent which were originally discounted as unsatisfactory, in that, when a patient presents himself to a doctor who assesses a need for therapy, the decision of the doctor as to the need for treatment and the type of therapy which is appropriate, would seem to shift the burden of proof to the litigant to show that the 'reasonable patient' would not have consented had the information been disclosed.

Equally, the patient wishing to sue in medical negligence cases is faced with the further difficulty of establishing that the doctor's behaviour fell below the accepted standard of practice.[64] The notion of standard practice is central to the attitudes of the British Courts in allegations of medical negligence,[65] and may affect the assessment of whether or not the intervention is lawful.   Gordon has pointed out that: 'To be lawful the operation must, of course, be one which is recognised by the profession as appropriate and be carried out in accordance with proper professional standards.'[66]

Thus, the notion of professional judgement, which has already been shown to be significant in deciding whether or not intervention is desirable, also becomes important in the decision as to what type of intervention is appropriate and the methods and standards of that intervention.   The use of this concept, sometimes referred to as 'clinical judgement', makes the doctor's choice of an alternative form of therapy or course of action less susceptible of comment from those who are not part of the medical profession.[67]   Equally, it may permit the doctor to explain his apparent failure to make certain facts known to the patient on the grounds that standard practice does not demand such disclosure.   As Walker has said:

It may be negligent to fail to warn the patient of the risks inherent in a proposed course of treatment, but only if proper practice is to give a warning in such circumstances and the patient would not have consented to the treatment.[68] (Emphasis added.)

The decision as to what is reasonable in these terms is largely based not on what the patient regards as reasonable, but on an apparently objective test of normal or proper medical practice. However, since exposition of 'normal practice' depends on the evidence of fellow medical practitioners, the test may be less objective than at first appears.   The problems inherent in permitting standards to be set by fellow professionals have been much discussed, and it has been pointed out that 'Respect for a patient's right of self-determination on particular therapy demands a standard set by law rather than one which physicians may or may not impose upon themselves.'[69]

In any event it would seem that:

In most general terms, the goal of health care as it pertains to such fundamental human values relates to the maintenance of the integrity, of the coherence of the human person, with specific reference to the physical substrate of that integrity.[70]

This appeal to personal integrity is not unusual in medical practice, nor is it unusual in other disciplines such as social work, where it has been claimed to be the major aim of a professional service.[71] This concept and related ones such as autonomy and self-determination, have often been recognised as potentially problematic.   Thus, social workers, who see themselves as aiming at 'enhancing a client's self-determination' or 'respecting his or her autonomy', have wondered how it is possible to be professionally involved with a client at all, since notions such as advising, guiding, and directing, seem to them to be notions which conflict with the idea of free rational agents making their own informed choices and decisions, which is what self-determination is seen as involving.

However, in medical cases, discussions relating to consent,

and particularly to the problems of disclosure, would seem to indicate that, although 'prima facie it is the patient who should decide whether or not to take the benefit of surgery attended by definite risk',[72] nonetheless both practitioners of medicine and courts of law will probably hold the decision to be one which, at least in some cases,[73] will fall within the professional competence and clinical judgement of the doctor.[74]

It is important for any theory of consent that the reasons for obtaining it are clear. It has been suggested that:

The professions, both medical and legal, are in danger of losing sight of the fact that the object of consent, written or oral, is to protect the medical practitioner against the risk of an action for assault being formulated against him.[75]

This statement seems to display a fundamental misconception of the purpose for which consent is sought, even although it may be a reflection of the views of some medical practitioners. While it may be a result of obtaining consent that a doctor cannot be sued for failing to obtain it, it is hardly the justification for obtaining it. That must surely be found in the right of the individual to choose or refuse medical treatment, or certain types of treatment, and to assess his own situation and reach a rational conclusion in his own terms as to what intervention he is prepared to authorise.

While it may be true that: 'The difficulties presented by the law in this area probably result from the adaptation of ill-fitting criminal law and tort concepts to an area with its own particular problems',[76] it is equally clear that medical practice cannot be entirely exempt from the restrictions placed on other groups in the community, nor does it necessarily benefit from finding itself in a special position.[77]

If 'informed consent' is taken as a description of a necessary extent of disclosure, and a reflection of certain rights which are necessarily held by all patients and which need not be dependent on purely medical risks, rather than as implying understanding of complicated medical techniques, then it can be seen that it is possible to provide adequate guidelines which will safeguard both the doctor and his patient. These would involve recognition by the doctor of the patient's right to refuse treatment in view of the risks which he, the patient, regards as unacceptable, and would entail a modification of the esteem in which the therapeutic model is presently held. Further, the operation of such guidelines would involve the courts in assessing the behaviour of the individual doctor in respect of a specific patient, rather than assessing his behaviour solely as part of a professional group. Since it is already clear that a doctor may well be unaware of the factors which may be regarded by any given patient as important in shaping his decision whether or not to undergo therapy, this would seem to argue for a fuller disclosure than may be made at present, although it would not necessarily prevent the doctor from employing the 'Prevention of Harm Argument' in appropriate cases.

For the moment, however, it would seem that there is a shift to seeing the obtaining of consent as part of a doctor's general duties to his patient, which will be assessed on the basis of the approach taken by his colleagues, and the test which will be applied in these circumstances is likely to be that of the 'reasonable doctor'. This provides the medical profession with considerable scope in the setting of standards and allows that their fellow professionals will be largely responsible for assessing the extent of the disclosure which doctors should make.

It could be argued, then, that although it may be convenient for courts to view a failure to obtain consent as a breach of the doctor's duty, this attitude, as presently interpreted, offers little protection for the patient's right to self-determination and may even display a fundamental misconception of the very reason for obtaining consent. It can also be claimed that the assessment of what amounts to 'real' consent cannot rationally be based on the established practice of those who are seeking, rather than providing, consent.

Robertson convincingly argues that:

the doctrine of informed consent ought to be accepted and developed by the courts in this country so as to ensure that patients are given the information which they require to exercise their right to decide whether to undergo proposed medical treatment,[78]

but, somewhat sadly, concludes that 'it is...judicial policy, rather than the patient's right to determine his own medical treatment, that will dictate the future development of the doctrine of informed consent in this country.'[79]

If this is so, then the courts will almost certainly prefer to view failures in disclosure as breaches of the general duty of the doctor to the patient, presumably partly because it is simpler to assess the behaviour of the 'reasonable doctor' than to attempt to conceptualise the 'reasonable patient', who may, as has been seen, be influenced by a variety of personal factors outwith the knowledge of the doctor. This attitude, unless it is used in a discriminating manner by courts, will inevitably protect the doctor, since therapy is often seen as a good in itself, and will also protect the doctor's clinical freedom perhaps to the detriment of the patient's rights to self-determination. To assess the doctor's behaviour in terms of that of his fellows is perhaps a less satisfactory approach - particularly in this highly sensitive area - than to view each case on its own merits, which would permit the interests of each individual patient to be taken into account. To accept that the choice of when and how to intervene lies primarily, or even exclusively, with the doctor rather than the patient seems, however, accurately to reflect the assumptions underlying the present legal approach to medical practice.[80]

It might appear, therefore, that the patient is better protected by the emphasis on his interests which is a feature of the assault based action, which necessitates proof only that real consent was not given, rather than by the current development of the negligence action which reflects such intangible and subjective notions as 'clinical judgement' and 'standard practice', and focuses the attention of the law on the practice of the doctor, as part of a professional group, rather than on the interests or rights of the patient. However, any form of action which concentrates the issue exclusively on one party's attitudes or interests may well be suspect in this particular area. Both the assault based action, and the negligence action as currently used, present problems if the aims of health care, the interests of the patient and the expertise of the doctor are to be protected. It is submitted however, that the negligence action, used discriminatingly, could serve to highlight both the rights of the patient and the duties of the doctor, by reflecting an acceptance that decision-making in this area is a joint process, and if anything should be weighted towards the rights and interests of the patient rather than being seen as exclusively the prerogative of the doctor, although the patient will, of course, be guided to some extent by the advice of the doctor. It has already been pointed out that certain groups are excluded from the provision of consent because they do not have the capacity to make understanding choices,[81] and if it is indeed this capacity which differentiates the 'normal' patient from these groups, then the 'normal' patient will be in a position to give real consent only where an attempt has been made to offer him sufficient information to make an informed choice. Unless the negligence action develops along the lines proposed above, thereby expanding the use of the concept of consent in medicine, the patient's right to choose may be inadequately protected both by the doctor and by the law.

S.A.M. McLean
A.J. McKay

NOTES

1. For a definition of rape and discussion of the nature of the offence, see Gordon, G.H., The Criminal Law of Scotland, (2nd Ed.), Edinburgh, W.Green & Son Ltd., 1978, ch. 33; see also, Williams, G., Textbook of Criminal Law, London, Stevens and Sons, 1978, ch. 8.

2. c.f. R v. Morgan [1976] A.C. 182; R v. Eatch [1980] Crim. L.R. 651.

3. Devlin, P., The Enforcement of Morals, London, Oxford University Press, 1959, at p. 8. (From the Proceedings of the British Academy), Vol. XLV, London, Oxford University Press.)

4. For discussion of the application of this doctrine see Walker, D.M., The Law of Delict in Scotland, Edinburgh, W.Green & Son, 1966, at pp. 351 et seq; The implications of this doctrine are succinctly expressed in Watson, A.A., and McLean, A.M., 'Consent to Treatment - A Shield or a Sword', 25 Scott. Med. J., (1980), 113, where they state (id.).'It is a cardinal tenet of the common law that when a person has freely and voluntarily given consent to a particular course of conduct by another, he cannot sue that other for damages arising from that consent.'

5. Walker, op.cit., at pp. 351-2.

6. id.

7. Cusine, D.J., 'To Sterilize or Not to Sterilize?' 18 Med. Sci. & Law, 120 (1978), at p. 381.

8. Williams, op.cit., at p. 566.

9. Mason, J.K., Forensic Medicine for Lawyers, Bristol, John Wright & Sons Ltd., 1978, at p. 381.

10. Quest, I.M., 'Recent Developments in Medical Negligence', 1 I.J.M.L., 483 (1980).

11. Skegg, P.D.G., '"Informed Consent" to Medical Procedures', 15 Med.Sci. & Law, 124 (1975), at p. 127.

12. For discussion, see Singer, P., Democracy and Disobedience, Oxford, Clarendon Press, 1973.

13. ibid., at p. 110.

14. Skegg, loc.cit., (1975), suggests at p. 124 that: 'The term "informed consent" is seriously misleading when it is used in

a way which suggests that there is a single doctrine of informed consent.' However, this assertion is convincingly challenged in Robertson, G., 'Informed Consent to Medical Treatment'. 97 L.Q.R., 102 (1981).

15. [1980] 7 Current Law 44.
16. Lee, R.G., 'Consent to Medical Treatment: Some Current Difficulties', 1 I.J.M.L., 493 (1980), at p. 501.
17. Skegg, loc.cit. (1975), at p. 127.
18. For discussion see Hoggett, B., Parents and Children, London, Sweet & Maxwell, 1977, at pp. 13-15; Williams, G., op.cit., at pp. 525-528; Gordon, op.cit., at p. 830; Skegg, P.D.G., 'Consent to Medical Procedures on Minors' 36 M.L.R. 370, (1973). In the case of non-therapeutic intervention it is even more certain that those purporting to offer consent would have their decision closely scrutinised, c.f. Re D (a minor) [1976] 1 All E.R. 326.
19. For discussion of these problems see for example Cohen, C., 'Medical Experimentation on Prisoners' in Medical Responsibility, Robison, W., and Prichard, M., (eds), Clifton, New Jersey, 1979. The prison population has been of particular concern in this area where they are requested to participate in medical research. It has been suggested that by the nature of their position, they cannot be other than exploited by researchers, and cannot choose 'freely' to participate in experiments since they may be influenced by factors which would not be present in the minds of other members of the community. Of course, the possibility of being influenced by non-rational factors is also open to those outside the prison population and it may be that doubts about the way in which prisoners might be used should be extended to them also.
20. c.f. H.M.A. v. Rutherford 1947 J.C. 1, and in particular the judgement of Lord Cooper, where he stated (at p. 5): '...if life is taken under circumstances which would otherwise infer guilt of murder, the crime does not cease to be murder merely because the victim consented to be murdered.'; see also Rex v. Donovan [1934] 2 K.B. 498.
21. See Williams, op.cit., at p. 531, where he states that: 'If a doctor, to speed his dying patient's passing, injects poison with the patient's consent, this will be murder...'. This situation must, however, be differentiated from that where a doctor treats a terminally ill patient with e.g. massive doses of pain-killers, knowing that this will hasten death but also that it is the only means by which the patient can tolerate the level of pain. Gordon points out, op.cit., at p. 765 that although there may be doubts about the appropriate charge in cases of euthanasia (i.e. murder or culpable homicide), nonetheless there is no doubt that euthanasia remains a form of unlawful killing.
22. op.cit. at p. 531.
23. See however, Skegg, P.D.G., 'A Justification for Medical Procedures Performed Without Consent', 90 L.Q.R., (1974), 512, and particularly at p. 518 where he states that: '...a doctor is justified in proceeding, without consent, with any procedure which it would be unreasonable, as opposed to merely inconvenient, to postpone until consent could be sought.'

24.   Gordon, op.cit., at p. 828.
25.   Watson and McLean, loc.cit., at p. 113.
26.   Brazier, M. 'Informed Consent to Surgery', 19 Med.Sci.& Law, 49 (1979).
27.   See Buchanan, A., 'Medical Paternalism', 7 Philosophy and Public Affairs, 340.   The following paragraphs owe much to the arguments developed by Buchanan.
28.   ibid., at p. 377.
29.   infra, p. 98.
30.   loc.cit., at p. 386.
31.   Robertson, loc.cit., at p. 111, where he further asserts that American Courts have tended to rely on the notion of 'reasonable disclosure' rather than concentrating on protecting the patient, and that the development of the doctrine in America has mirrored the desire to compensate more patients by extending the field of medical liability in this way.
32.   464 F. 2d 772 (1972).
33.   ibid., at p. 780.
34.   Lee, loc.cit., at p. 503.   The author also refers here to the Canadian case of Chrichton v. Hastings (1973) 29 D.L.R. (3d) 692, where it was held to be negligent to fail to warn of the possible side-effects of a drug.
35.   For discussion see Robertson, loc.cit.;   Rozovsky, L.E., 1 Leg.-Med. Q., 162 (1977).
36.   Rozovsky, loc.cit., at p. 165.
37.   For discussion see Rozovsky, loc.cit.
38.   154 Cal.App. 2d 560 (1957).
39.   ibid., at p. 578.
40.   [1957] 2 All E.R. 118.
41.   per McNair, J., at p. 214.
42.   'The Times' 2 July 1954.
43.   Canterbury v. Spence, supra, at p. 789.
44.   For discussion see Lee, loc.cit., where he states at p. 497. 'If the medical staff cannot obtain consent either because the patient is unconscious and no relative is readily available, or because of a refusal to consent by the parent of a child, then the law will cease with this requirement [of obtaining consent] providing there is an immediate necessity.'
45.   'The Times' 29 July 1978.
46.   [1981] 1 All E.R. 257.
47.   ibid., at p. 264.
48.   ibid., at p. 265.
49.   For definitions of assault see Gordon, op.cit., and Williams, op.cit.
50.   For discussion see Skegg, loc.cit., (1975).
51.   Skegg, loc.cit., (1975), at p. 124.
52.   ibid., at p. 265.
53.   loc.cit. at p. 483.
54.   Annas, G.J., Glantz, L.H., Katz, B.F., Informed Consent to Human Experimentation: The Subject's Dilemma, Cambridge, Mass., Ballinger Publishing Co., 1977, at p. 28.
55.   loc.cit., at p. 117.
56.   see infra, ch. 7.
57.   Skegg, loc.cit., (1975) at p. 128.
58.   It was stated in this case that '...you might well take the

view that unless the plaintiff has satisfied you that he would not have taken the treatment if he had been warned, there is really nothing in this point', per McNair, J. at p. 214.

59.   (1978) 2 Leg.Med. Q. 72.

60.   ibid., at p. 75.

61.   Hatcher v. Black, supra; Bolam, supra.

62.   For discussion of the general principles of law applied in negligence cases see Wilson, W.A., 'The Analysis of Negligence', in Introductory Essays on Scots Law, Edinburgh, W. Green & Son, 1978.

63.   infra, p. 99-100.

64.   For discussion see McLean, S.A.M., 'Negligence - A Dagger at the Doctor's Back?', in Robson, P., and Watchman, P., (eds) Justice, Lord Denning and the Constitution, Gower Publishing Co. Ltd., 1981. See also infra ch. 7.

65.   It was suggested in Hatcher v. Black, supra, that a doctor who is not criticised by his fellow professionals should not be criticised by the courts. For discussion of this case see Denning, The Discipline of Law, London, Butterworths, 1979. In Hunter v. Hanley 1955 S.C. 200, it was further stated that, even if a doctor does deviate from a standard practice, he will not be negligent unless there is evidence that a doctor acting with due skill and care would not have deviated from that practice.

66.   Gordon, op.cit., at p. 828.

67.   McLean, S.A.M., loc.cit.; Denning, loc.cit.

68.   op.cit., at p. 1055.

69.   Canterbury v. Spence, supra.

70.   Fried, C., Medical Experimentation: Personal Integrity and Social Policy, North-Holland Publishing Company, 1974, at p. 95.

71.   For discussion see McDermott, F.E., (ed), Self-Determination in Social Work, London, Routledge & Kegan Paul, 1978.

72.   Brazier, loc.cit., at pp. 53-4.

73.   This decision may be based on the vulnerability of the patient in question and/or the need for the particular therapy: see Re D (a minor), supra.

74.   Brazier, loc.cit., suggests at pp.52-3 that: 'In principle...what must be sought is a balance between the right of a sane, adult person to understand the true nature of what is going to happen to him, and the inevitable fact that the final judgement must be that of the medical staff.' Here again the therapeutic model would seem to be regarded as of prime importance, since otherwise there can be no grounds for suggesting that the ultimate decision rests anywhere other than with the patient.

75.   Quest, loc.cit., at p. 483.

76.   Lee, loc.cit., at p. 504.

77.   Indeed, when considering the basis of liability in medical negligence cases, the Royal Commission on Civil Liability and Compensation for Personal Injury, Cmnd 7054/1978, expressly declined to alter the nature of liability in these cases since it would place doctors in a different position from the rest of the community - see para 1344.

78.   loc.cit., at p. 126.

79.   id.

80.   See McLean, S.A.M., loc.cit.
81.   infra, p. 98.

9 Medical Progress and the Law
D. Soutar and S. A. M. McLean

The majority of medical ailments are susceptible to a wide variety of treatments. Established methods of therapy have the advantage that their benefits and disadvantages are well documented; they are 'tried and tested', whereas there is often no statistically valid proof regarding the efficacy of newer methods. Such proof can only be attained following use in a clinical situation and there is understandable concern that patients should not be used as 'guinea pigs' for clinical research purposes. There has been much concern over human experimentation for some considerable time, and many examples of (often quite bizarre) experiments.[1] Experiments may be therapeutic (i.e. directly for the benefit of the patient), or non-therapeutic,(i.e. for the advancement of knowledge or the benefit of future patients), but whatever their motivation they raise ethical and legal problems which must be weighed against the interests of medical science in developing and improving therapies and techniques.

Guidelines regarding the ethics of human experimentation were laid down by the World Medical Association in the Declaration of Helsinki in 1964, revised in 1975, which states:

1. In the treatment of the sick person, the doctor must be free to use a new therapeutic measure if, in his judgment, it offers hope of saving life, re-establishing health or alleviating suffering.

2. The doctor can combine clinical research with professional care, the objective being the acquisition of new medical knowledge, only to the extent that clinical research is justified by its therapeutic value for the patient.[2]

In addition, both Declarations stress the importance of obtaining consent following a full explanation of the proposed treatment,[3] and provide the ethical basis for experimentation on human subjects, the major dilemmas in which concern the obtaining of valid consent from the subject, and the justification in using new techniques and therapies. The question of consent is considered elsewhere in this book,[4] and thus this chapter will concern itself primarily with the problems of justification for new therapies and the problems of control in this area.

Experimentation, whatever its problems, is essential to the development of medical science, and through this medium to the health of the community. As Klass has said:

...human medical experimentation must continue, or progress in drug treatment will cease. This is the kind of experimentation that must inevitably take place when the first, the very first, course of treatment with a new drug is carried out on a human, or the first surgical operation promising an improvement over the previous one is attempted.[5]

While it should be noted that: 'Under a broad definition [of experimentation], recognised medical treatment might be classified as experimental owing to the peculiarity presented by any given patient's case',[6] this chapter will be concerned with the use of new medical products or new techniques, and since the problems surrounding the justification of the use of new products and techniques are essentially different they are better considered independently.

TREATMENT INVOLVING A NEW MEDICAL PRODUCT.

In the code of practice for the pharmaceutical industry the present situation regarding new medical products is succinctly stated:

Before a medical product is placed on the market, the manufacturer will have accumulated considerable toxicological, pharmacological and clinical evidence and will have met all the statutory requirements for the testing, manufacture and marketing of that product. Comprehensive legislation has been introduced to safeguard the public by ensuring that all products meet the standards of quality, efficacy and safety which are acceptable in the state of present knowledge and experience.[7]

However, the initial clinical trials of new drugs rarely produce ideal information, since they are primarily geared towards meeting the legal requirements. The law has intervened in the control of the marketing and production of new drugs via the establishment of the Committee on Safety of Medicines,[8] with overall responsibility for supervision in this area, and for the control of pre-marketing research and trials. The Committee requires that certain tests are carried out before a new drug is marketed or given a limited trial, and these tests will include animal tests, although there is some concern as to the efficacy of such tests given that the response of any drug on the human metabolism may vary considerably from that on an animal.[9] No matter the extent of animal experimentation carried out, there is inevitably a risk when the product has its first trial on a human subject, but equally such experiments will provide valuable, if not infallible, information.[10]

In conjunction with the work done by the Committee on Review of Medicines[11] which was established to consider the effects of drugs produced before the establishment of the Committee on Safety of Medicines, an effort is also made to scrutinise the reported side effects of drugs once they are on the market. Recently published figures of the number of reports of suspected reactions received over the past five years by the Committee on Safety of Medicines show the number of suspected reactions reported to them, of which about 75 per cent were notified through the yellow card system.[12]

1975	5,052
1976	6,490
1977	11,255
1978	11,873
1979	10,840

They concluded that:

The voluntary reporting system, despite manifest drawbacks is still the most effective method of detecting a serious new hazard in a recently marketed drug. When combined with continuous surveillance of world literature, it also provides an effective means of monitoring drug safety.[13]

In addition to these Committees, the media exert a powerful influence in monitoring drug safety, as can readily be seen by the influence of the 'Daily Mail' and the 'Sunday Times' in the case of Thalidomide.[14] There can be little doubt that, but for their intervention, the children concerned might yet be awaiting compensation, and indeed given the uncertainty of the law at that time in respect of this type of case and the problems of proof, it may be that no compensation would actually have been awarded in any event.[15]

It is thus essential that clinical trials are carried out before a drug will be given a licence for marketing on a large scale, and these trials are organised and controlled by the manufacturers once the protocols have been approved by the D.H.S.S..[16]   There is available a wide variety of clinical trials, using healthy volunteers or patients, in both therapeutic and non-therapeutic clinical research programmes.   Trials may be randomised,[17] or controlled,[18] and the most valid clinical results are obtained in 'blind' and 'double blind' trials.[19]   The most helpful information when trying to justify a new treatment, comes from comparative trials[20] where one method of therapy is evaluated against another but unfortunately such trials are rarely, if ever, performed prior to marketing a new product.

Further, most manufacturers retain control over publication of the results of their clinical trials.   This protects them from competitors by preventing premature release of information and, in the event that the product proves of little or no value, avoids public and professional humiliation.   Not surprisingly, there is considerable concern as to the advisability of permitting the manufacturing industry this freedom in controlling the only sources of clinical data concerning a new medical product, and the recent controversy over the clinical information presented by the company in the marketing of Debendox/Bendectin is a case in point.[21]   This is not to suggest that all, or even many, companies will deliberately disguise unfavourable information regarding a new product, and in recent times at least one major company has accepted significant financial loss rather than market a product concerning whose safety there were serious doubts.[22]

However, as in any industry, economic factors are of prime importance to companies, which invest a considerable proportion of their substantial income in researching and developing new drugs.[23]   As Klass points out:

> ...in the industrial world it is 'mission-orientated'
> research that dominates.   There the aim is to discover
> something of practical value, such as some advance in the
> treatment of a specific disease or the alleviation of a
> particular symptom.[24]

Prima facie, this aim is laudable but Klass continues that although it would be a mistake to control the marketing of such new products thoughtlessly, nonetheless this should not 'blind one to the very serious and often unnecessary risks involved in the commercially profitable exploitation of new drugs.'[25]

Equally, financial considerations often mean that companies tend to promote trials in medical centres where there are relatively large numbers of suitable cases for inclusion in the trial, thus obtaining the requisite number of cases for analysis in a relatively short time and speeding up the process towards eventual marketing of their product.   In defence of the system, the centres chosen have a good reputation, particularly regarding research and publication.   Here again, however, there are mixed motives since the manufacturer will obviously choose medical centres of high repute to ensure that the trial is carried out according to the protocol and that it is completed satisfactorily to meet the statutory requirements.

Direct or indirect financial assistance to those performing clinical trials, is an additional moral and ethical problem.   Such assistance can be used to persuade doctors to carry out clinical trials or to 'try out' the product following market release and here society is totally dependent on the moral and ethical codes of the individual manufacturers and doctors concerned. It could be argued that it is immoral for a manufacturer to finance or 'buy' a clinical trial, but should analysis and investigation require expensive and sophisticated equipment or specialised technical help, then perhaps the manufacturing industry should be responsible for providing these, even although this may amount indirectly at least to financing the project.   Since often, in such cases, the specialised knowledge and equipment remain available for the medical staff concerned and thus benefit the National Health Service, it may be felt that the overall benefits of this practice outweigh the potential disadvantages.

Certainly, if doctors apply their ethical codes to the expected high standard, then problems should be minimised, although it has been suggested that the pressures on doctors are such that '...events...have diminished an honourable profession [medicine] to the level of a junior partner in an immensely powerful industrial-medical complex'.[26]   Such is the concern over the use of the clinical trial that, following the Declaration of Helsinki, supra, a number of local medical groups issued their own guidelines on the matter of experimentation.   For example, the Royal College of Physicians and Surgeons of Glasgow issued a set of guidelines in 1972,[27] which state that: 'In selecting volunteers and in elaborating projects, the doctor has to consider his duty to patient, to colleague and to the National Health Service',[28] bearing in mind that patients may be influenced in favour of participation in any research project by their relationship with the individual doctor.[29]

Concern over the use of volunteers in medical research led to the setting up of Research Ethical Committees,[30] which now exist in virtually every hospital in which clinical investigation is carried out.   Their influence is such that it is now almost impossible to obtain financial support for research without their sanction, and subsequent publication of any results will normally only be possible in a reputable journal where such approval has been given.   By stipulating lay representation on such Committees[31] it was hoped that a balanced approach to clinical research could be obtained. However, a recent survey of Research Ethical Committees in Scotland[32] suggests that:

There is a considerable and confusing lack of uniformity in arrangements for the different types of ethical committees. Even at the same level they vary dramatically in size, composition, remit and mode of operation.   Some serve as little more than debating forums, while others seek to maintain quite strict supervision of research.[33]

Thus, while apparently offering a further scrutiny of the ethics of experiments, the Committees may require to tighten up their own standards before they can offer a valuable and uniform means of controlling at ground level the nature and extent of acceptable experimentation.[34]   Concern as to the potential adverse side-effects of drugs has also led recently to the establishment of a drug surveillance research unit at Southampton University, which will initially scrutinise a limited number of drugs on the market, as an additional check to that carried out by the Committee on Review of Medicines.[35]   The hope is that this unit's results will 'reveal quite slight side-effects of drugs', which might escape the attention of the doctor in other circumstances, or which he may not feel to be sufficiently important to justify the use of the 'yellow card' system.

By the time a medical product reaches the market, then, it must have met all the statutory requirements, its clinical trials will have been subject to some form of scrutiny at local level, and it has, in effect, been 'passed' by the government.[36] This indirectly confers a legal right on a medical practitioner to use the product and, provided he complies with the information given in the data sheet,[37] there can be no question of negligence. The recent controversy surrounding the widespread use of Tagamet[38] would, however, suggest that doctors are not always entirely vigilant in their adherence to the contraindications outlined on the data sheet.

However, although this may appear prima facie to amount to negligence, it should be borne in mind that courts have traditionally supported the right of doctors to exercise their clinical judgement in the practice of medicine, which may have the result that his choice, even of a potentially dangerous drug, may not be legally criticised. One area, however, where it has been suggested the position is more clear, is in the case of the provision to a pregnant woman of known teratogens.[39]

The law, therefore, attempts to perform a double role - on the one hand attempting to protect the public and on the other, effectively shielding the medical profession from subsequent litigation by demanding a certain standard of safety and efficacy.

The major problem for the doctor is whether there is sufficient information to justify the use of a new medical product. This problem is a medical rather than a legal one since it is the doctor who has to explain in detail the proposed treatment to the patient, and should therefore have access to sufficient information to make this explanation. This must to some extent be dependent, not only on the clinical information provided in respect of the trials of a new drug, but also on the receipt of information as to the reported effects of the drug once it becomes generally available. However, apart from the restrictive control which the manufacturer can exert on the initial clinical trials, obtaining valid clinical data is further made difficult by the lack of controlled post-market surveillance. There is no statutory surveillance once a new product has been released, except for production and manufacturing quality controls. Society is dependent on a voluntary reporting system with doctors notifying adverse reactions to treatment to the Committee on Safety of Medicines using 'yellow cards', and on the action subsequently taken by that Committee.

This system has its drawbacks, despite the confidence in it expressed by the Committee on Safety of Medicines. Thus, even although the Committee may have evidence that other countries have experienced problems with a particular product, whatever the evidence accumulated there is no obligation on the Committee to withdraw a drug or even to recommend limiting its use. Therefore, in the Debendox/Bendectin example, although the Food and Drug Administration in the United States[40] instructed doctors after one successful legal action that, in view of the emerging evidence of teratogenesis, this drug should not be prescribed except in extreme cases, the C.S.M. has only very recently made a similar recommendation although couched in very much more restrained terms.[41]

Thus, there are further risks in the use of new drugs which relate not simply to the voluntary nature of the reporting system and the effective control of trials by the industry itself, but also to the time-lag in the reporting of adverse effects. It is the medical literature which eventually provides the most valuable clinical data, since this may include some of the manufacturers' clinical trials in addition to research performed by independent workers. Of particular value in aiding a doctor to decide on a method of treatment are reports on comparative trials, but all this information requires the use of the product in the clinical situation and since there is obviously a considerable delay between the marketing of the product and the availability of good clinical data, the product will continue to be used until sufficient evidence becomes available to demonstrate the nature and extent of the risks involved.

Clinicians vary as to the amount of clinical information they require before commencing treatment. Here, marketing by the manufacturer can influence the doctor, by providing him with quotations from selected sections of published articles in promotional material, obviously intended to be favourable to the product. Such quotations can be unrepresentative and may even be misleading, but, coupled with the other information provided almost exclusively by the pharmaceutical company, may amount to the total information which is in the possession of any doctor prior to his initial use of a drug. This will make his assessment of the risks and benefits of any particular therapy necessarily inadequate, since, in carrying out any course of therapy, it is essential that both the doctor and the patient are satisfied that the proposed treatment is safe and that it may prove of benefit to the patient.

The doctor's responsibility is to his individual patient, and through him to the community at large. If he confines himself to the treatment of the individual patient, the clinician can, to some degree, diminish conflicts surrounding human experimentation. His greatest dilemma lies in the fact that he is totally dependent on second-hand information and not on his own personal clinical experience. He is, in fact, at the mercy of the manufacturing industry and statutory controls for the extent and content of the necessary clinical information. This also highlights the major difference between the use of new medical products in treatment, and the use of new techniques.

Quite apart from the problems which new drugs pose for the medical profession, there are major problems for the patient attempting to obtain compensation having been damaged as a result of the use of such products. These problems exist both where the patient is involved in the clinical trials of a new drug and also where he is the recipient of a drug which, although passed as 'safe' by the Committee on Safety of Medicines, is nonetheless new to his doctor.

In the situation where the patient is involved in a trial of a new product, assuming that he has validly consented to participate, there will be no question of the doctor being liable unless some negligence exists. Equally, there is unlikely to be evidence of negligence on the part of the company concerned. Thus, given the present system on which liability in personal injury cases operates, there is considerable concern as to how a volunteer could receive compensation for damage in these circumstances. In their evidence to the Royal Commission on Civil Liability and Compensation for Personal Injury[42] (Pearson Commission), the Medical Research Council indicated that, should such damage occur, they would seek the authority to make an ex gratia payment to the patient or his dependents.[43] The Pearson Commission considered such an approach to be unsuitable, and stated that:

We think that it is wrong that a person who exposes himself

to some medical risk in the interests of the community should have to rely on <u>ex gratia</u> compensation in the event of injury. We recommend that any volunteer for medical research or clinical trials who suffers severe damage as a result should have a cause of action, on the basis of strict liability, against the authority to whom he has consented to make himself available.[44]

Thus, were the recommendations of the Pearson Commission to be implemented (which now seems unlikely), then the volunteer who is seriously injured would be able to claim compensation merely by demonstrating that the damage was the result of his participation in the research, and there would have been no need to establish that any person or organisation was at fault. Clearly, the implementation of these proposals would provide two major benefits for the volunteer and for medical research itself. First in compensating him without the need for complicated, costly and perhaps unsuccessful legal action, and secondly, hopefully by thus encouraging volunteers. However, implementation of these proposals would not have been entirely without problems. It was argued by the medical profession in their evidence to the Pearson Commission that the tortious/delictual action should be retained, since, it was claimed:

Liability was one of the means whereby doctors could show their sense of responsibility and, therefore justly claim professional freedom. If tortious libility were abolished, there could be some attempt to control doctors' clinical practice to prevent mistakes for which compensation would have to be paid by some central agency.....this could lead to a bureaucratic restriction of medicine and a brake on progress.[45]

The Pearson Commission, although eventually agreeing that the basis of liability should continue to be fault, were nonetheless largely unimpressed with this line of argument.[46] However, it may seem to be in the abstract a more powerful argument in the area of experiments since, if he is not to be blamed for his practice and the patient can readily obtain compensation, then the doctor may be less inhibited about experimentation. Nonetheless, there can be little doubt that, despite some shortcomings, the practice of the doctor in this area is already much circumscribed and his opportunity for unnecessary or frivolous experimentation is thereby limited.

Where the injuries result not from involvement in research but from the prescription of a drug which has received a product licence, but with which the doctor is unfamiliar, the problems are equally complicated. It is necessary in such a claim both to establish fault (generally negligence) and causation, and to identify the appropriate party to sue. There are considerable problems in the first but equally there may be special difficulties attached to the second, since, although the decision to use new medical products rests finally with the doctor, there is considerable debate as to the party who should be held responsible in the event of complications or adverse reactions occurring as a result of treatment.

To a great extent, the use of new therapies will depend on the extent to which the doctor becomes aware of them by keeping himself up-to-date with developments in medical science, and his liability may well be dependent on this also. It is undoubtedly the professional responsibility of the doctor to be well informed so that he can properly advise his patient, but should he follow the guidelines, however inadequate, provided by the drug company, he is unlikely to be successfully sued in negligence and since the drug used by the doctor has been been granted a product licence, there is little basis for arguing that the doctor should not have prescribed it.

The question of liability, however, remains. In view of the inherent risks of the production and marketing of new drugs, it might be thought that the manufacturing industry must accept increased responsibility. It was stated in the case of <u>Glasgow Corporation</u> v. <u>Muir</u>,[47] that those involved in inherently risky situations were legally required to demonstrate a higher than average standard of care, and it would seem not unreasonable to apply this to the pharmaceutical industry, and indeed some States in America have imposed a system of strict liability in this area.[48] Where damage does occur in these circumstances, there may also be an element at least of moral responsibility to be shouldered by the committee which approved its use on human beings, or perhaps a good argument for changes in the legislative controls.

It is clear, however, that the patient attempting to sue in these circumstance will have special difficulties in establishing negligence either on the part of his doctor or on the part of the drug company involved. This means that many patients will either remain uncompensated, or will have to depend on the company making an <u>ex gratia</u> payment. This was eventually the outcome in the Thalidomide situation, and it is obvious that for the patient to be put in a situation of relying on the desire of the pharmaceutical company to avoid bad publicity or to accept a certain moral blame, is of dubious value to any of the parties likely to be concerned. Although some companies may show themselves willing to settle a case out of court,[49] this is unsatisfactory for several reasons. First, it may mean that the patient receives less compensation than he/she might otherwise have done, and the pressures to accept out of court settlements, even given that this is the case, may well be great.

In the second place, the effect of such settlements is to preclude courts from assessing the liability of companies, and thereby from establishing whether or not the link in causation and the degree of negligence are sufficient, at least for legal purposes. This has the effect of leaving any other victim or potential victim uncertain as to the likely success of any claim which he may choose to raise, and also prevents the companies and the medical profession from being in a position adequately to assess the likely consequences of continued use of a drug. In other words, it may serve to suppress valuable information.

Certainly, while the system of compensation continues to require evidence of fault, then there may seem <u>prima facie</u> to be insurmountable problems in successfully suing in respect of a drug passed for marketing.[50] The uncertainties of the reporting system, and the lack of proper post-marketing surveillance, will further present the pursuer with substantial barriers to a successful action, since proof of causation, also necessary in this type of action, will be hampered by an inefficient method of scrutiny, and an inadequate scheme for noting and recording such effects. Although it would seem that the company rather than the doctor (unless otherwise negligent) is the appropriate defender in such actions, since the manufacturer carries the responsibility for production of the substance in question, there is little doubt that the individual attempting to challenge a wealthy and experienced company is at a great disadvantage.

However, since there would seem to be little chance in the near future of the system of compensation being altered to, e.g. one of strict liability which would not require proof of fault,[51] there are problems for the patient who is injured which could be ameliorated by both medicine and the law by ensuring that clinical trials are subject to tighter controls from outwith the industry itself.

Greater legal control could be effected over clinical trials by ensuring that research and development programmes are carried out in independent government controlled centres, and by exerting a greater control in the organisation and monitoring of clinical trials set up by the manufacturer. Greater emphasis could also be placed on the government's role in post-market surveillance, perhaps by producing annual reports on every new medical product, which could include a review of the world literature and a report from the Committee of Safety in Medicines on adverse reactions to treatment. Powers already exist to require further investigation to be carried out by companies on new products before a licence is granted should this seem to be necessary,[52] and the careful use of these powers can only be beneficial.

The Committee on Review of Medicines, is already in a position to carry out at least part of these functions. This Committee has the benefit of hindsight in that all the drugs in question will have been available and used, probably in a fairly substantial number of cases, for some considerable time. Thus, adverse side-effects are likely to have been reported, for example in the medical literature, and a certain statistical validity in respect of the effects will have been attained. There would seem then to be no major legal or scientific obstacle to tightening the surveillance of side-effects of drugs, nor to providing a more efficient means of identifying side-effects than the voluntary reporting system. Thus, the manufacturing industry, which at present controls much of the clinical data, could be made more accountable by government, perhaps by the introduction of statutory post-marketing surveillance, as for example in the regulations in the United States of America, where the manufacturer has to maintain full and detailed information concerning his products.[53]

However, the damage caused by drugs will not necessarily become immediately evident, and it may take many years of extensive use before adverse reactions become apparent. Doctors may have to become more alert to the possible side-effects of therapy, but even in the case of Thalidomide, which caused one of the most major public responses to the question of liability in this area, only some 400 children were damaged in the United Kingdom (an estimated 10,000 world-wide)[54] and even had doctors been more alert, the evidence with which they were confronted may not have seemed sufficiently significant to merit withdrawal of the drug.

In any event, it is perhaps regrettable that the final step of prescribing treatment lies in the hands of the doctor, who will have had no control over the production or investigation of the product, but on whose shoulders the burden of alertness to adverse effects and the general problems of patient care will rest. His responsibilities are great, and it has been said that:

> ...the physician has come to stand as the guardian for his
> patient, protecting him from the thousands of offered and
> advertised remedies that range from the harmless to the
> dangerous, produced by those who seek wealth.'[55]

What is clear is that, unless a new system of liability is introduced or the controls are tightened, the problems of compensation will

remain major, and the patient largely unprotected. However, it is
not just in the accumulation of evidence that the patient wishing to
sue in these circumstances may be prejudiced. In all cases where
damage is drug-based there may be a considerable time-lag between the
taking of the drug and the eventual conclusion that the damage was
caused by it, or between the taking of the drug and the harm actually
occurring. This will be particularly true where the effects of the
drug are teratogenic,[56] but even in other situations it may present
problems. For example, some Americans and Australians hoping to sue
in respect of damage allegedly caused by their exposure to dioxin
(used as the defoliant 'Agent Orange' by troops in Vietnam) have been
judged to be out of time, i.e. they can no longer raise an action for
personal injuries since the time limit for raising an action of this
sort has passed.[57] Whereas it may be that the operation of a bar
on proceedings of this sort will operate unfavourably to the pursuer
in other situations, it is likely to be particularly problematic in
cases of drug-based damage. The likely and appropriate legal
response to this situation will be that the time-limit runs from the
time at which the damage becomes evident,[58] but it may be that the
patient whose injuries are in this category will note the emergence of
a problem long before there is any medical or scientific reason for
tying it up with the taking of a drug. The law allows that
exceptions may be made to the general rule in respect of
time-limits,[59] but this remains at the discretion of the courts, who
may be loath to use it. The best solution in this situation might be
for the law, rather than regarding such situations as being unusual,
to assume that it is often the case in damage of this sort, and
expressly to exclude such cases from the time-bar, particularly since
the problems of accumulating convincing evidence are clear, and the
average patient cannot reasonably be expected to make the link in
causation when first he recognises the harm.

TREATMENT INVOLVING NEW TECHNIQUES

It is not only in the prescription or use of new products that
experimentation takes place. It is clear that:

> Medical science relies on research and experimentation, as do
> all other sciences, to advance its knowledge in man's fight
> against sickness and disease. Inevitably, such
> experimentation must utilise human subjects if it is to have
> primary significance. For any new therapy, drug or
> treatment there must always be the first patient or
> subject.[60]

Doctors may, then, attempt 'deviational, unpractised or unaccepted
treatment' which the law has 'classed, often imperfectly, as
experimentation'.[61] Although there are no statutory requirements
covering the choice of technique in treatment, it is already clear
that some scrutiny is maintained by the law in this area by the use of
the negligence action where the doctor is shown not to have acted with
due skill and care.[62] By and large, however, the decision as to
types of therapy and the responsibility for success or failure rest
entirely with the clinician.

When justifying the use of a particular technique, the clinician
must be convinced that he is personally competent to carry out the
procedure and that the technique offers the patient some benefit over
alternative methods. In cases where complications arise as a result

of such treatment, the onus in law remains with the pursuer who, in order to succeed, must establish negligence on the part of the doctor, i.e. that the doctor in question is guilty of such failure as no doctor of ordinary skill would be guilty if acting with ordinary care.[63]   This may be extremely difficult for him to establish, particularly where the technique is one which has been described in the medical literature, thereby implying that both the author and the editorial board of the medical journal concerned deem the technique worthy of approval.   It is insufficient for the complainer merely to show deviation from normal practice.   As the court said in Hunter v. Hanley[64]:

> To establish liability by a doctor where deviation from normal practice is alleged, three facts require to be established.   First of all it must be proved that there is a usual and normal practice; secondly, it must be proved that the defender has not adopted that practice; and thirdly (and this is of crucial importance), it must be established that the course the doctor adopted is one which no professional man of ordinary skill would have taken if he had been acting with ordinary care.   There is clearly a heavy onus on the pursuer to establish these three facts and without all three, his case will fail.   If this is the test, then it matters nothing how far or how little he deviates from the ordinary practice for the extent of the deviation is not the test.
> The deviation must be of a kind which satisfies the third of the requirements just stated.[65]

This last caveat should be borne in mind by doctors who are tempted only to use established methods of treatment, since it would appear that his choice of innovative therapies will be protected providing that there is no other evidence which would tend to suggest that he has been negligent.   In the case of the use of new drugs, proof that the doctor had observed, for example, the contraindications, or that in his clinical judgement, and with the consent of the patient, the risks involved in new therapies were worth taking, then it is unlikely that a successful claim could be made against him.   Some doctors may choose to remain 'safe' by restricting treatment to older established methods of therapy, perhaps because they have failed to keep up-to-date by reading sufficient medical literature, and although established treatment may be safer, there is in this approach a risk of denying patients alternative methods which may prove more beneficial.

However, the pressures on him to remain safe are largely imagined since there is considerable evidence to the effect that any deviation from 'standard practice' will generally not be negligent.   This test of standard or reasonable behaviour may not in any event require that the doctor is particularly well-informed, even in his own specialism.   It would clearly be difficult to ensure that any doctor was up-to-date in all areas of medicine, since, if he were to keep abreast of developments, this might well involve him in a full and continuing educational programme.   It is, however clearly unreasonable to assume that a doctor engaged in a demanding clinical practice can be, or should be, well read in all fields of medicine, covering an ever-expanding field of new products and new techniques. Although recommendations have been made as to the continuing education of doctors,[66] there is at present no legislative provision for it, and although such education is desirable, it may be impracticable. To maintain a general practitioner fully educated in a wide variety of specialties would require a continuous programme of educational courses that could well require fifty two weeks in every year, and although the doctor may be regarded as professionally blameworthy should he fail to keep abreast of developments, he is unlikely to be the recipient of legal liability in these circumstances.

One further difficulty in this area is the establishing of a balance between the possible (or even likely) benefits to his patient from the choice of a new therapy, and the possible legal liability which the doctor may incur should the treatment fail or the patient be damaged.   Since, unlike treatment involving a new medical product, there is no third party to be held responsible, it is clear that any liability which does follow will be that of the doctor whose duty it remains fully to inform his patient as to the possible treatments available.   Failure to do so must be regarded as a grave error in professional judgement, although it will not necessarily be criticised by the courts, who have stated that a doctor need not disclose certain risks,[67] and even that he may lie to a patient about the risks of treatment,[68] even where the doctor was selecting one from the available therapies.

However, the doctor may, despite the evidence supra, remain tempted on the grounds of personal safety to use only tried and tested therapies, as a result of which he is unlikely to be criticised unless there is other evidence of negligence.   However, this type of 'defensive medicine' is perhaps unlikely to occur to any extent in the United Kingdom, where by and large the interest of the doctor in helping his patient is still paramount.   Indeed, doctors have shown themselves prepared to carry out risky therapies, e.g. in heart transplants, even although the chance of success is very limited.

When considering the case to be made for a heart transplantation programme, for example, there is no doubt that from a clinical point of view, patients proposed for heart transplant have a poor prognosis;   the alternative being certain death.   Nonetheless, the doctor, in pioneering this new technique, has shown himself to be largely unconcerned with potential liability, even although it is possible to argue that the therapy remains experimental at the present time.   This may partly be due to the enormous public goodwill surrounding this particular enterprise, which may in turn reflect the attitudes of society to experiments carried out in terminal illnesses.   The same cannot necessarily be said when considering the treatments available for non-terminal illnesses.

In any event, in the less glamourous parts of medical experimentation, it is clear that the rule outlined in <u>Hunter</u> v. <u>Hanley</u>, supra, will prove beneficial to both medicine and the patient, since it not only protects the doctor's right to make a reasonable deviation from accepted practice, but also allows that medical practice will not be inhibited in such a way as to be detrimental to patients who have found accepted therapies or techniques unhelpful.

These tests, combined with the necessary provision of consent by the patient, should serve to ensure that the doctor is not entirely inhibited from therapeutic experimentation by threat of legal liability.   Thus both the doctor and the interests of the public will be protected, providing that doctors do not opt for new therapies for their own sake where there is a 'safe' and efficient alternative therapy available, unless there are good medical reasons for so doing, and real or 'informed' consent has been obtained by disclosing not only the relative risks, but also the availablility of alternative therapy.[69]

CONCLUSION

In addition to the medical and legal aspects of new treatment, medicine is becoming increasingly subject to the inhibitions and stresses of economic and political factors, and it is clear that these pressures may be substantial. The National Health Service is the major consumer of medical products in the United Kingdom, and also promotes the use of new techniques more than any other medical system, particularly the private sector which is bedevilled by litigation cases. It has been said that:

It is incumbent upon those who demand that medical care of the highest quality be universally provided as a matter of right to explain how this can be done. And if it cannot, which would they dispense with; equity or the lives that could be saved by selective use of expensive technology?[70]

The same author continues:

The only way a nationalized program can realistically hope to keep costs in line is to enforce strict schedules of permissible treatments for all illnesses. These would be established on the basis of empirical studies detailing cost-effectiveness - assuming that political pressures to act otherwise are avoided. Therapeutic measures failing to come up to the stipulated benefit per dollar level would simply be disallowed.[71]

There is little doubt that doctors, politicians and society in general are increasingly aware of the cost of various methods of treatment. Nonetheless, it remains essential that the doctor's prime concern should lie with the individual patient and not directly with society at large or political and economic pressures. This may explain to some extent the willingness of doctors to attempt heart transplants, which, if successful, would prove enormously beneficial. On the other hand, such operations are extremely expensive and although benefiting the patient initially, they have not been proved to prolong life dramatically. There are, as yet, no long-term survivors of heart transplantation surgery in Britain. Can society justify a programme of heart transplantation on medical, economic, political, ethical or social grounds? The financial support such programmes have received would appear to indicate widespread approval by many sections of society, although this is not necessarily a satisfactory justification in the long run for continuing such programmes in view of shortages of finance elsewhere in the Health Service. Thus, although ideally the doctor should not concern himself with such matters, nonetheless there can be no doubt that he will become increasingly aware of such difficult choices as the Health Service continues to run short of adequate funding.[72]

Whatever the external pressures on the doctor, it is clear that: Medical science has conferred great benefits on mankind, but these benefits are attended by considerable risks. Every surgical operation is attended by risks. We cannot take the benefits without taking the risks. Every advance in technique is attended by risk. Doctors, like the rest of us, have to learn by experience; and experience often teaches in a hard way.[73]

Every form of therapy used in medical treatment involves a degree of risk to the patient, and there can be no precise standards of safety because of the very nature of medicine, which relies largely on clinical experience and personal clinical judgment. Medicine is not an exact science and there are no absolute standards: a group of doctors presented with the same patients may well agree on the clinical diagnosis, but will often differ regarding appropriate treatment. There is usually no 'right' or 'wrong', and provided that there is no negligence, the freedom of the doctor to treat a patient to the best of his ability is largely accepted by the medical and legal professions and the public, even where it involves the use of new therapies.

Even if established treatment is effective, this should not impede progress towards finding alternative methods which might prove equally or, hopefully, more beneficial. To limit treatment to a single effective form of therapy presumes that the disease will remain static - i.e., that the pattern of the disease and the pathological processes will be unaltered, both by the passage of time and/or by treatment. This is a most dangerous and inaccurate presumption as can be seen when one considers the role of antibiotics in the control of infection. The pattern and natural history of many infective diseases have radically altered following the discovery of penicillin in 1928. The contribution of this antibiotic agent is in no doubt, but infection has also altered during this time as a result of improved social living standards and increased medical knowledge, allowing a wide variety of infective organisms to be identified. Many of these organisms have proved to be insensitive to penicillin, requiring newer and more effective antibiotics. Furthermore, the use of penicillin itself has altered the nature of many infective processes by permitting resistant strains of bacteria to evolve. These resistant organisms remain capable of producing severe infective disease which requires alternative forms of antibiotic therapy.

The constant search for medical advancement remains a necessity and with increased knowledge and understanding of illness and therapy, new methods of treatment will develop. If medicine is to keep apace with disease and hopefully even advance, then some measure of human experimentation is essential. This should not however, conflict with general patient care and the key appears to be the doctor - patient relationship, as so much depends on full explanation and understanding of the various treatments available, and the essential trust between doctor and patient. The doctor should, as far as possible, avoid all outside political and economic pressures and confine himself to the treatment of each individual patient, thus preserving his clinical freedom to treat patients to the best of his ability. Medicine in any event, has a special role in the community which may require its independence from economic pressures. As Lomasky says:

Medical care is not simply one consumer good among others; because it bears so directly on life itself as well as the ability to lead a good life, medical care cannot be left to the vagaries of the market.[74]

It can be seen, therefore, that there may be considerable pressures, intellectual, medical and political, on the doctor to advance medical science by using new therapies and perfecting new techniques. Whether such experiments are therapeutic or non-therapeutic the doctor will continue to be bound by his high ethical standards, and restrained to some extent by the possibility of legal liability. The ethical conduct of medical experiments requires the scrutiny of the law and society, but also the independence of medicine. Society is therefore, largely dependent on the doctor himself in these situations, and it has been suggested that where:

...truly knowing and voluntary consent of the patient or

subject has been obtained prior to any medical experimentation, the primary concern of the law has been satisfied and...the law should thereafter be concerned only with the method in which the experimentation is carried out and its effect or result...[75]

However, although this approach has superficial charm, the result of it may be to leave the doctor uncertain and perhaps even vulnerable. The obtaining of consent is not necessarily an adequate protection for the doctor in the use of a new therapy, since one cannot consent to negligence, and it may be that the doctor's choice of therapy could be deemed to be negligent. The law must therefore accept a certain responsibility for ensuring that the doctor knows what his position is and what potential liability there may be. Equally, although the doctor may only choose alternative therapies when he feels these to be directly for the benefit of his patient, medicine must protect the patient more stringently, particularly in cases where their illness is not life-threatening, by balancing the advancement of medical science and the right of the patient to expect that the doctor will not experiment on him when there is a 'safe' and reliable therapy practised, documented and available. However, he should also be in a position to expect that the doctor will not be so inhibited by the likelihood of legal liability as not to attempt, where established therapies are inadequate or have failed, a soundly based alternative.

In the experimental stages of the production and use of new drugs, the doctor may seem to be unreasonably pressured by the vested interests of the pharmaceutical industry, and insufficiently protected by the law in its regulation of the production, marketing and surveillance of drugs. In this situation, the doctor is dependent not on his own skill and judgement, but on second-hand information, and there would thus seem to be little justification for imposing liability on him. However, since there is a need to allow for compensation in this area, it may be that the imposition of strict liability on drug companies whose profits are generally substantial[76] coupled with the tighter controls advocated supra, would be the most efficient means of ensuring both that medical science develops and that the necessary volunteers for medical research are forthcoming and are adequately compensated for damage suffered.

D. Soutar
S.A.M. McLean

NOTES

1. For examples, see Katz, J., Experimentation with Human Beings, New York, Russell Sage Foundation, 1972.
2. Declaration of Helsinki, Part II, paras. 1 and 2. Although this declaration was updated in 1975, the same terminology is used in Part II, paras. 1 and 6.
3. Declaration of Helsinki, id. This appears in the revised version in Part I, paras. 9 and 10.
4. See infra, ch. 8.
5. Klass, A., There's Gold in Them Thar Pills, Penguin Books, 1975, at p. 31.
6. Meyers, D.W., The Human Body and the Law, Edinburgh

University Press, 1970, at p. 72.

7. Data Sheet Compendium 1980-81, Association of the British Pharmaceutical Industry, Introduction at p. vi. This is an annual publication.

8. Set up as part of the Medicines Commission created by the Medicines Act 1968. For further discussion of the functions of the Committee, see infra chs. 3 and 11.

9. For discussion, see 'The Guardian' 7 August 1980; Smyth, D.H., Alternatives to Animal Experiments, London, Scolar Press, 1978. See also, infra ch. 5.

10. See Smyth, op.cit., and infra ch. 5.

11. This Committee was established in November 1975.

12. This refers to the cards issued to all doctors on which they should notify any adverse side-effects of any drugs prescribed or used by them.

13. Current Problems No.5., February 1981, Committee on Safety of Medicines, London.

14. For an excellent discussion of this influence, see Teff,H., and Munro,C., Thalidomide: The Legal Aftermath, Saxon House, 1976, at pp.13-25.

15. For further discussion, see infra ch. 11.

16. The Committee on Safety of Medicines analyses all laboratory and animal tests carried out by the manufacturer, and the protocols of proposed clinical trials are studied before a Clinical Trial Certificate can be issued.

17. These are trials carried out on a totally unselected group of patients, and are of doubtful scientific value since the results cannot be correlated with important perameters, e.g. age and sex, unless vast numbers of cases are accumulated.

18. Such trials are selective, either in terms of the groups of patients chosen, or in the nature of the trial, or both.

19. 'Blind' trials involve the use of a placebo for some patients and the patients are unaware of whether or not treatment is actually being given. It nonetheless remains possible for the observer to influence the results since he is aware of which patients are receiving the treatment. 'Double Blind' trials also involve the use of a placebo, but in this case neither the patient nor the observer are aware of which patients actually receive the treatment.

20. These trials compare the efficacy of one treatment against another in a controlled clinical trial situation.

21. For discussion, see 'The Guardian' 22 December 1980; see also infra, ch. 11.

22. It was reported in 'The Guardian' 14 January 1981 that, after clinical trials, Fisons had withdrawn Proxicromil, a drug which it had been hoped would relieve much distress in patients suffering from asthma. The same report pointed out that immediate reaction to this withdrawal was that Fison's shares dropped dramatically and that Fison's had spent an estimated £12 million on the development of this drug before animal tests showed unacceptable risks.

23. For discussion, see Klass, op.cit., particularly at pp. 72-73.

24. op.cit. at p. 29.

25. op.cit. at p. 30.

26. Klass, op.cit. at p. 11.

27. R.C.P.S. (Glasgow), 'Concerning Responsibility in Research Investigations on Human Subjects', May 1972.

28. ibid. at p.3.
29. ibid. at p.2.
30. These Committees were established after the publication by the Medical Research Council of 'Responsibility in Investigations on Human Subjects', Brit. Med. J., 1963, iv., pp. 177-178, and subsequent recommendations from the Royal College of Physicians of London.
31. The need for lay members was reinforced by the British Medical Association in a recent statement on the powers of R.E.C.s; see 282 B.M.J., 21 March 1981.
32. Thompson, I.E., et al., 'Research Ethical Committees in Scotland', B.M.J., 28 February 1981, 718.
33. ibid. at p. 719.
34. This seems to have been recognised by the statement of the B.M.A. referred to in note 31, supra, which was expressly designed to strengthen the Committees, and further to extend their scope to cover experiments carried out in situations other than hospitals, e.g. by general practitioners.
35. For a fuller discussion of the aims of the unit, see 'Times Higher Education Supplement', 23 January 1981.
36. Teff and Munro, op.cit., in discussing the means by which product licences are obtained point out, at p. 116, that: 'Technically the licence is granted by the Minister and an appeal from a refusal lies to the [Medicines] Commission, but so far the advice of the Committee [on Safety of Medicines] has always been followed.'
37. Under the Medicines Act 1968 s.96, data sheets are supplied to medical practitioners in respect of all drugs. The sheets are prepared by the manufacturers and must follow the requirements of the Medicines (Data Sheet) Regulations 1972. They will contain information in respect of presentation, contraindications, uses, dosage and administration, pharmaceutical precautions, package quantities, warnings and product licence numbers.
38. The Data Sheet in respect of this particular drug specifically states that before treatment is commenced, 'malignancy should be excluded as treatment may alleviate symptoms and delay diagnosis.' However it was alleged in a report in 'The Sunday Times' 11 January 1981, that the drug, designed primarily for the treatment of peptic ulcers, was used for uninvestigated digestive complaints without prior testing for malignancy. Indeed, it was further alleged that Tagamet may actually be linked to the risk of developing stomach cancer, (although this is strenuously denied by the manufacturers).
39. Scottish Law Commission, Liability for Ante-Natal Injury, Cmnd 5371/1973, para 10.
40. For discussion of the powers of the F.D.A., see Teff and Munro, op.cit. at pp. 119-125.
41. Reported in 'The Sunday Times' 22 February 1981.
42. Cmnd 7504/1978.
43. ibid. para 1339.
44. ibid. para 1341.
45. ibid. para 1342.
46. ibid. para 1343.
47. 1943 S.C.(H.L.) 3.
48. For discussion, see Teff and Munro, op.cit., ch.5.

49.   For example, in the recent case of Quixalin, a drug closely
      related to Enterovioform which has been banned in some
      countries having caused blindness and paralysis in an
      estimated 10,000 Japanese but which continues to be marketed
      in countries which permit it.   For discussion, see 'The
      Sunday Times' 22 February 1981.   This was of course also the
      evntual form of settlement in the Thalidomide case.
50.   For discussion, see infra ch. 6.
51.   For discussion, see infra ch. 6.
52.   For discussion of the powers of the Medicines Commission, and
      in particular the Committee on Safety of Medicines, see Teff
      and Munro, op.cit., at pp. 116-118.
53.   Act of October 10, 1962, Public Law 87-781, s.103.
54.   Teff and Munro, op.cit., at p. xi.
55.   Klass, op.cit., at pp. 20-21.
56.   As was the case in Thalidomide.   Klass, op.cit., at pp.
      70-71 also cites the case of Diethyl Stilboestrol (DES) which
      was fed to beef cattle in order to increase their yield of
      meat.   Neither the animal nor the pregnant woman was damaged
      by the drug, but the female children of these mothers are 'at
      risk of developing a hitherto excessively rare tumour: cancer
      of the vagina.'   Equally, drugs whose effects are not
      teratogenic may not show adverse side-effects for some time;
      see for example, the controversy over the neuroleptics,
      reported in 'The Sunday Times' 26 October 1980, and Valium
      reported in 'The Observer' 24 February 1980.
57.   'The Guardian' 31 December 1980.
58.   In Scots Law the Prescription Limitation (Scotland) Act 1973,
      sets a three year time limit on raising claims in personal
      injury cases, ss. 17-19.   In England, the time limit of
      three years is set by the Limitation Act 1975 s. 1, which
      inserts s. 2 (a) into the Limitation Act 1939.   This period
      runs from the date at which a cause of action accrued or from
      the date (if later) at which it came to the plaintiff's
      knowledge.
59.   Under the 1973 Act, there was no such discretion in Scots
      Law.   See, for example, McIntyre v. Armitage Shanks 1980
      S.L.T. 112;   Campbell, J.R., 'Limitations of Actions in
      Personal Injury Claims', 1980 J.L.S.S. 60 and 95.   An
      open-ended discretion was introduced into Scots Law by the
      Law Reform (Miscellaneous Provisions) (Scotland) Act 1980 s.
      23, which allows courts to rehear cases which were previously
      time-barred if that was the sole ground for the action
      failing.   Discretion in English Law was provided by s.1 of
      the 1975 Act, which inserted s.2(d) into the 1939 Act setting
      out the grounds for the exercise of discretion.   English
      Courts have held that this amounts to a more or less
      unfettered discretion;   c.f. Ferman v. Ellis [1978] 2 All
      E.R. 851, and Simpson v. Norwest Holst (Southern) Ltd. [1980]
      2 All E.R. 471.
60.   Meyers, op.cit. at p. 70.
61.   ibid. at p. 73.
62.   For discussion of the application of this test, see infra ch.
      7.
63.   c.f. Whitehouse v. Jordan [1981] 1 All E.R. 267; Roe v.
      Ministry of Health [1954] 2 Q.B. 66.
64.   1955 S.C. 200.

65.   ibid. at p. 206

66.   Report of the Committee of Inquiry into the Regulation of the
        Medical Profession (Merrison Report) Cmnd 6018/1975.   This
        report states at para. 129 that 'general practice requires
        specific knowledge and skills just as do other areas of
        practice.   It follows that we believe there to be a need for
        specific specialist training in general practice, and that
        general practice should be recognised as a speciality...'

67.   Bolam v. Friern Hospital Management Committee [1957] 2 All
        E.R. 118.

68.   Hatcher v. Black 'The Times' 2 July 1954.

69.   For discussion, see infra ch. 8.

70.   Lomasky, L.E., 'Medical Progress and National Health Care',
        Philosophy and Public Affairs, Vol. 10, No. 1, (1981), at pp.
        68-69.

71.   ibid., at p. 71.

72.   For further discussion, see infra ch. 3.

73.   Roe v. Ministry of Health, supra, at p. 83.

74.   Lomasky, loc.cit., at pp 65-66.

75.   Meyers, op.cit., at p. 76.

76.   For discussion of the profits of the pharmaceutical industry,
        see Klass, op.cit., at pp 72-77.

10 Medical Genetics and the Law
M. A. Ferguson-Smith

Approximately 3 per cent of liveborn children are born with a significant congenital malformation or genetically-determined disease,[1] and a further 2 per cent will develop a genetic disorder later in life. These numbers have not changed appreciably over many years, but are now more apparent as perinatal and infant mortality decreases with improvements in medical and nursing care. Severely disabled infants now tend to survive the first few critical weeks to live lives of varying quality, sometimes wholly dependant on their families and on health and social services.

These changes in the past twenty years have occurred alongside important developments in medical genetics. Chief among these have been improvements in the clinical diagnosis of genetic syndromes due not only to chromosomal aberrations visible under the microscope, but also to gene mutations inherited in a classical Mendelian manner. McKusick[2] catalogues some 2,800 different single gene disorders which are now sufficiently well characterised to be identified by current methodology, but it is clear that there are many more similar conditions which still await adequate characterisation. The diagnosis of many of these genetic syndromes requires special expertise, and it is not surprising that the speciality of medical genetics has arisen to help cope with the problem and to develop strategies for prevention. The most useful preventive measures to be developed are genetic screening (including prenatal diagnosis), and genetic counselling. Both have moral, social and legal implications and are therefore relevant to any discussion on legal issues in medicine.

GENETIC SCREENING

The purpose of genetic screening is to identify either those affected by genetic disease, or those at risk of having children with genetic disease, in time to allow appropriate action. Thus populations of apparently normal persons are tested as part of a routine public health procedure equivalent, for example, to immunisation.[3] The appropriate action depends on the type of screening programme and some of the more usual examples are described in the following sections.

1. Neonatal Screening

Infants are tested shortly after birth with the objective of identifying conditions such as phenylketonuria (PKU) and cretinism (hypothyroidism), in which prompt treatment immediately after birth can prevent irreversible brain damage. A sample of the infant's blood is taken by heel prick, usually on or about the 6th day of birth (after feeding is well established), and spotted onto a filter paper (Guthrie card) which is allowed to dry before being sent by post to the screening laboratory. The method of collection is simple and reliable. For example, in 1979 the screening laboratory which serves all Scotland received a Guthrie card from 99.87 per cent of all liveborn infants, i.e., all but 88 of the 68,352 born that year. In a small proportion of cases, the sample is inadequate for testing and fresh samples have to be obtained. For some of the conditions tested the methods are less specific than for others and false-negative results are occasionally obtained. This is quickly identified during the follow-up investigation.

In Scotland, the prevalence of PKU at birth is about 1: 8,000. Without treatment, affected children become grossly mentally handicapped and develop neurological abnormalities including seizures. Restriction of phenylalanine in the diet for the first 10-12 years entirely prevents this, and almost all affected children detected by neonatal screening and subsequently treated have normal I.Q.'s. Congenital hypothyroidism occurs in 1: 3,800 newborn, and maintenance of treatment with thyroid hormone from birth can prevent progressive mental deterioration. The screening test depends on detecting elevated levels of thyroid stimulating hormone in the blood spot and is extremely sensitive and specific. Other less common treatable conditions such as galactosaemia, maple syrup urine disease, homocystinuria and tyrosinaemia may be detected by neonatal screening, but not all centres test for all these conditions. Incurable disorders such as Duchenne muscular dystrophy and cystic fibrosis may also be identified by neonatal screening in order to provide early symptomatic treatment and to warn families about the risk of recurrence. However, the current practice is not to recommend screening for such disorders until effective treatment or prenatal diagnosis is available, in view of the high false-positive rates encountered and the anxiety created by investigating asymptomatic children.

Although parents are free to decline testing on behalf of their children, the compliance rate for neonatal screening is clearly high, and cases are seldom missed. The major hazard is the occurrence of a false-negative result which leads to an affected child not receiving appropriate treatment in time to prevent irreversible brain damage. Such occurrences could result from both technical and clerical errors, but, if this has happended, there appears to be no record of legal proceedings in the United Kingdom. However, if such errors did occur as a result of fault, and the child is damaged as a result, then theoretically an action in negligence is possible[4] although it may be difficult to establish.

2. Carrier Detection

Screening of young couples to detect the carrier state of autosomal recessive conditions like Tay-Sachs disease and sickle-cell anaemia, is designed to identify marriages in which both partners are carriers and in which the future offspring have a 25 per cent risk of being affected with a serious genetic disease. This information helps couples to plan their families and to choose options such as prenatal diagnosis and selective termination, artificial insemination using donor semen,(AID) or sterilisation.

An excellent example is Tay-Sachs disease, a progressive neurological degenerative disease of infancy in which blindness, deafness and seizures are prominent and death occurs before the age of four years. The condition is rare except in Ashkenazic Jews, where it occurs in 1: 3,600 live births. This means that the carrier rate among Ashkenazic Jews is 1: 30 and the proportion of marriages in which both husband and wife are carriers is about 1: 900. Carrier detection depends on plasma hexosaminidase A activity, and this is a simple and reliable test except during pregnancy. Screening is recommended for late teenagers or newly married couples. Where both husband and wife are shown to be carriers, prenatal diagnosis in subsequent pregnancies is available so that the couple may plan to have only healthy children.

Failure to provide screening for Tay-Sachs disease has resulted in an action for damages against an obstetrician in the United States.[5] The court did not allow the parents to recover damages for their own suffering, but did not exclude the possibility of allowing damages for the suffering of their affected child.

To be successful, carrier detection screening programmes require the careful provision of educational, counselling and back-up services, so that couples are adequately informed about the significance and implications of the results of screening. Considerable distress and harm have resulted from inadequate programmes for the detection of carriers of sickle-cell disease in the black community in the United States. Some of those found to be carriers of this common disease wrongly felt themselves stigmatised and sometimes have even found themselves penalised in obtaining life insurance and employment. Carriers tended to suppress information about their carrier state from their future spouses, and the effect has often been to increase feelings of guilt and anxiety rather than to promote appropriate family planning measures. Because of these difficulties, carrier detection programmes have not found the same acceptability as neonatal screening and are largely limited to high risk populations in North America and in countries bordering the Mediterranean.

If such measures were applied in the U.K., they could effectively reduce the prevalence of a few conditions in selected groups of the population. For example, they could be used for the prevention of beta-thalassaemia in the Cypriot, Italian and Greek communities; of Tay-Sachs disease among Ashkenazic Jews; of sickle cell anaemia among black Africans; and of alpha-thalassaemia and glucose-6-phosphate dehydrogenase deficiency among the Chinese. Probably the only conditions which would be appropriate for mass carrier detection in the native British community are cystic fibrosis and X-linked Duchenne muscular dystrophy. These serious conditions occur in 1: 1,600 and 1: 3,000 newborn respectively, but, unfortunately, there are as yet no reliable tests for the detection of carriers.

3. Prenatal Screening

One of the provisions of the 1967 Abortion Act allows termination of pregnancy on the grounds that there is a substantial risk that the foetus is severely handicapped.[6] Since then, prenatal tests have been developed for the diagnosis of foetal abnormality early enough in pregnancy to allow selective termination if the foetus is affected. This development has allowed many thousands of normal pregnancies to continue which would otherwise have been terminated on the grounds of uncertain risk rather than the definite diagnosis of foetal abnormality. Pregnant women at substantially higher than population risks for chromosome aberrations, neural tube defects (mainly spina bifida cystica and anencephaly), metabolic disorders and numerous other rare congenital abnormalities, can now be given the option of prenatal screening. These women may be identified as being at particular risk because they have had an affected child previously, because of their age in the case of chromosomal disorders, because they have an elevated level of alphafetoprotein (AFP) in their blood, or because they have been found to be carriers of a genetic disorder. It is estimated that approximately 8 per cent of all pregnancies can be considered to be at risk for a detectable foetal abnormality.[7] The principal techniques used for prenatal screening are amniocentesis, foetal ultrasonography, foetoscopy and foetal sampling.

(a) Amniocentesis. This is the procedure whereby a sample of the amniotic fluid surrounding the foetus is withdrawn by a needle inserted through the mother's abdominal wall. It is recommended that the optimum stage of pregnancy for this procedure is the 16th week of gestation, as this is the safest time for mother and foetus, and the best time for obtaining viable amniotic cells for culture. Ideally, amniocentesis should be performed by a skilled doctor with the experience of at least 100 amniocenteses per annum, in a recognised genetic centre, and with the aid of a real-time ultrasound scanner to localise the placenta and to identify a safe portal of entry into the amniotic sac.[8] An MRC assessment of the hazards of amniocentesis[9] estimated the increased foetal loss rate resulting from the procedure as between 1 to 1.5 per cent. Other studies suggest that this is an overestimate,[10] and the results from centres with most experience indicate that a more reasonable estimate would be less than 0.5 per cent.

(b) Foetal Ultrasonography. Ultrasound scanners are now widely available which may be used to visualise the foetus and placenta, measure parameters such as crown-rump length, diameter of foetal head, limb length, body circumference, and so on. The stage of gestation may be determined and it is possible to detect multiple pregnancy, foetal death and a wide variety of developmental malformations including anencephaly, hydrocephaly, spina bifida, polycystic kidneys and gross skeletal defects. Research is continuing on the detection of other disorders, and there is hope that a proportion of severe congenital heart defects may also be diagnosable in the near future.

(c) Foetoscopy. This procedure allows direct visualisation of the foetus by a fine fibre optic telescope inserted through the abdominal wall. It is a highly specialised technique only available in a few adademic research centres. Its main use is in the sampling of foetal blood from a placental vein under direct vision for the prenatal diagnosis of the haemoglobinopathies and haemophilia. The foetal loss rate following the procedure is high, averaging between 5-10 per cent, and so its use should be restricted to pregnancies with a 25 per cent or higher risk of severe foetal disorder, undetectable by other means. Its most important application at present is in the diagnosis of beta-thalassaemia.

Prenatal screening is used mostly for the detection of chromosomal aberrations and neural tube defects and the main indications are illustrated in Tables I and II.[11] Advancing maternal age is the commonest indication for numerical chromosome abnormalities of which the most important is Down's syndrome due to an extra chromosome 21 (trisomy 21). In Scotland, for example, it can be estimated that 37 per cent of Down's syndrome infants are born to the 5.4 per cent of mothers aged 35 years of age and older. If all such women had

136

prenatal diagnosis followed by selective termination, an equivalent reduction of Down's syndrome births would be achieved, plus a reduction in other chromosomal syndromes (trisomy 13, trisomy 18, XXY Klinefelter's syndrome, etc.), which also occur with increased frequency in older mothers. Risks increase steeply with maternal age, so that there is a tendency to offer prenatal diagnosis particularly to women 40 years of age and older. However, the number of such women having children is comparatively small and has, in fact, declined steadily over recent years, so that the reduction in Down's syndrome achieved by confining screening to women 40 years of age and over would be only about 10 per cent. In the U.K., many obstetricians do not offer amniocentesis to patients under 38, 39 years and even 40 years of age, and so the effects of the introduction of screening have been disappointing. In 1979, there was an overall reduction of Down's syndrome births of 13.6 per cent in Scotland, due to screening 23.6 per cent of women aged 35 years and over (Table III).[12] No national figures are available for other countries.

The occurrence of neural tube defects shows considerable geographic variation and where prevalence is high, as in Scotland and South Wales, prenatal screening programmes based on the estimation of maternal serum AFP levels have been introduced. Mothers with an elevated AFP determined by the screening test are referred for further diagnostic investigation including amniocentesis and the estimation of amniotic AFP, which is currently the best available diagnostic test for open neural tube defects.[13]

The optimum time of pregnancy for the serum AFP test is between 16-18 weeks, and as serum AFP levels normally rise steeply between 15 and 25 weeks, accurate means of 'dating' the pregnancy are essential. This can be achieved by determining foetal head size by ultrasound examination. Elevated maternal serum AFP levels are found in other types of foetal abnormality (e.g., exomphalos, nephrosis, etc.), in twin pregnancies, and are associated with certain complications of pregnancy which may lead to small-for-dates babies and premature delivery. The interpretation of serum AFP results and the investigation of elevated levels is thus a specialised procedure, best accomplished by an experienced team. More than 95 per cent of anencephalic foetuses and about 80 per cent of spina bifida foetuses can be detected by prenatal screening, and in regions where a high proportion of mothers are screened, there has been a marked reduction in affected births,[14] and in the number of infants admitted to hospital for the surgical treatment of spina bifida.[15] For example, in 1979 in Scotland 68.1 per cent of all pregnancies were screened at between 16 and 20 weeks gestation leading to a 36 per cent overall reduction of neural tube defects births. Unfortunately, those mothers most at risk because of their socio-economic circumstances tend not to be screened as they frequently come too late to the antenatal clinic. With an increasing proportion of pregnant mothers coming forward for screening in 1980, a much larger reduction in neural tube defect births has been observed in the West of Scotland.

Comment is required about some of the other listed indications for prenatal diagnosis in Tables I and II,[16] particularly those in which the observed incidence of abnormal results is similar to or less than the overall population incidence. Mothers who have had a child with Down's syndrome or other numerical chromosome abnormalities are generally unwilling to attempt a further pregnancy without prenatal diagnosis even although the risk is identical with the population risk, and for these reasons amniocentesis is regarded as justified.

There is no need, on the other hand, to recommend amniocentesis when there is a more remote family history of Down's syndrome, provided that the parent with the affected relative has been excluded as a carrier of familial (translocation) Down's syndrome. This is easily accomplished by chromosome analysis from a blood sample. Similarly, maternal anxiety on its own is not a reasonable indication for amniocentesis as the likelihood of hazard to the foetus from the procedure is far greater than the occurrence of a detectable abnormality.

Prenatal diagnosis is occasionally required to determine the sex of the foetus when the mother is a known carrier of a severe X-linked disease, e.g., Duchenne muscular dystrophy. This enables the mother to have an unaffected female child and avoid the 50 per cent risk of an affected infant should the foetus be found to be male. For every male infant terminated there is an equal chance that a normal foetus has been sacrificed, and there is an urgent need for a reliable 'prenatal diagnostic' test in such cases.

There is widespread acceptance that prenatal screening should be available to couples who wish to use it, and that this should be part of regular antenatal care provided within the National Health Service. Prenatal diagnosis should be regarded in the same way as other forms of family planning, and those with moral, religious or other objections to the selective termination of abnormal foetuses should be able to exercise their own wishes. In one hospital in the West of Scotland, the numbers of mothers declining the serum AFP test, when this is offered to them at the antenatal clinic, has remained at about 7 per cent over the past three years. Information about the availability of prenatal diagnosis is given by the doctors at the clinic and in leaflets which the patients take home. Women who are not likely to accept termination are discouraged from having the tests. There is clearly no purpose in needlessly putting the foetus to the risk associated with amniocentesis, however slight, if the results of the test are to be ignored. Despite this, a few patients change their minds about accepting termination when a foetal abnormality is diagnosed. This freedom of choice is to be jealously guarded, although it means that a considerable burden, financial and other, may later be imposed on the family and social services. The argument that a handicapped person ought not to have escaped prenatal diagnosis and abortion, or that the parents are in some way negligent not to have agreed to abortion, is rightly repugnant to a caring society. In this context it is considered fortunate that the Congenital Disabilities (Civil Liability) Act 1976[17] allows no cause of action for damages claimed by a handicapped child against its parents for 'wrongful life'.[18] There appears, however, to be a real possibility that such actions may succeed in the United States.[19]

In view of the legal issues which arise from the practice of prenatal diagnosis, it seems appropriate to comment on some of the problems which may sometimes occur so that the limitations of prenatal diagnosis can be appreciated.

1. The Safety of Amniocentesis. Reference has already been made to the risk of foetal loss associated with amniocentesis which, in experienced hands, is likely to be less than 0.5 per cent. To this should be added a slight increase in infant mortality resulting from premature delivery and respiratory difficulties. It follows that patients should be advised of these risks before having amniocentesis,

so that they may weigh the risks of foetal abnormality against the risks of foetal loss. In some circumstances, couples may well accept a much greater risk of foetal loss, as many would regard the birth of a severely handicapped child more seriously than a miscarriage. Each case must be regarded on its merits, and rigid guidelines imposed by the medical profession as to what degree of risk constitutes a justifiable indication for amniocentesis are likely to cause difficulties.[20] As with all other aspects of medical practice, the risks of amniocentesis should be explained in order that 'informed consent' may be given, and in these situations the evaluation of risks must be made by the parents rather than the doctor.

2. Failure to advise about the availability of prenatal diagnosis.

Although regions differ in the quality of obstetric and laboratory facilities available for prenatal diagnosis, absence of facilities can no longer be used to excuse the doctor who fails to raise the possibility of prenatal diagnosis in a mother at risk of a diagnosable foetal abnormality. All Regional Health Authorities in England, and equivalent regions in Scotland, Wales and Northern Ireland, now have access to prenatal diagnostic laboratories and facilities for amniocentesis.

A doctor who has religious or other objections to prenatal diagnosis would be expected to refer his patient to a colleague prepared to give the necessary advice. At least on case claiming negligence on the grounds that the doctor failed to inform his patient of the availability of prenatal diagnosis, when this was clearly indicated, has been successfully raised in the United States,[21] and might also be difficult to defend in the U.K.

3. Results of prenatal diagnosis.

Patients should be informed that it is sometimes not possible to arrive at a prenatal diagnosis, that prenatal diagnosis cannot be expected to detect all foetal abnormalities - only those for which the test is designed - and that amniocentesis may have to be repeated. There are numerous causes of failure. Amniocentesis may be unsuccessful (a 'dry tap'), urine rather than amniotic fluid may be obtained inadvertently, the amniotic cell culture may not be successful (most centres achieve a success rate of at least 95 per cent), maternal cells may grow in the culture, and the amniotic fluid culture may be lost because of bacterial or other contamination. These occurrences need not result from negligence and, in fact, occur from time to time in the most experienced centres.

4. Erroneous diagnoses.

Errors in diagnosis have occurred on average in 1: 500 pregnanaices tested.[22] Some of these have been due to maternal cell contamination in which the maternal karyotype has been reported instead of the foetal karyotype. False-positive and false-negative amniotic AFP results have occurred in approximately 1: 1000 pregnancies at risk for neural tube defects. These are likely to become even rarer with the increasing use of confirmatory tests and detailed ultrasound scanning.

Another potential problem of foetal chromosome analysis is the occasional occurrence of a chromosome aberration which arises during amniotic cell culture. Such 'pseudo-mosaic' cases can usually be distinguished from true mosaics, as the latter are invariably evident in separate cultures.

5. Fortuitous Diagnoses. Sometimes unexpected foetal abnormalities are detected during the course of prenatal diagnosis, and this can lead to difficulties if there is uncertainty about the clinical significance of the finding. For example, when foetal chromosome analysis is undertaken to exclude Down's syndrome, one of the sex chromosome aberrations (e.g., 47,XXY; 47,XYY; 47,XXX) may be found fortuitously. Mild mental handicap is not uncommon in some of these sex chromosome disorders, but some affected individuals live a 'normal' unremarkable life as accepted members of society. Some doctors advise withholding information about the karyotype from the parents in these cases, on the grounds that this information may lead to parental anxiety, is open to misinterpretation, and may have a detrimental effect on normal family relationships.[23] The more usual action is to discuss the findings carefully with both parents so that they may be helped to understand the prognosis and make an informed decision about continuing the pregnancy. An alternative course which has been suggested, is to have available within the Genetic Centre, a written statement of policy about such cases for all prospective amniocentesis patients to read, so that they may decide beforehand whether or not they wish to be informed of such fortuitous findings.

A similar situation may occur in the prenatal diagnosis of neural tube defects, with the unexpected detection of an umbilical herniation (exomphalos), associated with elevated levels of amniotic AFP. These malformations range in severity from those which are surgically correctable to those which are incompatible with survival. The difficulty is to distinguish the surgically correctable type in utero, although this may sometimes be achieved by ultrasonography. To complicate the issue even further, exomphalos may be associated with severe chromosome aberrations.

The occasional occurrence of an unexpected diagnosis should not deter the prenatal diagnostic laboratory from giving the most complete service possible. Many centres, including the West of Scotland Genetic Centre, examine all amniotic fluid specimens for both amniotic AFP and chromosome aberrations irrespective of the primary indication for amniocentesis. As the mother has undergone the risk (and trouble) of amniocentesis, it is felt that the fluid should be tested for the common severe foetal abnormalities. Other centres are unable to provide foetal chromosome analysis in every case because of the cost. Tables I and II [24] show that the population frequency of chromosome aberrations and neural tube defects is to be expected, and that the birth of an appreciable number of severely malformed infants can be avoided.

6. Choosing the sex of offspring. The fact that there is a small but appreciable risk of foetal loss associated with amniocentesis, should be sufficient to deter the use of prenatal diagnosis for non-clinical indications. There is mounting evidence, however, that a small section of the community wish to be able to choose the sex of their child by prenatal sex determination followed by the abortion of those of the undesired sex.[25] In fact, there is evidence of cases where prenatal diagnosis has been obtained fraudulently for this purpose by misrepresenting the indication, followed by a termination of pregnancy at another centre. The identification of foetal sex is a by-product of foetal chromosome analysis, and many centres now omit details of the sex chromosome constitution in their written reports simply to avoid the possibility that this information may lead to the

abortion of a normal child; information on foetal sex is only provided if the obstetrician specifically requests it. It should be emphasised that the sex of the foetus cannot be considered legal grounds for termination under the Abortion Act, 1967, unless the mother is at risk of producing a male child affected by a severe X-linked disease.

GENETIC COUNSELLING.

The first genetic clinics in the United Kingdom were established after the second World War, and since then a network of genetic centres has gradually developed so that each region in the country has at least one centre to which patients and their families can be referred for genetic advice. Their main purpose is to determine the risk of a genetic disorder or malformation syndrome occurring in a future pregnancy, so that couples may make sensible and informed decisions about planning their family.

As the prior requirement for reliable genetic advice is an accurate diagnosis, medical geneticists must be fully-trained in medicine and have a full range of diagnostic facilities available to them. Training programmes for medical geneticists have now been established and a system of accreditation is in operation in the U.K. Genetics clinics are usually sited in a teaching hospital, often in association with specialised genetic laboratories and together they provide a comprehensive genetic service for an average population of about three million.

For many straight-forward medical conditions, adequate genetic advice may be provided by doctors who have not specialised in medical genetics but have received some instruction in genetics in their undergraduate course. In fact, it would be wholly impossible for the small number of consultant medical geneticists to cater for all patients' questions concerning genetics and reproduction. Non-specialists should, however, appreciate the limitations of their experience and refer patients to their regional genetics clinic if the problem is complex, or the diagnosis unclear.[26]

Ignorance of basic genetics has not prevented practitioners in the past from offering advice about risks of recurrence of quite complex disorders and every medical geneticist has the regular embarrassing experience of hearing from their patients about totally inappropriate advice given previously by a colleague. Often, this misleading advice takes the form of a bland assurance that as the disorder is extremely rare it is unlikely to recur in a subsequent child. In other cases, the original diagnosis is incorrect, or the mode of inheritance mistaken. It is hoped that with the more widespread introduction to undergraduate curricula of formal teaching in medical genetics, and with the growing use of regional genetic services, these common mistakes will decrease. Meanwhile, cases where the doctor has failed to give genetic advice, or has given the wrong advice, are increasingly the subject of litigation both in the U.K. and United States. Accounts of some of the more usual problems related to genetic counselling are given below.

1. Failure to understand advice. Consideration of some of the patient's accounts of previous genetic advice makes it clear that they have misunderstood what they have been told. Often they have been given this advice in inappropriate circumstances, e.g., in a busy ward

or clinic, after a recent bereavement, or at the time they have been told the nature of their child's serious illness. Genetic counselling is best accomplished when the parents have recovered from these traumatic experiences and sometimes this recovery may take weeks or months. It has been the experience of the West of Scotland Genetics Clinic that parents find it helpful to have the main conclusions of the advice they have received at the clinic summarised in the form of a letter. This helps to reinforce the advice they receive and may assist them in making sensible decisions about family planning later, and may reduce the amount of subsequent litigation.

2. Sterilisation and Contraception. If parents find that the risk of recurrence of a genetic disease is too high to contemplate a further pregnancy, they may choose the option of sterilisation.[27] Occasionally the operation is not successful and this may be grounds for an action in negligence should a further affected child result.[28] Actions of this sort are recorded in the United States, including one where an error in dispensing led to a mother receiving an ineffective drug instead of a contraceptive. There are also occasional difficulties in obtaining sterilisation, either because the couple are young (for there is a general reluctance among obstetricians and urologists to sterilise patients under the age of 30 years), or because of the patient's religion. One patient with no chance of having a healthy baby because she was a carrier of a chromosomal translocation between homologous chromosomes, had to bear three affected stillbirths before receiving dispensation from her Church to be sterilised.

3. Genetic Heterogeneity. One common difficulty in genetic counselling is to determine the appropriate mode of inheritance, for there are many clinically identical conditions which have different modes of inheritance in different families. Blindness due to retinitis pigmentosa is one example where in some families the condition is autosomal recessive (both parents of the affected child are carriers of the abnormal gene); in other families the condition is X-linked, i.e., carried on the X chromosome and transmitted to affected males through carrier females. The risk of a sister of a patient with the autosomal recessive type having affected children is small and depends on her marrying a carrier of the same gene. However, if the disorder is X-linked and inherited from a carrier mother, a sister will have a 50 per cent chance of being a carrier also, and a 25 per cent risk of having a son affected. In these cases a genetic consultation is essential if mistakes are to be avoided.

4. The right of relatives to know the results of genetic studies. A genetic consultation differs from other medical consultations in that the whole family is often the patient and not simply the person affected with the genetic disease. Genetic investigation often reveals that multiple members of the family are either at risk of disease, or at risk of having affected children. It is clearly in the interests of relatives to have these risks explained to them so that they may take appropriate action. Occasionally, patients do not wish their relatives to be given confidential medical information about themselves, and it is sometimes difficult to ensure that all relatives at risk are properly advised. With care, the individual patient's right to confidentiality can almost always be preserved and

it is usually possible to contact relatives through their family doctors without breaking this confidence. It is not known if breach of confidentiality has been successfully claimed in these circumstances, nor how such claims would be considered by the courts. However, it is clear that a doctor is entitled to make disclosure of confidential information to the appropriate authority where he feels himself to be under a social duty to do so, and that in such cases the doctor may be able to claim a qualified privilege.[29]

5. Genetic Registers. Anxiety about the confidentiality of patient records which are placed on computerised files, has led to the formulation of guide lines by the Clinical Genetics Society.[30] Genetic registers are very helpful in ensuring that members of families obtain correct genetic counselling as they reach the age of reproduction, and several centres have developed local registers in which patients with a specific disorder can be linked with other patients in the same pedigree. These local registers are kept in 'dedicated' computer files accessible only to the Consultant in charge of the Genetic Clinic. They have considerable value in the prevention of genetic disease in the community and the various safeguards which are currently used should ensure that they are not abused. However, the storing and handling of information has been the subject of some recent concern, as have questions relating to access to the information maintained on such records. Unfortunately, recommendations from the Committee on Data Protection,[31] which would have set up a Data Protection Authority to supervise the use and handling of such computerised records[32] thereby ensuring the absolute confidentiality and correct usage of such information, now seem unlikely to become legislation.

6. Consanguinity. Patients who plan to marry cousins or other blood relatives may wish to seek advice regarding the risk of producing abnormal children. In general, provided that there is no family history of genetic disease, the advice given can be reassuring, and the increased risk over the general risk is usually regarded as being acceptable. In cases of incest, however, the risk becomes unacceptably high,[33] and it has been found, for example, in follow-up studies of children born of brother-sister and father-daughter unions, that fewer than half of the children are normal.[34] Rare recessive disorders are found in addition to a high incidence of mental retardation and a smaller increased incidence of congenital malformations.[35]

7. Artificial Insemination using Donor Semen (AID).[36] When both parents are known carriers of a rare autosomal recessive disease which cannot be detected prenatally, the option of AID should be considered. Experience shows that parents who have already lost children with severe recessive disease are even more suitable as condidates for AID than where the father is infertile. Another important indication is where the husband is at risk for transmitting the gene for Huntington's Chorea. This severe type of progressive dementia associated with involuntary movements and ataxia is inherited as an autosomal dominant trait, but the disease does not usually become apparent until the third decade by which time the patient may have already completed his family and passed the condition to half of his children. Individuals who have an affected parent can only be advised not to have children. As they may not be regarded as

suitable surrogate parents by adoption societies, the only alternative to risking an affected child is to have a pregnancy by AID. Of course, this is only applicable where the husband is at risk of carrying the gene.

One unsolved problem relating to AID is the fact that children born following it are required to be registered as illegitimate. It seems likely that many families choose to ignore this, and instead register the child as the husband's. Although illegal, this may be realistic in view of the high proportion of children born out of wedlock who are not registered as illegitimate, and in any event it serves to reflect the attitude of the parents to the child. Nonetheless, it is clear that for such a child to be registered as illegitimate may cause severe problems, and that some change in the law is long overdue.[37]

Another aspect of AID which requires some reconsideration is the choice of donors. They cannot be regarded as a random selection of the population as most centres seem to rely on medical students. It is also not clear how far donors are screened to exclude genetic defects. The minimum that is necessary should include chromosome analysis to exclude translocation, the obtaining of a careful family history, particularly to exclude dominant or common autosomal recessive conditions, and blood group analysis to determine the Rhesus status.

However, at the present time there seems to be no identifiable standard practice in the screening of donor semen, and in the long run the extent and nature of screening may well depend on non-medical factors such as the ready availability of diagnostic procedures or the pressure to achieve a successful pregnancy. In view of this, it would seem that it is unlikely that a doctor failing to screen for a particular defect will be regarded as having been negligent unless the defect is so common that the reasonable doctor would have screened for it. As a standard practice emerges, however, the doctor may become more vulnerable to allegations of negligence as a result of such failure to screen, although it should be borne in mind that, while the position in Scotland may be open to debate, the Congenital Disabilities (Civil Liability) Act 1976 expressly states that a doctor will not be liable to any subsequent child simply because he deviated from normal or standard practice.[38] In other words, the reasonableness of any deviation will be taken into account.

There is an unfortunate tendency to destroy donor records in order to preserve anonymity, but this may not be in the best interests of the children particularly when semen is banked in liquid nitrogen for multiple use. The occurrence of a genetic disorder (e.g., cystic fibrosis) in the child might mean that further use of the particular donor is contraindicated.

CONCLUSION

Medical genetics is a comparatively new discipline in medicine and as yet there is little in the way of case law relating to some of the problems peculiar to it which are illustrated in this chapter. Problems common to other specialities, for example, the meaning of informed consent[39] are not discussed here and the newer areas of medical genetics, such as in vitro fertilisation, gene therapy and genetic engineering are at too early a state of development to be usefully considered. It is hoped, however, that the brief description of genetic services currently available to the community will be helpful both to those concerned with providing legal advice when misunderstanding or mistakes occur, or when services fail, and also to those who provide medical advice in such cases.

M.A. Ferguson-Smith

NOTES

1. For further discussion, see infra ch. 11.
2. McKusick, V.A., Mendelian Inheritance in Man, (5th Ed.), Baltimore, Johns Hopkins University Press, 1978.
3. For further discussion, see infra pp. 35-7.
4. For further discussion, see infra, chs. 7 and 11.
5. Howard v. Lecher, quoted in Milunsky, A., and Annas, G.J., Genetics and the Law II, New York, Plenum Press, 1980, at p. 63.
6. s. 1(1)b.
7. Ferguson-Smith, M.A., et al., 'Avoidance of duencephalic and spina bifida births by maternal serum alphafetroprotein screening', Lancet i, 1330-1333, (1978).
8. Hamerton, J., and Simpson, N.E., 'Prenatal Diagnosis: Past, Present & Future', Prenatal Diagnosis, 1 (Special Issue), (1980).
9. Medical Research Council Working Party on Amniocentesis, 'An assessment of the hazards of Amniocentesis', Brit. J. Obstet. Gynaec., 85, Supplement No. 2, 1978.
10. Hamerton, J., Simpson, N.E., loc. cit.
11. See infra, pp.147 and 148.
12. See infra, p. 149.
13. For further discussion on this general subject, see Report by the Working Group on Screening for Neural Tube Defects, D.H.S.S., 1979.
14. Ferguson-Smith, et al., loc.cit.
15. Moussa, S.A., Scobie, W.G., 'Effect of antenatal screening for neural tube defects on the number of new spina bifida cases presenting to a paediatric surgical unit', Z. Kinderchir, 28, 307, 1980.
16. See infra pp. 147 and 148.
17. This Act extends to England and Wales, but not to Scotland. where such cases will be dealt with at common law.
18. For further discussion, see infra chs. 6 and 11.
19. Milunsky, A., Annas, G.J., loc. cit.
20. For further discussion, see infra ch. 8.
21. For example see the case discussed in 3 Leg. Med. Q., 97, (1979). For further discussion, see infra ch. 11.
22. Ferguson-Smith, M.A., et al., 'The provision of services for the prenatal diagnosis of fetal abnormality in the United Kingdom', Bulletin of the Eugenics Society, Supplement No. 3, (1978).
23. This 'Prevention of Harm Argument' is often used by doctors although it can be, and has been, convincingly criticised. For further discussion, see infra pp. 99-101.
24. See infra pp.147 and 148.
25. Even although technically termination on such grounds is not

directly sanctioned by the terms of the Abortion Act 1967 which allows termination in the following circumstances:

s. 1(1)(a)   that the continuance of the pregnancy would involve risk to the life of the pregnant woman, or of injury to the physical or mental health of the pregnant woman or any existing children of her family, greater than if the pregnancy were terminated; or

(b)   that there is a substantial risk that if the child were born it would suffer from such physical or mental abnormalities as to be seriously handicapped.

26.   It is generally asserted that doctors should identify and refer to specialists those cases which are outwith their competence, otherwise they may be deemed to be negligent. See, for example, Martin, C.R.A., Law Relating to Medical Practice, (2nd Ed.), Pitman Medical, 1979, at p. 377.

27.   For further discussion, see infra ch. 13.

28.   However, this will only be negligence if the failure of the sterilisation is the result of some fault on the part of the doctor, or perhaps where the patient has not given proper consent, i.e. was not told of the risks of sterilisation failing, or was not in a position to give proper consent. For further discussion, see infra ch. 8.

29.   For further discussion, see infra pp. 19-22.

30.   Emery, et al., 'A Report on Genetic Registers: Based on the Report of The Clinical Genetics Society Working Party', J. Med. Genetics 15, 435, (1978).

31.   Cmnd 731/1972.

32.   ibid.

33.   This argument strongly influenced the Scottish Law Commission, in a recent assessment of the law of incest in Scotland, see Memorandum No. 44, The Law of Incest in Scotland, April 1980.

34.   For further discussion, see Gibbens, et al., 'Siblings and Parent-Child Incest Offenders' 18 Brit. J. Criminol., 40, (1978).

35.   'Lancet' i, 250, (1981).   See also, Roberts, 'Incest, Inbreeding and Mental Abilities', B.M.J., 336, (1967).

36.   For further discussion, see infra ch. 12.

37.   See infra ch. 12.

38.   s.1 (5).   For further discussion, see infra pp. 152-4.

39.   For further discussion, see infra ch. 8.

TABLE I
INDICATIONS FOR PRENATAL CHROMSOME ANALYSIS:
RESULTS OF WEST OF SCOTLAND SERIES, 1969-80 INCLUSIVE.
PREVALENCE OF UNBALANCED CHROMSOME ABNORMALITY IN NEWBORN = 0.44%.

INDICATION	NO. OF PREG. TESTED	CHROMOSOME ABNORMALITY NUMBER	%	TRIS-21	TRIS-18	TRIS-13 SEX CHR. ABN.	OTHERS
MATERNAL AGE - 40	912	27	3.0	17	4	5	1
MATERNAL AGE 35-39	1428	12	0.8	7	3	2	-
PREVIOUS TRISOMY-21	268	1	0.4	1	-	-	-
PARENTAL TRANSLOCATION	54	4	7.4	-	-	-	4
PARENTAL MOSAICISM	5	0	0	-	-	-	-
PREVIOUS ANEUPLOIDY (EX.21)	50	0	0	-	-	-	-
FAMILY HISTORY DOWNS	224	1	0.4	-	-	-	1
MATERNAL ANXIETY	197	0	0	-	-	-	-
RAISED SERUM AFP	815	9	1.1	1	6	-	2
AMNIOTIC FLUIDS DRAWN FOR OTHER INDICATIONS	1758	5	0.3	3	0	1	1
FETAL SEXING FOR X-LINKED DISORDERS	37	11*	30.5	-	-	-	-
	5748	70	1.2	29	13	8	9

* MALE INFANTS

TABLE II.
PRENATAL DIAGNOSIS OF NEURAL TUBE DEFECTS:
RESULTS OF WEST OF SCOTLAND SERIES, 1969-80
(PREVALENCE AMONG TOTAL BIRTHS = 0.58%)

INDICATION	NUMBER OF PREGNANCIES TESTED	ABNORMAL NUMBER	ABNORMAL %	ANENCEPHALY	OPEN SPINA BIFIDA	EXOMPHALOS	OTHER
PREVIOUS NEURAL TUBE DEFECT	1407	50	3.6	28	21	1	-
FAMILY HISTORY OF N.T.D.	138	1	0.7	1	-	-	-
ELEVATED MATERNAL SE AFP	815	256	30.5	141	95	19	1
MISCELLANEOUS INDICATIONS	188	42	22.3	36	5	1	-
AMNIOTIC FLUIDS DRAWN FOR OTHER INDICATIONS	3191	13	0.4	8	4	1	-
TOTALS:	5739	362	6.3	214	125	22	1

148

TABLE III.

PRENATAL DIAGNOSIS OF CHROMOSOME ABERRATIONS:
NUMBER AND PROPORTION OF SINGLETON PREGNANCIES SCREENED IN 1979.

HEALTH BOARD	SCREENING CENTRE	TOTAL BIRTHS	TOTAL BIRTHS MA -35 YEARS	NO.SCREENED MA-35 YEARS	PERCENT SCREENED	TERMINATIONS TRIS.21	TERMINATIONS OTHERS	TERMINATIONS-35 TRIS.21	TERMINATIONS-35 OTHERS	% TRIS.21 DETECTED.
GRAMPIAN ORKNEY SHETLAND	ABERDEEN	7049	300E (4.2%)	29	9.7	0	1	0	1	-
TAYSIDE	DUNDEE	4879	205 (4.2%)	55	26.8	0	0	0	0	-
LOTHIANS BORDERS	EDINBURGH	13843E	623 (4.5%)	242	38.8	2	1	1	4	15.5
AYRSHIRE AND ARRAN ARGYLL AND CLYDE GREATER GLASGOW LANARKSHIRE FORTH VALLEY DUMFRIES & GALLOWAY	GLASGOW	35505	211E (5.9%)	478	22.6	6	4	2	0	16.6
WESTERN ISLES		397	50(12.6%)	0	0	-	-	-	0	-
HIGHLAND	INVERNESS	2811	82(6.5%)	22	12.1	1	0	0	0	25.6
TOTALS		64487	3471 (5.4%)	826	23.8	9	6	3	5	13.3

11 Ante-Natal Injuries

S. A. M. McLean

Every year many children are born in the United Kingdom suffering from congenital defects, but despite advances in medical science and technology it is often impossible to pin down the major cause of such disabilities. Whereas some defects are apparently the result of faulty genetic material, there are a number which offer no ready explanation - for example, those allegedly induced by the ingestion by the pregnant mother of certain drugs, or by the inhalation of chemicals which form part of our environment or which are artificially produced by man in the development of, for example, weed killers. In response to the complications of drug based damage, medical science now recognises pharmacogenetics as a distinct discipline. In its purest sense, it is said to be concerned with '... genetically determined variations which are revealed <u>solely</u> by the effects of drugs,' but it is now taken by some investigators to include '... those hereditary disorders in which symptoms may occur spontaneously but are often precipitated or aggravated by drugs'.[1]

Although both medicine and, of course, the public have long been aware that some children will be born with congenital defects, the legal world appeared largely uninterested in this problem and its causes until the tragedy of Thalidomide aroused public concern in the early 1960's.[2] It has since been estimated that there are approximately 1500 drugs having known teratogenic effects,[3] and it cannot be assumed that this is by any means the complete picture. Despite the fact that it is largely uncertain which drugs may have teratogenic effects, it has been estimated that some 82 per cent of pregnant women take prescribed drugs during pregnancy with approximately 65 per cent taking self medication.[4] (Of course, since it is within the first eight weeks of pregnancy that the damage is most likely to occur, the above estimates tell us nothing about the potential risk to the developing foetus. Nor do they tell us the necessity for taking such drugs to preserve the life of the mother and/or the foetus).

However, apart from damaging an estimated 10,000 children throughout the world and some 400 in the United Kingdom,[5] Thalidomide had the effect of ringing two major changes in the legal response to ante-natal injuries. First, and importantly from the point of view particularly of the marketing and production of new drugs, it resulted in the setting up of the Medicines Commission,[6] under whose auspices were created the Committee on Safety of Medicines (replacing the Committee on Safety of Drugs), with responsibility for the regulation and control of the introduction and trials of new drugs and the Committee on the Review of Medicines with responsibility for monitoring the effects of drugs already on the market.[7] In any comparison, however, these Committees lack the authority and apparently the efficiency of their counterpart in the United States, the Food and Drug Administration, which has been granted substantially greater powers in successive legislation since the 1930's.[8] It is to a large extent these powers which guarantee the apparently superior abilities of the Food and Drug Administration, particularly in the control of new drugs. However, it has further been suggested that any such apparent difference in controlling the marketing and production of drugs is not simply based in the nature of the regulations, but on the entirely different approach to clinical freedom in the two countries concerned:

In Britain greater reliance is placed by the Committee on Safety of Medicines upon professional freedom, to enable the clinician a wide latitude of judgement regarding new drugs.
In the United States on the other hand the Food and Drug authorities are curtailing professional freedom to a degree by a more restrictive approach to new drugs.[9]

Whatever the reason, it is the case that between 1962 and 1971, nearly four times as many new drugs became available in the United Kingdom as in the United States,[10] although it can reasonably be assumed that, since the Committee on Safety of Medicines started operating, these figures would not necessarily any longer represent a true picture. In fact they represent the control exercised by the Committee on Safety of Drugs which apparently failed initially to appreciate the appalling hazards of Thalidomide (which was available in any one of some 37 drugs in this country as the sole or active agent, some of these drugs being available over the counter without prescription), whereas the Food and Drug Administration refused a licence for the production of Thalidomide in the U.S.A. Although this refusal was due largely to the efforts of one doctor who accumulated evidence worldwide, nonetheless, a clinical trial licence was refused by the F.D.A. and a major disaster averted.[11]

The second major result of the Thalidomide tragedy, and perhaps the more interesting from the legal point of view, was the realisation that there was a remarkable degree of uncertainty as to whether or not there was a right of action by which compensation could be sought on behalf of those damaged as a result of being injured prenatally. In the event, it was largely due to media pressure that ex gratia payments were made in this country by the Distillers group of companies who marketed the drug in the United Kingdom and who at no point accepted liability.[12] Indeed, the Royal Commission on Civil Liability and Compensation for Personal Injury,[13] (Pearson Commission), maintained that it is doubtful whether or not the case would have been established if it had been judicially considered. [14] The legal response to the Thalidomide situation can best be described as confused and resulted in the Law Commissions of both Scotland and England considering the question of whether or not children in this position did have a right to sue.

The Scottish Law Commission, which reported in 1973,[15] concluded that: 'In Scotland...the right to reparation is general in its nature, based on the existence of a fault for which the defender is responsible and which has caused foreseeable harm to the pursuer.'[16] The test which would normally be applied in such circumstances would be that of the reasonable man,[17] and the reasonable man could be assumed, according to the Scottish Law Commission, to 'take account of the risk of causing injury to a child in the womb....'.[18] The Report continued that although it was not possible to predict all the situations where a duty might exist, nonetheless: 'An obvious example would be where a doctor, prescribing a drug for a pregnant woman, selected one which was commonly known to have teratogenic effects'.[19]

Essentially the conclusion of the Scottish Law Commission was that a right to sue existed on the application of two principles commonly used in Scots Law:- firstly, the equitable principle that a child, if subsequently born alive, should be regarded as having been alive whenever it is to its advantage to do so; and secondly, the principle applied in Donoghue v. Stevenson,[20] that 'the fault or breach of duty persists until the damage is suffered, or at any rate emerges as a wrong at that stage.'[21] Any suggestion that since a child in the womb cannot attract legal rights no action could therefore be available, clearly falls on the combination of these two principles.[22]

The English Law Commission which reported in 1974,[23] concluded that the situation under English law was uncertain and recommended legislation to clarify the matter. They pointed out that there were no Scottish or English cases directly in point although reference was made to a case at Liverpool Assizes in 1939 in which a settlement was achieved out of court.[24] Although the Law Commission felt that: '...it is highly probable that the common law would, in appropriate circumstances, provide a remedy for a plaintiff suffering from a pre-natal injury caused by another's fault...',[25] nonetheless they concluded that legislation was necessary to clarify the situation and to ensure that a right of action did lie where a child was born alive, and where the pre-natal injury was caused intentionally, negligently or by a breach of statutory duty.[26] The Report of the Committee included the draft of a Bill, now the Congenital Disabilities (Civil Liability) Act 1976, which does not apply to Scotland.[27] The Act provides that a person who is responsible for an occurrence which affects the parent of the child, and causes a subsequent child to be born disabled, will be liable to the child if he would have been liable in tort (delict) to the particular parent who was affected.[28] The terms of the Act enshrine the fault principle which is the traditional basis for attracting liability in personal injury claims.[29] However, the Act was regarded as potentially an interim measure since the Pearson Commission was then sitting and was expected to report fully on the basis of liability in tort in the foreseeable future. Although, like all permissive legislation, the Act is essentially also restrictive, in that it delineates areas in which an action is possible, and restricts those parties who may sue or be sued,[30] it should ensure that the situation which arose in the case of S v. Distillers Company,[31] where liability had to be settled by agreement between the parties, should not recur. The provisions of the legislation provide an exception to the general rule in relation to remoteness of damage laid down in the Wagon Mound (No.1),[32] in that the defendant in any action cannot successfully escape liability by claiming that he didn't know that the mother was pregnant, nor that the damage to her child was not foreseeable.

Thus it is clearly established that, although there are some differences in respect of details, the situation in both Scotland and England is that a child born suffering from a congenital defect does have a right of action where he or she can prove two things:

(1) fault, which is generally negligence or breach of duty on the part of one person or organisation who owes a duty of care to the parent(s) or the child before or after conception; and

(2) causation, i.e., the chain of cause and effect between the breach of the duty of care or negligence and the subsequent damage to the child.

It should be remembered however that there are two groups of children who may be born suffering from congenital defects. While one group may be damaged by the exposure of the parents to radiation or harmful chemicals or the ingestion of drugs, the other group may be born suffering from a defect which is not apparently caused by any of these but by genetically transmitted disease. However, many genetic problems are readily identifiable, and medical science is developing apace in this area.[33] In some cases, therefore, when the legal standard of proof 'on the balance of probabilities', which is the test used in non-criminal allegations, is applied it may be relatively simple to establish the likelihood of a defect being the result of some genetic rather than environmental problem. Causation is therefore comparatively simple, and there is clearly no question of the damage being anyone's fault, so no action would lie simply because the damage occurred.

Genetic defects, while the result of factors outwith control, may nonetheless be legally problematic for the doctor. While genetic screening of <u>all</u> pregnant women is not standard practice, a woman attempting to <u>sue</u> a doctor after the birth of a damaged child, would (unless other negligence exists) be unlikely to succeed. However, in those groups where screening is becoming the norm, the doctor may be more vulnerable in line with the decision in <u>Hunter</u> v. <u>Hanley</u>.[34] This vulnerability relates to the fact that the concept of 'standard practice' is much relied on in assessing the professional behaviour of the doctor.[35] Deviation from standard practice does not, however, amount to negligence <u>per se</u> and it was stated in <u>Hunter</u> v. <u>Hanley</u>, supra, that for a doctor to be accused of negligence on the basis that he deviated from normal practice, it was necessary to prove three things. First, that there is a normal practice (in the case of intensive genetic screening this is unlikely at the moment); secondly that the doctor deviated from that practice; and thirdly, and most importantly, that no reasonable doctor acting with due skill and care would have deviated from that practice.

However, as a normal or standard practice evolves, the doctor may become liable for any unreasonable deviation from that practice, although there are clear difficulties in assessing what might amount to an unreasonable deviation. It is at this stage that the notion of 'clinical judgement' becomes relevant,[36] and courts may well have problems in assessing what the 'reasonable doctor' might have done in any given circumstances. In <u>Hatcher</u> v. <u>Black</u>,[37] Lord Denning suggested that a doctor's behaviour would ultimately be judged by the attitude of his fellow practitioner to it. The assessment of what is unreasonable deviation would therefore, almost certainly be largely based on the evidence of other practitioners, although the court would also lay great stress on other evidence, e.g., the known history of the family, the age of the mother, and so on.

Doctors in this country may well, however, be interested in a recent American decision in which a doctor, who had failed sufficiently to inform a woman of the availability/risks of amniocentesis, and she subsequently gave birth to a damaged child, was held to be responsible for the maintenance of the child up until the age of majority.[38] However, this would appear to amount to an action for 'wrongful life', and the United Kingdom has always been wary of anything which looks like that sort of action; attempts to compensate for injuries which were not caused by the fault of, for example, the doctor and which, in any event, could not have been prevented and could only have been avoided by termination of the pregnancy, are unlikely to be successful in this country.[39] However, it would seem that courts in this country would also be prepared to impute fault in such cases since the woman concerned was in the 'high risk' group of older women.[40] It is worth noting, however, that should genetic screening become standard practice in all women, for example over a certain age, then any unreasonable deviation from such screening could, in line with Hunter v. Hanley, supra, amount to negligence and result in a successful claim against the doctor[41] based on his negligence in respect of the woman, however, rather than on his duty to the child.

Nor do the doctors' problems end there. In their efforts to ensure that infertile marriages may be productive, medicine has refined the practice of donor insemination.[42] Although the mechanics of this technique have been carefully developed, it is not yet sufficiently used for there to be an apparent normal practice in the screening of donor sperm, although it is becoming increasingly clear that certain tests should be carried out.[43] However, since there is at present no normal practice, an allegation such as that made in Hunter v. Hanley, supra, would clearly fail, but where a woman is inseminated with sperm which is in some way defective, for example carrying of venereal disease, the damage to any resulting child might found the basis of a successful action under the 1976 Act or under common law in Scotland, since the doctor owes a duty of care to the mother, and a breach of the duty of care will give to the child a right to sue where it is born damaged. In the United States of America, recent cases would suggest that in that country in certain situations, e.g. blood donation, any liability imposed on doctors and hospitals might be strict rather than based on proof of fault.[44] In the United Kingdom however, such a move is unlikely, and the situation remains that, although, where the congenital defect is the result of genetic problems, causation may be relatively easy to establish, proof of fault which is still necessary in negligence actions, will be extremely difficult, and will only be possible in respect of the failure to screen. Thus, in view of the fact that the 'wrongful life' action is precluded, only the parents would have any chance of success if their claim was based on their suffering or grief.

The problems involved in suing as a result of a suspected drug or chemical based injury are, if anything, even greater. Since the Committee on Safety of Medicines is now well established and has regulated carefully the tests required to be carried out (including tests on pregnant animals)[45] in order that a new drug can be marketed, it is clear that drugs companies will require to follow these or suffer the rejection of a licence for a new drug on which they may have spent considerable time, expertise and of course money.[46] It would be not unreasonable therefore were companies to claim in these circumstances that, if they have conformed to tests required by the Committee on Safety of Medicines, there is at least prima facie evidence that they were not negligent or at fault. Proof of fault where the drug has been on the market for some time may be even more difficult.[47]

Equally problematic in this case is the question of establishing causation. Even assuming that fault can be proved, there is still the need to link this with the subsequent damage, i.e., the need to establish that the defect did not arise spontaneously or as the result of the defective genetic inheritance of the child, but was in some way attributable to the particular drug. In this situation a scientist attempting to establish causation may require a high level of probability, whereas a court will seek an answer on the balance of probabilities. However, although this test is apparently lower, as the Pearson Commission pointed out: 'Our consultations have led us to the conclusion that, as the boundary of knowledge increases, so does

the area of uncertainty'.[48]   They continued:
> We received no evidence that causation is becoming easier to
> establish.   On the contrary, we understand that birth
> defects do not all have the same basis.   The effect of a drug
> may be to cause a pre-existing and latent genetic defect to
> become manifest rather than to act directly on the unborn
> child.[49]

Equally, of course, any given drug may only react adversely where
it is combined with other drugs, and the problems of multiple drug
therapy are already becoming evident in the United States of
America.[50]   It is also impossible to overlook the importance of an
idiosyncratic response to a particular drug or chemical.   Indeed, it
has been pointed out that:
> With any new drug, even when most of the risks involved are
> known, or knowable, there is always an undiscovered element
> of risk not yet known to anyone.   Until the drug has been in
> wide use for a number of years, adverse effects may occur,
> but remain unknown.[51]

In establishing causation, the role of the doctor cannot be
underestimated.   Certainly, the responsibility for assessing the
relationship between cause and effect in such situations cannot be,
and is not, left with the individual doctor whose only previous
experience of a new drug will be the scientific and advertising
information with which the drug company has provided him.[52]   Such
information, of course, is aimed at ensuring that the doctor will use
and continue to use the drug in question, and cannot necessarily be
regarded as altogether unbiased.   That this is the case is now
clearly shown by the recent controversy over Debendox/Bendectin.[53]

In scrutinising the side effects of drugs newly produced, or which
have been on the market for some considerable time, the Medicines
Commission has a supervisory function which is generally the only
efficient way in which a picture of the pattern of side effects can be
collated, although this picture may not be particularly accurate given
the lack of efficient post-marketing surveillance and the voluntary
nature of the reporting system.[54]   It is largely dependent on the
vigilance of the individual doctor who may see only one case of an
unpleasant side effect and who is 'not surprisingly...reluctant to
ascribe a patient's illness or death to therapy'.[55]   In 1974 the
Committee on Safety of Medicines received 4818 notifications, but in
the Annual Report they expressed the view that 'the numbers....still
only represent a small proportion of those which actually
occur'.[56]   Further, Teff and Munro report that during 1965 and 1966
only six deaths of asthmatics were reported as likely to be due to the
use of aerosol bronchodilators, during which time 'it has now been
reliably estimated they led to 1700 deaths'.[57]

To compound the situation and its problems even further, it is not
only the pharmaceutical industry in its production of drugs which may
damage the developing foetus.   A recent case in point is the
controversy surrounding the possible teratogenic effects of
dioxin,[58] which is produced during the chemical process when the
weed killer 245-T is made, and which could be removed from the product
before it is used by the public.   It is known that dioxin attacks the
DNA molecule but it is not clear how this occurs.   Nonetheless animal
tests have shown that an extremely low dosage of dioxin (as small as
one part per million to body weight in rats, and 0.1 parts per billion
in mice embryos) is teratogenic in these and other animals.   Whereas
the United States Government's National Institute for Occupational

Safety has, on the basis of such figures, declared dioxin to be a suspect human teratogen, the Pesticides Advisory Committee in the United Kingdom continues to insist that 245-T is insufficiently dangerous to justify a ban. This despite the fact that there are presently several thousand claims in progress in the United States alleging that exposure to dioxin (either as part of the infamous 'Agent Orange'[59] or in weed killers for domestic use[60]) has resulted not only in an increase in cancer amongst those exposed to it, but in a dramatic increase in the number of children subsequently born suffering from congenital defects. The 'New Statesman' recently reported that whereas the national average rate of births of deformed children in Australia is one per thousand, the comparable rate amongst Australian ex-Servicemen exposed to 'Agent Orange' is one in four.[61]

The dangers of lead in the atmosphere have also recently come under scrutiny in the field of pre-natal injury,[62] and the practice of feeding beef cattle with the hormone diethyl stilboestrol (DES) in order to increase their profitability when slaughtered has been shown to be almost certainly connected with the increase in vaginal cancer (previously almost unkown) amongst the daughters of those who were fed DES-fattened beasts during their pregnancies.[63]

Confronted with this morass of scientific and medical evidence, the Pearson Commission sought to provide an adequate system of compensation for all children born with congenital defects. As Teff and Munro point out: 'The legal significance of the thalidomide litigation stretches far beyond its particular facts. It has highlighted some fundamental shortcomings of the tort system...'.[64]

The Commission received evidence that significant birth defects may be seen in 30 per thousand births but the medical evidence contended that this may in the end prove to be a conservative estimate.[65] They further pointed out that:

In considering ante-natal injury, we found that the cause of such injury could rarely be established with certainty.
There are some 90,000 severly handicapped children whose condition is due to congenital disability, but only those whose condition is caused by injury before or at birth are within our terms of reference. These children cannot be distinguished from those whose condition is caused by genetic abnormaliity or disease, and it is simply not feasible to devise a separate scheme of compensation for the children who are within our terms of reference. The question is whether provision should be made for none or for all.[66]

In these circumstances, the Pearson Commission attempted to provide a system of compensation for all children who were born 'severely handicapped' on the grounds that only a minute proportion of those born with congenital defects would be in a position 'to establish causation and prove that it was due to negligence'.[67] In view of the retention in the 1976 Act of the tortious action, Lord Pearson was moved to write to 'The Times' on 28 January, 1976 expressing his concern about the reliance on the operation of the tort action in the field of ante-natal injuries. His concern centred around the difficulties of proving fault and causation, but he also pointed out that there would still be delay and expense where the delictual or tortious action was the only method of compensating such children and that the effects on family relationships and on relationships between doctors and patients in such cases could be extremely damaging.[68]

Accordingly, in an attempt to alleviate these problems, the Commission recommended the introduction of a new allowance in the form of a disability income (non taxable) of £4 a week from the age of two, which would supplement the other allowances presently available.[69] (The sum of £4 it should be noted, was calculated at January, 1977 levels and would doubtless be considerably higher by today's standards). This allowance would be paid to those suffering from severe handicap (which would be assessed by doctors and other members of the health care professions) and administered by the D.H.S.S.[70] They further recommended that mobility allowance, which is presently paid, should be available in future from age two[71] and that the category of children presently included in this allowance might be extended.[72] In this way, the only proof required for a form of compensation would not be the difficult and technical ones required in the tortious/delictual action, but would simply be the existence of severe handicap.

The idea of all children receiving increased benefits where they are 'severely handicapped' has a number of obvious attractions. Nonetheless, as is discussed infra,[73] the problems of establishing liability in the area of medical and pharmaceutical products will still confront those who wish to take advantage of the residual right of action on the traditional grounds of delict or tort. It should be clear that in the vast majority of cases, the right of action embodied in general principles of Scots Law and in the 1976 Act, is largely useless. It may, however, be necessary that some do attempt to use the residual action since the agreed definition of what amounts to 'severe handicap' may not equate with the reality of their own situation, and in any event a weekly allowance will scarcely serve to satisfy the needs of many of the handicapped. The Pearson Commission itself recognised that such needs may be diverse and expensive. The report pointed out that:

> The forms of support required have a wide range. They can include special needs such as wheel chairs, adaptations to houses, extra clothing and bedding and also such needs as holidays and portable television and radio sets.[74]

Thus, although the recommendations are satisfactory at one level, they have done nothing to ease the burden of those who require (and surely merit) substantial damages in order to fulfil the basic function of compensation which, apart from the elements for grief, loss of life expectation and so on, is generally concerned to restore the person to the position he would have been in but for the damage, inasmuch as this is possible. While this is particularly difficult in the case of a child who has clearly never had a 'normal' life with which to make a comparison, it is nonetheless by no means impossible. Damages have been awarded in two such cases in the Commonwealth,[75] cases which both Law Commissions and the Pearson Commission considered in their assessment of the difficulties of pursuing an action for damages in this situation.

A number of American States have attempted to circumvent some of the problems of the fault-based action by imposing strict liability where drug-based injuries are alleged, thus effectively removing the need for proof of fault, which as has been seen is particularly problematic the more carefully the development and production of drugs are regulated.[76] Although the establishment of causation will still remain a problem even where strict liability is applied, at least one major difficulty will have been removed. However, in the case of vaccine-damaged children, to whom such a system has been instituted, the removal of fault from the equation seems to have simply resulted in the requirement that a serious disability is

established.[77]   This assessment is also problematic and simply
seems to replace one burden (proof of fault) with another (proof of 80
per cent disability).

   Not surprisingly, drug companies have protested that to impose
strict liability is to restrict the development of medical science,
and it has been suggested, not unreasonably, that:

   ...in this field of professional activity where the law's
   relations with medicine and science are so uneasy, all three
   callings will have to maintain a continuing scrutiny of the
   operation and effects of governmental controls if the effort
   to reinforce ethical obligations by legal duties is not to
   impair the progress of research and innovation in drug
   therapy.[78]

Some would also argue that to hold a company responsible for
injuries without requiring proof of fault is particularly unjust
in an area where the influence of unpredictable personal
idiosyncracies, accidental or deliberate misuse of drugs
otherwise safe, and the unforeseen and unforeseeable effects of
combinations of environmental hazards, other drugs and genetic
inheritance, cannot be taken account of.   However, as Teff and
Munro point out:

   ...if strict liability is to be significantly different from
   negligence, it surely ought to apply to precisely those cases
   where the defendant is either not at fault, or the task of
   proving that he is lies beyond the resources of most
   litigants.[79]

It is clear that in the form of action which would still exist
over and above the allowances which the Pearson Commission would make
available to these children, the problems of proof continue to be
great and show no sign of lessening, since this action continues to
require proof of fault and causation.   While it may the case that:

   By the accident that a wealthy company could be held
   responsible for their misfortune, they [in this case the
   thalidomide children] will become a tiny plutocratic elite
   while 8,500 children (many of them with disabilities just as
   grave as theirs) are condemned to lifelong incarceration in
   obsolete longstay hospitals,[80]

nonetheless, apparent inequality in terms of compensation is
unavoidable where manufacturers, of drugs or other commodities, are to
continue to be responsible for damage caused by their product.   It is
perhaps the most significant omission from the recommendations of the
Pearson Commission that, despite the disquiet expressed over the
almost insurmountable barriers to a successful claim and the retention
of the fault-based action in such cases, no recommendation was made
which would have eased the burden of the claimant who chooses, or is
forced by his personal circumstances, to take advantage of this
residual action.

It should, however, be clear that:

   ...there can be no all purpose formula for products
   liability.   The particular form it takes in any given
   industry needs to be worked out on the basis of as thorough a
   study as is practicable of the peculiarities of its market
   structure.[81]

Those who are involved in the manufacture and production of drugs are
in both a highly profitable and a highly risky (for the consumer at
least) business.   As a general rule of law, those involved in
inherently risky occupations or tasks are required to demonstrate a

higher standard of care,[82] and it is not perhaps out of proportion
to the risks (and the profits) of this particular industry that
companies should be required to act in a particularly (and even
unusually) careful manner.   Thus, were the basis of liability in such
cases to be changed to, for example, strict liability, although the
pursuer would still be required to establish causation, no proof of
fault would be necessary and compensation might become more readily
available.
    Certainly, it must be obvious that merely to provide for a right
of legal action is in itself insufficient to protect the vulnerable in
all cases.   The legal response to the Thalidomide situation was in
many ways welcome, although perhaps it was not as satisfactory as it
might have been.   The Member of Parliament introducing the 1976 Act
as a Bill saw it as potentially short-term in view of the imminent
report of the Pearson Commission.   However, this report failed to
live up to some expectations and is, as can be seen, inadequate in
some ways.
    Certainly, in easing the present burden of those with a right and
desire to sue, efforts are necessary on the part of medical science
and medical practitioners, and particularly the latter in the short
term.   The poor response to the attempts by the Committee on Safety
of Medicines to achieve substantial notification of side effects must
ultimately be the responsibility of these practitioners and will
reduce the chances of a successful action by exacerbating the problems
of proof of causation.   The delay in identifiying the link between
the high incidence of phocomelia and the use of Thalidomide must
largely be responsible for the delay in its withdrawal from the
market,[83] and for the number of children damaged.
    It has already been pointed out that doctors are loath to
attribute illness to therapy and also that their experience of a drug
will be extremely limited, particularly in the case of newer drugs.
They are, however, not required to be in a position to make such an
absolute link between an unpleasant side effect and a particular form
of therapy, since this is the statutory function of the Committee on
Safety of Medicines who can only function efficiently if they are
notified in all cases where the doctor is suspicious, not necessarily
certain.   This does not merely apply to new drugs but also is true in
the case of drugs which have been in use for many years.   The recent
findings in the case of Valium[84] have shown, if nothing else has,
that whatever their faith in a drug, the ultimate responsibility of
the doctor in this situation is to be alert on behalf of his patients
rather than to use his own confidence as an absolute guideline.

S.A.M. McLean

NOTES

1.   Emery, A.E.H., Elements of Medical Genetics, (5th Ed.),
        Edinburgh, Churchill Livingstone, 1979.
2.   For a thorough analysis of the Thalidomide case see Teff, H.,
        and Munro, C., Thalidomide: The Legal Aftermath, Saxon
        House, 1976.
3.   Report on Injuries to Unborn Children, Cmnd 5709/1974, para.
        21.
4.   id.

5.   Teff and Munro, op.cit., at p. xi.
6.   Medicines Act 1969 s.2.
7.   ibid., s.4.   For discussion of the operation of these
      Committees, see infra chs. 3 and 8.
8.   For discussion see Teff and Munro, op.cit., at pp.118-125.
9.   Klass, A., There's Gold in Them Thar Pills, Penguin Books,
      1975, at p. 129.
10.   Klass, op.cit., at p. 128.
11.   For discussion see Teff and Munro, op.cit., at p.120.
12.   See Teff and Munro, op.cit., at pp. 11-25.
13.   Cmnd 7054/1978.
14.   ibid., para. 1456.
15.   Liability for Antenatal Injury, Cmnd 537/1973.
16.   ibid., para 10.
17.   This was the test accepted in Donoghue v. Stevenson 1932 S.C.
      (H.L.) 31.
18.   Liability for Antenatal Injury, supra, para 10.
19.   id.
20.   Donoghue v. Stevenson, supra.
21.   ibid., para 8.
22.   For discussion of the legal personality of the unborn child
      see York, D.M., 'The Legal Personality of the Unborn Child',
      1979 S.L.T. (News) 158.   For an analysis of some
      philosophical problems see Campbell, T.D., and McKay, A.J.M.,
      'Antenatal Injury and the Rights of the Foetus',
      Philosophical Quarterly, January 1978, 17.
23.   Report on Injuries to Unborn Children, Cmnd 5709/1974.
24.   (1939) 83 Sol. J. 185.
25.   Report on Injuries to Unborn Children, supra, para 8.
26.   ibid., para 60.
27.   s.6 (2).
28.   s.1.
29.   For further discussion, see infra ch. 6.
30.   id.   For example, the Act expressly provides that a mother
      may not be sued (s.1 (1)) unless the damage occurs when the
      mother is driving a motor vehicle and 'knows (or ought
      reasonably to know) herself to be pregnant' (s.2), and is
      therefore covered by insurance.
31.   [1970] 1 W.L.R. 114.
32.   [1961] A.C. 388.
33.   For further discussion, see infra ch. 10.
34.   1955 S.C. 200;   S.L.T. 213.
35.   For further discussion, see infra, ch. 7.
36.   But see Re D (a minor) [1976] 1 All E.R. 326.
37.   'The Times' 29/30 June: 1/2 July 1954.
38.   See 3 Legal Medical Quarterly, 97, (1979).
39.   For a discussion of the possible liability of doctors after
      conception in potential cases of genetic defects see Lord
      Kilbrandon, 'The Comparative Law of Genetic Counseling' in
      Hilton, et al. (eds), Ethical Issues in Human Genetics,
      Plenum Press, 1973, 245, and in particular their discussion of
      the case of Gleitman v. Cosgrove 49 N.J. 22, 227 A. 2d 689
      (1967).   For further discussion of the 'wrongful life'
      action, see infra ch. 6.
40.   For further discussion, see infra ch. 10.
41.   But see the Congenital Disabilities (Civil Liability) Act 1976
      s. 1(5) which states: 'The defendant is not answerable

to the child, for anything he did or omitted to do when responsible in a professional capacity for treating or advising the parent, if he took reasonable care having due regard to then received professional opinion applicable to the particular class of case; but this does not mean that he is answerable only because he departed from received opinion'.

42. For further discussion, see infra ch. 12.
43. For further discussion, see infra ch. 10.
44. See 3 Legal Medical Quarterly, 96 (1979).
45. For further discussion, see infra ch. 5.
46. Teff and Munro, op.cit., at p. 104. It is estimated that drugs companies, who are among the world's most profitable companies, spend about 7% to 13% of total sales on the research and development of new drugs. Interestingly, it is equally alleged that they spend about 14% on advertising and promotion. For further discussion of the testing required prior to the production of new drugs, see infra ch. 9.
47. See, for example, the discussion surrounding Debendox/Bendectin, in the 'Sunday Times' 2 March 1980 and 21 September 1980. The attitude of the medical profession in this country would seem to be that since the drug has been in use for many years, it is unlikely, in the absence of large numbers of reported cases to be teratogenic. Thus, although the Food and Drug Administration have recommended its use in only the most extreme cases, the Committee on Safety of Medicines for some time left any curtailment of use to the discretion of the individual doctor by declaring Debendox to be 'not unsafe'. Only very recently did the doctor receive a formal warning as to the possible problems with this drug. For discussion, see 'The Guardian' 22 December 1980.
48. para 1449.
49. para 1450.
50. See Wood, C., (ed), The Influence of Litigation on Medical Practice, London, Academic Press, 1977, at pp. 131-148.
51. Klass, op.cit., at p. 125.
52. For further discussion, see infra ch. 9.
53. The 'Sunday Times' 2 March 1980 and 21 September 1980.
54. For further discussion, see infra p. 115 and pp. 122-3.
55. Teff and Munro, op.cit., at p. 109.
56. Annual Report for 1974 of the Medicines Commission, H.M.S.O. 1975.
57. See Teff and Munro, op.cit., at p. 109
58. See 'Poison Approved by Government' in 'New Statesman' 6 June 1980, at p. 842.
59. A defoliant used by American troops in Vietnam.
60. For example, the Trade Union whose members are most exposed to dioxin, has condemned the Advisory Committee on Pesticide's failure to 'take account of strong evidence' against 245-T, which evidence seems to have been accepted by the United States Environmental Protection Agency. See 'The Times' 28 April 1981.
61. 6th June 1980.
62. Wynn, M. & A., 'Lead and the Unborn' in 'New Society', 17 April 1980, at p. 104.
63. For discussion see Klass, op.cit., at pp. 70-71.
64. Teff and Munro, op.cit., at p. 129.

65.   para 1454.
66.   para 1488.
67.   para 1452.
68.   This letter is reproduced in full in the Pearson Report, para
    1432.
69.   para 1525.
70.   para 1526.
71.   para 1533.
72.   para 1534.
73.   see infra, chs. 6 and 9.
74.   para 1503.
75.   For further discussion, see infra pp. 35-7.
76.   Watt v. Rama [1972] V.R. 353 (Australia); Duval v. Sequin
    (1972) 26 D.L.R. (3d) 418 (Canada).
77.   For discussion see Teff and Munro, op.cit., at pp. 133-135.
78.   Cavers, D.F., 'The Legal Control of the Clinical
    Investigation of Drugs' in Freund, P.A., (ed),
    Experimentation With Human Subjects, London, Allen and Unwin,
    1972, at p. 242.
79.   Teff and Munro, op.cit., at p. 137.
80.   Crossman, R., 'The Times' 18 July 1973.
81.   Teff and Munro, op.cit., at pp. 146-7.
82.   c.f. Lord McMillan in Glasgow Corporation v. Muir [1943]
    A.C. 448, where he said at p.456, 'Those who engage in
    operations inherently dangerous must take precautions which
    are not required of persons engaged in the ordinary routine
    of daily life'.
83.   For discussion of the problems resulting from such delays,
    see infra, ch. 9.
84.   For discussion see 'The Observer' 24 February 1980.

12 Artificial Insemination
D. J. Cusine

It is usually stated that between 10 and 15% of all marriages are involuntarily childless[1] and in a significant number of these the cause may be that the husband is sterile or grossly subfertile.[2] In these circumstances, it may be appropriate to consider artificial insemination.

The semen which is used for artificial insemination may be obtained from the husband (homologous artificial insemination - referred to as 'AIH'), or semen from a donor (heterologous artificial insemination - referred to as 'AID'). The success rates for AIH are poor[3] and for that reason AID is more common. Sterility and infertility are the main reasons for contemplating AID,[4] but it may also be practised where there is a risk that the husband may pass some genetic defect on to his children.[5]

It is not possible in a short paper to discuss all the legal issues which arise from the practice of artificial insemination. This chapter will therefore concentrate on AID and largely ignore AIH which creates fewer legal problems, although AIH will be discussed in connection with the possible use of the husband's semen after his death.

The discussion of AID will examine first, the major issues of concern to the doctor, and second, those which affect the couple and the child. It should be noted that, unless the contrary is stated, it will be assumed that the woman receiving AID is married and that she has her husband's consent to this form of treatment.

A.I.D. AND THE DOCTOR

The doctor's involvement in AID consists in counselling the woman and her husband, in selecting the donors, and in performing the inseminations. He may carry out all of these unaided, but in some centres, he will be part of a team which may include nurses, social workers, secretarial staff etc.

Before the doctor proceeds to inseminate a woman, it should have been established that there is no bar to her conceiving, but that her husband is infertile or there is a risk, if he fathers a child, that he may pass some hereditary disease on to the child.[6] In most cases, the reason for performing AID is that the husband is sterile (azoospermia) or grossly sub-fertile (oligospermoa). Given the shortage of children available for adoption, the practice of AID is likely to become more popular as a means of solving the problems of infertile couples.

CONSENT

Having established these points, the doctor will counsel the couple and obtain the necessary consent. In the absence of statutory direction, it is probably not necessary to have the husband's consent, but the matter has never been decided in a court and clearly, from the doctor's standpoint, it would be extremely imprudent to proceed without it.[7]   A more important point is whether the consent should be in writing or whether oral agreement is enough.   While written consent is not required by law (except, as in some states in the USA, where a statute requires this), it is preferable to oral consent in that there is a record of what was agreed to.   If the written consent exists, it will be easier to establish that the consent was 'informed', which is what the law requires.[8]

In order to qualify as informed consent, a number of matters must have been mentioned by the doctor to the patient (and her husband).[9]   He must indicate the chances of their producing a child naturally, which are very low where the husband is infertile, and nil if he is sterile.   If the husband suffers or could be suffering from some heritably-transmittable disorder, the couple should be aware of the likelihood of the child having the disease.   If, for example, the disease is caused by a dominant gene eg. Huntington's Chorea, the sufferer has a 50 per cent chance of passing it on to his child.[10] The couple should be made aware of the alternatives to AID, eg. adoption, fostering, and of the risks and the likely outcome of the treatment.

The risks surrounding a pregnancy following AID are the same as in any other pregnancy; indeed they may even be fewer given the tests which the donors undergo, but pregnancy cannot be guaranteed and success rates vary quite considerably.[11]   Finally, the doctor should say something about the donors, who they are and in particular what tests they undergo.   He should naturally be prepared to answer any questions which the couple may have and, if that is done, there should be little doubt that the consent is 'informed'.   In this connection, obstetricians in the UK are fortunate in that the Royal College of Obstetricians and Gynaecologists has produced a booklet which gives a good explanation of what is involved in AID and which incorporates a consent form which practitioners would be well advised to use.

RECRUITMENT AND SELECTION OF DONORS

The doctor's other major responsibility is in the recruitment and selection of the donors.   At present the majority of donors seem to be recruited from among medical students and the husbands of obstetrics patients.[12]   Some people prefer as donors those who have demonstrated not only their fertility, but also their ability to produce children.[13]   In selecting possible donors, the doctor will ensure that they are healthy and that their semen is of good quality.   Some will also check on the medical history of the donor's family and some will attempt to match the donor's physical characteristics with those of the husband.[14]   The problem is that practice varies and there is no one practice which is uniformly adopted even in the UK.   So far as the writer can trace, only the New York City Health Code specifically lays down what tests the donor must undergo.[15]

It is clearly important that the doctor undertakes certain tests, if only to try to ensure that no legal action is raised as a result of the insemination.   If the child which is born as the result of AID has some mental or physical handicap, it might be suggested that this had been transmitted by the donor and that the doctor should have known of the condition and hence excluded the donor.   A number of points must be made about this. The first is that in order to attach liability to the doctor, it is usually necessary to prove that he had been negligent i.e. that he had failed to act in accordance with the standards laid down by his profession.[16] It is not enough to show that some other doctors would have acted differently, because there may be several schools of thought on one issue,[17] as in the selection and matching of donors. In order to succeed, it would have to be established that no reasonable doctor would have acted in the manner complained of.[18] Again, it must be borne in mind that while some tests can be carried out either on the donor or during pregnancy to eliminate disease, it is not possible as yet to eliminate all disabilities in this way and therefore any claim that because the child is born with a handicap this must be attributable to negligence or fault on the part of the doctor, is unlikely to be successful. In any event, no such action has ever been raised in AID cases,[19] although a recent American case held a doctor to be liable where, in a normal pregnancy, he had failed to inform a preganant woman of the availability of amniocentesis which could have predicted with reasonable accuracy a number of foetal defects, one of which did in fact exist.[20]

CONFIDENTIALITY

The last matter which it is necessary to mention in connection with the doctor's involvement is confidentiality. The doctor's ethical codes will require him as a general rule not to reveal anything he may learn from or about his patient in the course of their professional relationship.[21] Indeed some countries have provisions in their criminal law to this effect.[22] Thus, the doctor will regard himself as being under an obligation not to reveal the donor's identity to the woman or her husband and vice versa. It may be that if there was a serious risk that the identity of the donor or the couple would be revealed, fewer people, if any, would be prepared to be donors or undergo AID. However, it must be borne in mind that with few exceptions the doctor does not have any special position in law and a court may require him to reveal such information.[23] It would be only in very exceptional circumstances that this would be done, but the doctor would be under an obligation to disclose what was requested.

Not everyone aproves of the secrecy which surrounds AID, if only because it may make a proper study of the subject difficult, even impossible. This matter will be touched upon again when the status of the child is discussed.

THE COUPLE AND A.I.D.

Apart from the matters already discussed, the couple's main concern will probably be to know how the law will regard any child which is born as the result of AID. The child's status is extremely important in that it determines inter alia how the child's birth should be registered and whether it will be entitlted to succeed to the husband's estate on his death. Unfortunately, in many jurisdictions, the law on this point is confused and hence unsatisfactory.

In many countries, there is a presumption, where a child is born during the subsistence of a valid marriage, that the husband of the child's mother is also the father of her child, pater est quem nuptiae demonstrant. That presumption can be overcome if the contrary is proved; in Scotland, beyond reasonable doubt,[24] and in England, on the balance of probabilities.[25]

Where, therefore, a married woman gives birth to a child after undergoing AID, the child will have the benefit of the presumption pater est and because only the woman, her husband and the doctor know that she has had AID, it is highly unlikely that anyone else could successfully challenge a statement that the child was the husband's child. If, as some doctors recommend,[26] the parties continue to have intercourse during the AID there will remain in some cases the possbility, however remote, that the husband is the father.

If, however, it could be demonstrated that the child was conceived by AID, i.e. that the husband is not the father, the result is that the child would be illegitimate. Whether it is because of the presumption pater est, or because of the fear that the child's origins will be made known, or for some other reason, it is extremely rare for the birth certificate of such a child to have the space for 'father' left blank. Most husbands register themselves as the father despite the fact that to do so might be a criminal offence.[27]

In some countries, no distinction is drawn in law between legitimate and illegitimate children,[28] while in others, the remaining distinctions are few and of relatively minor importance,[29] but a legal stigma may still attach to an illegitimate child and there may also be a social stigma e.g. in a small village or other closely-knit community.

In most cases, neither the husband nor the wife will wish to suggest that the child is not the husband's child, but if the relationship between the spouses deteriorates, the husband may wish to argue that he is not liable to maintain the child or the wife may seek to have sole custody and prevent the husband having access. If the husband could demonstrate that he was not the father, then in Scots law, he would not be liable for maintenance,[30] but in England, if he had brought the child up as a member of the family, he could not rid himself of the obligation.[31] These issues have been considered on a number of occasions in the United States. In one case, Doornbos v. Doornbos,[32] the wife raised an action for divorce and sought custody of the child which was conceived as the result of AID, to which the husband had consented. The court held that the child was illegitimate and that the husband had no rights in the child, not even that of visitation. In Strnad v. Strnad,[33] the husband had been given visitation rights in a divorce action, but the wife later attempted to have these rescinded on the basis that the child was illegitimate. She admitted that she had undergone AID with her husband's consent, but the court held that the husband should retain his rights and that because the husband had consented, the child was not illegitimate. In the words of the court, the child had been 'potentially adopted or semi-adopted' by the husband. In a third case, Gursky v. Gursky,[34] the court held that the child was illegitimate, even although the husband had consented to the AID, but it further held that he was nevertheless liable to maintain the child on the basis of an implied contract or the doctrine of equitable estoppel.

As the result of these differing decisions, some American States have enacted legislation to deal with the status of the AID child[35] and a section of the Uniform Parentage Act is devoted to the issue.[36] These provisions vary, but in essence they provide that where a married woman is artificially inseminated with the husband's consent, the husband is deemed to be the father of the child. While these statutes solve the problem for children born after the passing of the Act, in only one state (Kansas)[37] is the legislation retrospective, and therefore there continues to be doubt about the status of children born before the Acts. Another problem posed by these provisions (except the legislation in Oregon[38]) is in determining what effect the absence of the husband's consent has on the child's status. Most doctors will not proceed without that consent, but the issue still remains. A court might decide that the husband is to be deemed the father, even although he has not consented, but it would seem rather unfair to saddle a husband with the paternity of, and responsibility for, a child if his wife has been inseminated without his consent and perhaps against his wishes. On the other hand, it would be unfair on the child if the husband sought to deny paternity, if for many years he had brought the child up as his own. In such a case, he might be faced with the doctrine of estoppel (personal bar) which would prevent his founding on the lack of consent.[39]

While the main thrust of legislative activity has been in the US, there has been some in Europe, but only three countries have legislation which has any bearing on the status of the child. These are The Netherlands, Portugal and Switzerland.[40] These jurisdictions prevent the husband from denying paternity of a child if he has consented to his wife being artificially inseminated. A Draft Recommendation from the Council of Europe[41] provides that the child shall be considered the legitimate child of the woman and her husband, if he consents, and that no-one shall be able to challenge paternity solely on the basis of the artificial insemination.

In 1977, a Bill was introduced into the UK Parliament which would have made AID children legitimate, but this move was not successful.[42] More recently the (English) Law Commission produced a Working Paper on Illegitimacy part of which is devoted to the AID child.[43] Their recommendation is that 'there should be a statutory provision deeming the mother's husband to be the father of her AID child unless it is established that he had not consented to the AID treatment which resulted in the child's conception.'[44] That suggestion follows the approach in the United States, but it cannot be taken as the Commission's final view on the matter which will be expressed in their Report due to be published in 1981.

SECRECY

The existence of these legislative provisions and the general practice of husbands registering themselves as the fathers obviously conceals the child's biological origins. It has been cogently argued that this practice deceives the child and society and makes the pursuit of truth difficult, if not impossible.[45] In particular, it is said that the practice undermines the science of genetic counselling which relies to a great extent on family history. The author making these objections agrees that any legal handicap affecting AID children should be removed, but he attacks the statutory 'deeming provision' on the basis that it makes words meaningless. Instead he says:

> Only a register of genetic identity, maintained alongside of the register of social identity, will serve. The practitioner would be bound to record and enregister the donor of the seed for each successful insemination; the

mixing of seed would, of course, be forbidden.... That register, though normally strictly closed, could be opened at the request of an adult person with a legitimate and serious interest .... Some may see in such a register a threat to civil liberties .... Others will see it as a threat to the donor; he may be held liable in law (unless the law is changed) for all a natural father's liabilities. So be it. We must choose. At present, we drift, and truth and justice go by default.[46]

While there is undoubted merit in that proposal, it would seem that even its author would concede that considerable difficulty and opposition would attend its implementation. It is not only in relation to AID that birth records are falsified, and one would have to consider what the effect would be on donors and children if their identities could be revealed to one another, and the potential liability of the donor, assuming that the law remainded unaltered, should be borne in mind. Perhaps the real problem lies in the nature of the legislative process which tends to accept that compromise is often necessary and that an 'all or nothing' approach will often produce only the latter. While, therefore, criticisms can be levelled at the form of legislation in respect of AID which exists in some countries, it is at least an improvement in that it removes the anomalous position of the AID child in these jurisdictions.

A separate, but related, problem is whether the child ought to be told of the circumstances surrounding its conception, rather than have it assume, in most instances erroneously, that the husband is the father. Opinions are devided on this issue. One school of thought argues that each person has a right and a need to know of his biological origins[47] and this has been accepted in UK in relation to adopted children who may ascertain who their natural parents were.[48] It has been argued that if the adopted child has this right, then it should not be denied to the AID child.[49]

While not seeking to deny the proposition that each person may have a need to know his/her origins, it is important to draw a distinction between the situation of the adopted child and that of the AID child. In the case of adoption, there is a good practical reason why adoptive parents should tell the child about the adoption, because if they do not, others probably will, given that the adoption will be reasonably well known among relatives and friends. This is not so with the AID child, where only the woman and her husband (and, of course the doctor) know the true position. There is not therefore the same practical need to tell the child of its origins.

However not everyone would agree on the need to know about one's origins. Another school of thought puts the emphasis on the existence of social or psychological parents and argues that they provide a stability for the child which is what it requires rather than accurate details about its parentage.[50] That school would presumably support the practice of not telling the child that it was conceived by AID. Some parents may however wish to tell the child and in some cases, it may be very important for the child to know that the husband is not the father. If the reason for AID is not that the husband is infertile, but that he suffers or may suffer from some inheritable disease, then the 'parents' may wish to reassure the child on this point. Take the case of Huntington's Chorea. The husband may have been told that there is a 50/50 chance that he will suffer from the disease. If he suffers, there would then be a 50/50 chance that he would pass it on to his child; hence the decision to undergo

AID. If therefore, the husband does suffer from the disease, it will be in the best interest of the child to be assured that he is not similarly afflicted.

IS A.I.D. ADULTERY?

One other matter which may concern some couples, but which is now unlikely to be of great legal importance is whether AID, especially where the husband has not consented, provides a ground for divorce, and in particular whether it amounts to adultery. Much ink has been spilled over this subject in the past,[51] but there are good reasons for supporting the view that the question is now settled in favour of the conclusion that AID does not amount to adultery, even where it is undertaken without the husband's consent. Another writer has put the matter more forcefully by saying, 'Identification of AID with adultery can no longer seriously be maintained.'[52] Although one must admit that if a married woman undergoes AID without her husband's consent, such an act would strike at the very basis of the marital relationship and would or should provide a ground for divorce on that basis, it is nevertheless not adultery. The arguments on this issue are fully explored elsewhere[53] and so only passing mention will be made of them.

The principal legal argument is that it is an essential element in adultery that the parties have sexual intercourse which requires penetration of the female organ by that of the male and this does not take place in AID.[54] AID will rarely be given to a married woman without her husband's consent, but some writers have attempted to equate consensual AID with adultery which is condoned. The absence of sexual intercourse destroys that argument, but a number of other differences are also obvious. Adultery is normally a clandestine activity which it is hoped will not be known to the other spouse whereas AID is generally undertaken with the knowledge and approval of that spouse. It is unusual for adultery to be committed in order to produce a child, but this is the only aim of AID. Lastly, adultery is normally regarded as indicative of marital breakdown, whereas AID is thought of as evidence of marital stability.

If AID were to be regarded as adultery, there would arise considerable problems in determining whether it had been committed by the donor whose semen was used or by the doctor who performed the insemination. If the donor is regarded as being guilty of adultery, then that guilt could continue after his death, because it is now possible to preserve human semen for considerable periods[55] and it may be used after the donor's death. If it is the person who performs the insemination that is to be regarded as committing the adultery, then one must face and solve the problem that that person may be female.[56] For these reasons, it is submitted that AID, even without the husband's consent, is not adultery. However such an act would now be a ground for divorce, at least in the UK.[57]

A.I.D. AND THE UNMARRIED WOMAN

Until now, it has been assumed that the woman who receives AID is married. Some of the implications of her receiving the treatment without her husband's consent have been examined, but it is now appropriate to consider the position of the single or divorced woman, in that there is no legal objection to either being given AID. This is equally true of a lesbian couple. Some doctors may refuse to treat these persons on ethical or other grounds, but when the British Medical Association discussed AID for lesbians, they concluded that it would not be unethical to give them AID.

The principal effect in law of unmarried women receiving AID is reflected in the status accorded to the child, which, in most jurisdictions, will be illegitimate. Accordingly, the child will not come within the ambit of the legislation in the U.K. or Europe, and even in the State of Oregon where the legislation permits AID for unmarried women,[58] the child will still be illegitimate, since before the child can be deemed legitimate, the woman must be married and her husband must have given his consent to the insemination.

SEMEN BANKING: A.I.H. AFTER DEATH OF THE HUSBAND

The possibility that human semen can be preserved does not create many additional problems where the semen used is that of the donor, but legal issues of some complexity could arise if the semen used was that of the woman's husband. In the 1960's there was a proposal to preserve the semen of astronauts in this way, and it could be contemplated that the semen of others involved in potentially hazardous activities could also be preserved in this way. The consequence would be that a woman could continue to have her husband's children long after his death, until she reached the menopause, and there is one example on record of a woman who gave birth to a child 16 months after her husband's death.[59] In this situation, the legal problems would be to define the status of such children and to determine what effect their birth would have on the administration and distribution of the husband's estate.[60]

In relation to the question of status, it can be argued quite properly that a marriage terminates on the death of either party, and that, if the marriage is terminated, any children conceived thereafter are necessarily illegitimate. Although that argument is perfectly sound, it has most often been used in order to determine the status of a child born after a divorce. The point at issue has been whether it was possible that the child was conceived during the marriage (by the husband), or whether the evidence suggests that it was conceived after after the termination of the marriage, in which case the child would be illegitimate. That point would not arise in connection with AIH after death since there would almost certainly be no doubt that the child had been conceived from the husband's semen, and indeed, it would often be admitted that this was the case.

It is difficult to think of arguments which could be used to support a contention that such a child is legitimate, but it might be suggested that the courts would favour the status of legitimacy (at least where the mother has not remarried), because the child, although not conceived during the marriage may be regarded as a child of the marriage. While one can have some sympathy for this view, any conclusion to that effect would seem to do considerable harm to the principles governing the attribution of status.

If such a child is legitimate, or deemed to be legitimate, it would be entitled to share in the husband's estate and that would therefore prevent the estate being wound up until the woman reached the menopause or until she remarried. However, even if the child is illegitimate, there are many jurisdictions, including the United

Kingdom, in which it would nonetheless be entitled to some share in the estate, perhaps along with legitimate children, perhaps only if there are no legitimate children. The only factor apart from status which would have a bearing on the question of succession would be any rule which prevents the accumulation of income for long periods of time and, in some jurisdictions, consideration might have to be given to the 'rule against perpetuities', the aim of which is to prevent land and other property being tied up indefinitely, usually within one family.[61] It can be seen therefore, that, although the practice of inseminating women with their husband's semen after his death is not yet commonplace, the issues which it poses are complex and would probably be best resolved by statute.

THE FUTURE

At this point, it is useful to look at how AID might develop and consider some related practices. Although it is unclear what form the future development of AID might take, it is possible from recent cases and proposals to speculate on at least some of the problems which might have to be faced.

As has been said, it is now possible to preserve human semen for lengthy periods without affecting its viability. Semen banks are usually used in connection with a hospital AID service or a similar service operating from a private clinic. However, there are several semen banks in the United States which operate a postal service and produce data which enable a person to select semen from someone with particular characteristics, although the identity remains undisclosed. However, the Nobel Prizewinner, Dr. Hermann J. Müller, advocated what he termed 'germinal choice', which would involve preserving the semen of 'superior' individuals,[62] and it has recently been reported that in Los Angeles several women have been fertilised by semen from a bank where all the donors are or were Nobel Prizewinners,[63] but their identities do not appear to have been revealed. As one report in 'The Times' put the matter, 'When the storm broke....it started an international controversy with critics suggesting the 'elitist' bank was comparable to Hitler's 'master race' concept.'[64] Müller's ideas have been, and continue to be, criticised and so their implementation would not be without opposition, but at present it is not contrary to the law of the United Kingdom or the United States of America to have such a bank, nor to have one where the identities of the donors are known to the recipient, which is what Müller advocates.

Hitherto, the discussion has centred on some of the implications of semen donation, but its counterpart - ovum donation - is also possible. A woman could donate an ovum which would then be fertilised and implanted into another woman. The medical and legal problem would be to determine whether the child was the child of the first woman or the second.[65] The woman who donated the ovum would thereby have dictated one half of the child's genetic make-up, but the other woman would have been responsible for nurturing the embryo until birth. The woman donating the ovum might have agreed that on birth the child should remain with the second woman, e.g. because she could not have children in the usual way, or it may be that the intention was to return the child to the first woman e.g. where she had been advised to avoid the risk of a further pregnancy, the second woman acting as a host mother. This practice has been forecast by Mr

Patrick Steptoe,[66] and Dr Robert Edwards[67] has said that in theory it would be easier to implant the ovum in a second woman rather than to re-implant it in the first. Given the possibility of freezing semen, it might be possible to preserve embryos in the same way.

Some might regard such developments as improbable or undesireable, but they might have to be faced in the not too distant future. The fact that the legal issues surrounding AID in what one might call its 'simple' form have not as yet been resolved provides a somewhat uncertain and unsatisfactory basis for discussion of future practices.

D.J. Cusine

NOTES

1. Behrman, S.J. and Kistner, R.W., 'A Rational Approach to the Evaluation of Infertility', in Behrman, S.J., and Kistner,R.W., (eds), Progress in Infertility, (2nd Ed.), Boston, Little Brown & Co., 1975, p.1; Newill,R., Infertile Marriage, Harmondsworth, England, Penguin Books Ltd., 1974, p.13.
2. Newton, J.R., 'Current Status of A.I. in Clinical Practice', in Artificial Insemination, Proceedings of the Fourth Study Group of the Royal College of Obstetricians and Gynaecologists, London, 1976, p.25; Stangel, J.J., Fertility and Conception, New York & London, Paddington Press Ltd., 1979, ch.4.
3. Dixon, A.E., et al, 'Artificial Insemination using Homologous Semen - A Review of 158 Cases', Fert. and Ster., 1976, 27, at pp. 647-654. (9.5% pregnancy rate); Newton, J.R., op.cit., p.29 (results poor); Guttmacher, A.F., 'The Role of Artificial Insemination in the Treatment of Sterility', Obs. and Gyn. Survey, 1960, 15, 767-785 (success rate low).
4. International Planned Parenthood Federation Handbook on Infertility, London, 1979, at pp. 52-53; Stangel, op.cit. at p.157; Dixon, R.E., and Buttram, V.C., 'Artificial Insemination using Donor Semen - A Review of 171 Cases', Fert. and Ster., 1976, 27, 130-134.
5. I.P.P.F. Handbook, p.49; Foss, G.L., in Artificial Insemination, R.C.O.G., op.cit., at p. 44.
6. For further discussion, see infra ch. 10.
7. For discussion, see infra, ch. 8.
8. Martin, C.R.A., Law Relating to Medical Practice, (2nd Ed.), London, Pitman Medical, 1979, at pp.68 et seq; Holder, A.R., Medical Malpractice Law, (2nd Ed.), New York, John Wiley & Sons, 1978, ch. VIII.
9. For further discussion of the nature and extent of the disclosure required in obtaining consent, see infra ch. 8.
10. Jones, A., & Bodmer, W.F., Our Future Inheritance: Choice or Chance?, Oxford University Press, 1974, at p.51.
11. Sulewski, J.M., et al, 'A Longitudinal Analysis of Artificial Insemination with Donor Semen', Fer. & Ster, 1978, 29, 527-31; Cuvie-Cohen, M. et al, 'Current Practice of Artificial Insemination by Donor in the United States', The New England Journal of Medicine, 1979, 300, 585-589; Steinberger, E. and Smith, K.D., 'Artificial Insemination with Fresh and Frozen Semen', Journal of the American Medical Association, 1973, 273,

778-783.

12. Joyce, D.N., 'Recruitment, Selection and Matching of Donors', in Artificial Insemination, R.C.O.G., at pp.60-69; Guttmacher, A.F., 'Artificial Insemination', De Paul Law Review, 1969, 18, 566-583.

13. I.P.P.F. Handbook, at p.50.

14. Joyce, D.N., op.cit., at p.67.

15. New York City Health Code: Artificial Human Insemination, 21:03; 21:05.

16. Roe v. Ministry of Health [1954] 2 Q.B. 66; Hunter v. Hanley 1955 S.C. 200; Whitehouse v. Jordan [1981] 1 All E.R. 267. Holder, op.cit., ch. II; Percy, R.A., (ed.), Charlesworth on Negligence, (6th. Ed.), London, Sweet & Maxwell, 1977, at pp.580-581.

17. Charlesworth on Negligence, loc.cit.

18. Hunter v. Hanley, supra.

19. For discussion, see infra, ch. 11; see also the Congenital Disabilities (Civil Liability) Act 1976 s. 1(5), which states that the doctor will not be liable to the child if he takes reasonable care, and that, even if he does depart from received opinion he will not necessarily be negligent.

20. For discussion, see infra ch. 11 ; The case is discussed in 3 Legal Medical Quarterly, 97, (1979).

21. See e.g. Hippocratic Oath; American Medical Association Principles of Medical Ethics, s.9.; International Code of Medical Ethics; Declaration of Geneva; Handbook of Medical Ethics, British Medical Association, 1980, at pp.56-64.

22. e.g. Michigan Statutes, s.14.533; French Penal Code Art.378; Dutch Civil Code Art.272(1); Italian Penal Code Art.622; also U.S. Model Code and Proposed Federal Rules.

23. Att.Gen. v. Mulholland and Foster [1963] 2 Q.B.477, per Lord Denning M.R. at p.489; Holden, op.cit., at p.274.

24. Clive, E.M. and Wilson, J.G., The Law of Husband and Wife in Scotland, Edinburgh, W.Green & Son Ltd., 1974, at pp. 464-5.

25. Family Law Reform Act 1969 s.26.

26. Finegold, W.J., Artificial Insemination, (2nd Ed.), Illinois, C.C.Thomas, 1976, at p.75.

27. Stone, O.M., 'English Law and Artificial Insemination', in Law and Ethics of A.I.D. and Embryo Transfer, Ciba Foundation Symposium 17 (New Series), Elsevier, Excerpta Medica, North Holland, Amsterdam, London, New York, 1973, at pp.70-72.

28. e.g. Ontario, The Children's Law Reform Act 1977, SO 1977, c.41; New Zealand, Status of Children Act 1969; Krause, H.D., Illegitimacy: Law and Social Policy, New York, The Bobbs-Merrill Co. Inc., 1971, App. A.

29. e.g. in the U.K.

30. There is no provision corresponding to the Matrimonial Causes Act 1973s 52(1), see footnote 27, supra.

31. Matrimonial Causes Act 1973 ss. 23, 52(1).

32. 12 Ill.App. 2d. 473; 139 NE 2d 844 (1956).

33. 190 Misc. 786; 78 NYS 2d 390 (1948).

34. 39 Misc. 2d 1083; 242 NYS 2d 406 (1963).

35. Georgia Cods Ann. s. 74-101.1; Oklahoma Statutes Ann. Title 10 s.551-553; California Civil Code Art.216; Colorado Uniform Parentage Act Art.6, 19-6-106; Connecticut General Statutes Title 45, Chapter 778b, ss.45-69f; Kansas Statutes Ann. s.23-128/30; New York Domestic Relations Law s. 73; North

Carolina General Statutes 49A-1; Oregon Laws 1977 s.686; Texas Code Ann. s.12-03; Virginia Code s.64.1-7.1; Alaska Statutes ch.20; Washington Uniform Parentage Act Ch.26:26:050.
36.   section 5.
37.   Kansas State Ann. s.23-128-130.
38.   Oregon Laws 1977 Ch.686.
39.   Chandler, H.S., 'A Legislative Approach to Artificial Insemination',Cornell Law Review, 1968, 53, 497-513 at p.513; Waynard, R.E.,'Artificial Insemination and the Law', University of Illinois Law Forum, 1968, 203-231 at p.230.
40.   Dutch Civil Code Art. 201.1; Portuguese Civil Code Art. 1799; Swiss Civil Code Art. 256 (3).
41.   Draft Recommendation on Artificial Insemination Proposed by the Council of Europe, 1978.
42.   A.I.D. Children (Legal Status) Bill, (No.144 of 1977).
43.   Working Paper No.74 Family Law: Illegitimacy, H.M.S.O. 1979, Part X.
44.   Paras. 10.11-10.16.
45.   Dunstan, G.R., 'Ethical Issues Relating to A.I.D.', in Artificial Insemination, R.C.O.G., 182, at pp.185-187.
46.   at p.186.
47.   Adoption Act 1958 s.22 (Scotland); Children Act 1975 s.26 (England and Wales).
48.   Isaacs, S., 'Fatherless Children', in Isaacs, S. (ed), Childhood and After, London, Routledge and Kegan Paul, 1948.
49.   e.g. Brandon, J., address at Seminar organised by the Medical Group of the Association of British Adoption and Fostering Agencies, reported briefly in The Eugenics Society Bulletin, 1979, Vol.11, No.1., at pp.5-7.
50.   Goldstein, Freud, and Solnit, Beyond the Best Interests of the Child, New York, Free Press, 1973, at pp.16-17.
51.   e.g. Tallin, G.P.R., 'Artificial Insemination' Canadian Bar Review, 1956, 34, 1-27, 166-186, 628-631; Hubbard, H.A., 'Artificial Insemination: A Reply to Dean Tallin', Canadian Bar Review, 1956, 34, 425-451; Hahlo,H.R., 'Is A.I.D. Adultery?', South African Law Journal, 1959, 76, at pp. 90-91
52.   Dickens, B., Medico-Legal Aspects of Family Law, Toronto, Butterworths, 1979, at p.7.
53.   See note 48, supra.
54.   Decision of Lord Wheatley in MacLennan v. MacLennan 1958 S.C. 105, at p. 113.
55.   Sherman, J.K., 'Synopsis of the Use of Frozen Semen since 1963 - State of the Art of Human Banking', Fert.& Ster., 1973, 24, 397-412.
56.   People v. Sorensen 62 Cal.Rep. 462; 66 Cal. Rep.7 per Justice McComb; MacLennan v. MacLennan, supra, per Lord Wheatley at p. 114.
57.   Matrimonial Causes Act 1973 s.1(2)(b) (England and Wales); Divorce (Scotland) Act 1976 s.1(2)(b).
58.   Oregon Laws 1977 ch. 686, s.3(1).
59.   'The Times' 11 July 1977.
60.   Cusine, D.J., 'Artificial Insemination with the Husband's Semen after Death', J.Med. Ethics, 1977, 3, 163-5; Sappideen, C., 'Life After Death - Sperm Banks, Wills and Perpetuities', The Australian Law Journal, 1979, 53, 311-319.
61.   Leach, W.B., 'Perpetuities in the Atomic Age: The Sperm Bank and the Fertile Decedent', American Bar Association Journal,

1962, 48, 942-944.

62. Müller, H.J., 'The Guidance of Human Evolution', <u>Perspectives in Biology and Medicine</u>, 1959,3,1-42.

63. 'Los Angeles Times' 29 February 1980.

64. 'The Times' 8 March, 1980.

65. Cusine, D.J., 'Some Legal Implications of Embryo Transfer', <u>New Law Journal</u>, 1979, 129, 627-629; A shortened version was published in <u>The Lancet</u>, 25th. August, 1979.

66. This forecast was part of his address to the annual meeting of the British Association for the Advancement of Science, 1979.

67. <u>Law and Ethics of A.I.D. and Embryo Transfer</u>, supra, at. p. 37.

13 Sterilisation

S. A. M. McLean and T. D. Campbell

Sterilisation of both men and women is becoming an increasingly common method of controlling reproduction. It has been asserted recently that 'more than 18 million persons have chosen surgery to end their fertility, thereby making sterilisation the most used method of contraception in the world.'[1] Nevertheless, there is a continuing debate in both legal and medical circles as to whether, and in what circumstances, the operation can be considered as lawful.

It has been argued that the operation would only be lawful where it was undertaken for the purpose of saving the life, or the physical or mental health of the patient. This test is an exact parallel of that used in the case of R v. Bourne,[2] in the late 1930's, where the issue was the legality of an operation to terminate a pregnancy. However, Gordon in The Criminal Law of Scotland[3] maintains that sterilisation would be treated in the same way as any other surgical intervention, and would therefore be lawful if carried out with the consent of the patient. In order to make sterilisation illegal, a new crime would have to be created, a situation which, as Gordon convincingly argues, is unlikely.[4]

To some extent the doubts regarding the legality of sterilisation centre round the ancient religious attitudes towards what might be regarded as maiming,[5] although a moral element also crept into the debate. Lord Denning, for example, in the case of Bravery v. Bravery[6] made the following point:

Take a case where a sterilisation operation is done so as to enable a man to have the pleasure of sexual intercourse without shouldering the responsibilities attaching to it. The operation then is plainly injurious to the public interest. It is degrading to the man himself. It is injurious to his wife and any woman whom he may marry, to say nothing of the way it opens to licentiousness; and, unlike contraceptives, it allows no room for a change of mind on either side. It is illegal, even though the man consents to it ....[7]

In this dissenting judgement, Lord Denning raised not only the question of personal dignity but also the prospect of promiscuity suggesting that the overall effect is harmful to the 'public interest', and thus sterilisation, as an encouragement to promiscuity in Lord Denning's terms, would be unlawful. To a large extent this judgement was based on the rule stated in Rex v. Donovan[8] by Mr. Justice Swift who pointed out that: 'If an act is unlawful in the sense of being itself a criminal act, it is plain that it cannot be rendered lawful because the person to whose detriment it is done consents to it.' [9] While this is regarded as good law, in both Scotland and England, nonetheless Lord Denning's dependence on this statement presumes that it is clear that sterilisation is in itself a criminal act. While some may agree that it is contrary to 'public interest,' and others may also agree that it encourages promiscuity, nonetheless, neither of these are criminal in themselves, and sterilisation cannot therefore be a criminal act in se simply because it may lead to either of these results.

In practice, of course, this legal or moral debate has been rendered largely obsolete by the fact that sterilisations are performed daily throughout this country on eugenic or birth control grounds as well as on the therapeutic ground of saving life or alleviating serious pain or distress. It can therefore be assumed that, in common with other surgical intervention, where the patient consents[10] (except in non life-threatening emergencies where consent may be unobtainable), and further assuming the doctor acts with due skill and care, then it is unlikely that legal consequences will follow which are in any way a threat to the doctor, or which are likely to pose problems in respect of the legality of the operation itself. Recent decisions in the United States of America have held that sterilisation is legal and not contrary to public policy where it is voluntarily performed with the consent of the patient.[11]

Consideration has also necessarily been given to the implications of sterilisation in respect of its effects on the institution of marriage. It has been argued that such surgery might form the basis either for annulling a marriage or for a successful action for divorce. It is however, clearly established that the ability to procreate is not an essential factor in considering whether or not a marriage has been consumated.[12] Thus, a marriage cannot be annulled simply because procreation is impossible.[13] This is the case even where the operation to sterilise took place before the marriage,[14] so that it does not affect the nature of the contract of marriage that a person is unable to procreate.

Of major concern to the medical profession, however, is the question of whether or not sterilisation should be performed on a married man or woman without the consent of their spouse. It would seem fairly clear that, since '...there is no absolute right to reproduction as an incident of marriage',[15] then no action raised for loss of consortium[16] could be successful.
It has, however, been suggested, that:

before a surgeon sets out to perform a primary sterilisation the written consent of the spouse should be obtained as well as that of the patient. A surgeon who performs a non-therapeutic sterilisation without the consent of the spouse runs the risk of being sued for damages by that spouse because the operation might be held to be an actionable interference with marital rights.[17]

In the United States it has been argued that a husband's consent should be sought before a wife has a pregnancy terminated at her own instigation, since men as well as women have the constitutional right to procreate. It is said that this right is meaningless in the case of men unless wives are willing to bear children, anything less than this amounting to 'constructive sterilisation'.[18] Any such right would apply a fortiori to actual sterilisation (of either husband or wife) since this would render further procreation impossible.

However, while there may be grounds for arguing that spouses should share in making decisions regarding the sterilisation of either party, in that both should be consulted and the available options fully discussed between husband and wife, this does not entail that either should have a veto over the sterilisation of the other. In particular, the idea that a husband should be able to prevent his wife from being sterilised, may reflect the now outmoded idea that a wife is the property of her husband, or involve the erroneous assumption that the agreement to bear children is part of the marriage contract.[19]

What is, however, clear is that sterilisation without the consent of the spouse, in the same way as the extended use of other contraceptive methods, may well amount to cruelty on the part of one spouse against the other, should it result in the ill health of the other spouse.[20]   The Divorce (Scotland) Act 1976 and the Matrimonial Causes Act 1973 make the irretrievable breakdown of marriage the sole ground for divorce, and allow that it can be established by, for example, showing that the defender has been behaving in a manner which makes it unreasonable to expect the pursuer to cohabit whether the behaviour is active or passive.[21]   Since it is clear that the sterilisation of one party without the consent of the spouse, leading to ill health and distress on the part of the spouse, would have amounted to cruelty, then there is little doubt that it would amount to 'unreasonable behaviour' under the new divorce legislation.

In Bravery v. Bravery, supra, the wife raised an action for divorce on the grounds of her husband's cruelty in having a vasectomy without her knowledge or consent, she alleging that her health had suffered due to their inability to have a family.   Although she was not granted a divorce, this was not on the basis of whether or not the vasectomy without consent would have amounted to cruelty, but on the grounds that the majority of the court did not believe that the wife had not consented.   Indeed, there was considerable evidence that she had known the nature of her husband's operation.   Evershed, M.R. and Hodson, L.J. in their judgement in this case did, however, say that:

It would not be difficult...to construct in imagination a
case of grave cruelty on a wife founded on the progressive
hurt to her health caused by an operation for sterilisation
undergone by her husband in disregard of, or contrary to, the
wife's wishes or natural instincts.[22]

From the doctor's point of view, then, while he is clearly not legally bound to obtain the consent of both spouses, good practice might dictate that he should do so, particularly where the party seeking the sterilisation is married and living in family with his or her spouse.

Sterilisation without the consent of the subject raises further problems. In the case of Re D (a minor),[23] which involved debate as to the lawfulness of sterilising a young girl on the basis of the consent of her mother (the girl being too young to consent legally, and perhaps incapax on other grounds), the court referred to sterilisation without the actual consent of the patient as involving '...the deprivation of a basic human right...to reproduce...'.[24] The European Convention on Human Rights gives to all citizens the basic right to marry and found a family.[25]   Prima facie the existence of such rights is an obstacle to compulsory sterilisation. The right to marry and found a family however, is circumscribed by the rights of the State to legislate in respect of these issues.   Thus for example, the State legitimately proscribes incestuous marriages and de facto limits or removes entirely these rights in respect of the institutionalised.   Not only can any right to procreate which does exist be regarded as alienable by the individual but it can also be varied by the State.   As Lord Kilbrandon has suggested:

It might well be...that the European Court would not condemn
"national laws governing the exercise of" the right to found
a family if these laws were designed to prohibit the willful
transmitting of genetic defects.   Such laws would stand on
exactly the same footing as those which, for genetic reasons,

forbid marriage and punish sexual intercourse between persons of particular degrees of consanguinity.[26]

This would seem to open the way for asserting that compulsory sterilisation could be imposed by the State[27] in the public interest, although it can be argued that this would make a mockery of the idea of a human right to marry and found a family. Clearly a crucial factor in disputes concerning compulsory sterilisation (and also in situations where consent is sought from a proxy), is the interpretation given to the alleged basic human right to reproduce. The precise meaning and implications of such a right are far from clear, both as regards what is being protected by this right and the extent of the protection that such a right should afford to the individual.

In the case of sterilisation, what is at stake is a person's capacity to perform the male or female part in procreation. This suggests that any such right could be interpreted as a right to retain the capacity to procreate rather than a right actually to have children. Such a right would rule out compulsory sterilisation (and castration) but would be compatible, for instance, with State control of parenthood.[28] However, while the right simply to retain the capacity to procreate may be important as part of a more general right to protect one's body against mutilation by others, it is hard to see what significance the mere capacity to procreate can have except in relation to its possible use (unless, of course, the loss of such capacity has undesirable physiological or psychological side-effects).

Taking, then, the right to procreate as involving the right of persons to become biological parents seems a more plausible approach. This right could be based, as are other human rights, on the existence of deep rooted and universal human desires and instincts,[29] in this case the desire to reproduce (which must, of course, be sharply distinguished from the desire for the sexual relationship normally required for procreation). Such a desire, however, is not limited to the goal of sexual reproduction, but extends to the care, upbringing and continuing enjoyment of the parent-child relationship. The desire to procreate does not terminate in the event of parturition. If there is a desire for no more than the condition of becoming a biological parent, then it is neither a very strong nor, it might be thought, a very important desire. Indeed, it seems rather ridiculous to suggest that there could be a right to procreate which was not intrinsically connected to the right to fulfil the role of father or mother in relation to the growing child. Such a right, if it is admitted, would clearly be readily overridden by consideration for the welfare of the children concerned or the constraints of public expenditure.

When courts refer to the 'basic right to reproduce' as in the case of Re D, supra, this should probably be interpreted therefore along the lines of Article 12 of the European Convention on Human Rights (1950), as the right to 'marry and found a family'.[30] 'Founding a family' may suggest setting up a home or entering into some domestic arrangement whereby children are cared for and enjoyed. In this case the right to reproduce could be construed as applying only to those who are capable of forming the human relationships and participating in the domestic organisation required for the existence of a family unit of one sort or another. While this could hardly be taken to exclude from parenthood persons who do not, at the time of fertilisation, have the material prerequisites for homemaking, it could rule out those who, by reason of mental or physical deficiency, are unable to participate in the rearing of children. This would mean that the simple biological capacity to procreate, without the human abilities needed to play a parental role within a family, would not be sufficient to qualify a person for the right to procreate.

Already, this is to make the right something less than a human right (in the sense of universal right [31]) which applies to all men and women. Moreover, such rights have to be seen in the context of the obligation of States in terms of the Universal Declaration of Human Rights,[32] to give special protection to the family, which could involve the obligation to provide material aid for families under stress, a form of assistance which is - theoretically at least - standard in developed societies. There is no reason why societies should not make it easier for an 'inadequate' person to sustain a family life by the provision of personal and financial services, nor why courts should not take this into account in assessing a person's capacity to found a family.

However, the level of ability could be pitched extremely low thus making it almost universal. Further, if the right to found a family is taken to correlate with an obligation, on the part of the State, to assist the individual to enter into and sustain family life, this duty could be extended to the duty of providing medical services for those who are infertile, where the condition is treatable.[33] However, while this is doubtless a desirable goal where it does not run up against objections as to its expense, or arguments relating to over-population, to regard such medical treatment as part of the basic right to reproduce does seem to dilute the right by making it vulnerable to considerations of cost and relative priorities. Including such positive obligations with respect to the right to reproduce might therefore tend to weaken the stringency of the less controversial negative obligations which have been discussed and open the way for purely economic and administrative considerations to affect the much more protectable right to retain the existing capacity to reproduce.[34]

Sterilisation which is compulsory in the sense that it is carried out against the wishes of the subject is to be distinguished from that which is carried out without reference to the subject's wishes, as in Re D, supra. In this case, the disability of the child was not such as to raise problems for her future rights as an individual, e.g. she would have the legal capacity to marry. However, it is more problematic where a person (be he a minor or an adult) does suffer from mental problems or retardation, that is where he is regarded as being incapax at law. Clearly there are situations where sterilisation of the mentally unsound may seem to be in their best interests. As with all forms of intervention in such a case, the patient is by definition scarcely in a position to offer 'informed' consent, or indeed any form of consent which the law would regard as sufficient.[35] The moral problems raised by permitting proxy consent, particularly in situations like this, are legion, and raise the vexed question as to what is the power of the parent or guardian in respect of a child or ward. It is uncertain what rights parents actually do have in respect of their child or by implication what rights legal guardians have in respect of their ward.[36] It is clear, however, that in wardship proceedings parents rights can be superseded by the court, although the court '.....will not do so lightly....'.[37]

As far as the institutionalised are concerned, a policy of

intervention has already been adopted in their lives.   In such situations, if it is indeed possible, as it would appear to be, for a person voluntarily to consent to sterilisation, then it is likely that the person given the right to take major decisions on behalf of another, as always acting on their best interests, can in fact take such a decision where there is no likelihood of the person being in a position to do so themselves.   The extent to which such intervention is possible, may however be circumscribed by the nature of the role played by the person whose consent is sought, and will depend on the nature and extent of the powers awarded to the proposed proxy.   In Scotland, for example, it is clear that the curator bonis has powers only to protect the estate of the incapax but has no general power over his person,[38] although the award of custody generally does include a constituent element of control over the person, particularly in relation to welfare.[39]   Cusine has suggested that:

> Where the patient is an adult but is incapable of giving consent, treatment can be justified only if it is necessary.   In all other cases, the guardians would require to seek permission from the courts.[40]

In this situation, necessary treatment is probably that which is necessary to safeguard the physical/mental health of the person concerned   The case of Re D, supra, would seem to suggest that the same restriction obtains where the patient is a minor.   Certainly, the law has traditionally protected both the adult incapax and the very young by, for example, limiting the powers of these groups in respect of entering into contracts and by requiring that in any dispute their interests will be regarded as overriding.[41]

However, there is a further, and some would say more sinister, side to this particular problem.   This relates to the intervention of the State in sterilisating those who are not in a position to give consent, and on whose behalf there is no-one to speak.   It has been said that:

> In the case of mental abnormality, and particularly if it is likely to be passed on, there is an added reason for preventing pregnancy.   Indeed from society's point of view it is rational to encourage sterilisation not only of the mentally abnormal, but other groups of disadvantaged individuals, especially where they can be identified as being likely to produce abnormal children.   This in a way is the logical end point of genetic counselling...we have to weigh the advantages to society and to the individual of sterilisation against the loss of the individual freedom to have a child.[42]

This appeal to the benefits of the community, is made on the basis that the State will benefit by the reduction in the breeding of those likely to require institutionalisation or special help.   If this is a decision about the quality of life of any subsequent child, then it is one which is already taken where Section (1) of the Abortion Act 1967 is used.[43]   However, a major difference is that in the abortion situation, the person on whom the surgery is to be performed is able to consent and indeed is required to consent, whereas in the example of sterilisation this consent is not being given because it cannot be.   If however, the decision is one based on financial and resource-based difficulties with which the State would be confronted, then one might well, using the abortion example again, suggest that (quite apart from the morality of such decisions) the State in order to be consistent, should require rather than permit the termination of all other pregnancies which are shown to involve a seriously damaged foetus. However, both law and medicine are in fact concerned in these situations rather to offer support than to encourage termination.[44]

If it is assumed that all but the severely handicapped have the basic right to found a family, the question remains what protection does this offer against the sort of competing considerations which have been used to justify sterilisation without the actual consent of the person concerned? The point of establishing rights in general, and human rights in particular, is to protect the individual against being used as an instrument of public policy.[45] Only in the most extreme instances does the 'common good' serve to override human rights unless this common good is itself taken to involve the protection of the basic rights of others. Thus the expense and trouble of caring for the children of inadequate parents cannot be used as a ground for denying such persons a chance to become parents if they have a human right to do so.

Although human rights are, in theory at least, not defeated by an appeal to the common interest they might, of course, have to yield to other human rights where these come into conflict.[46] Compulsory sterilisation might therefore be compatible with the right to reproduce where the exercise of this right interferes with the, perhaps more basic, human rights of others. Thus, if the actual survival of society was threatened by the unlikely occurrence of a rapid genetic decline, control of the reproductive process could be justified.

More realistically, the rights which are most likely to stand in the way of these potential parents are the rights of the children who would be born to parents unable or unwilling to take care of them, or those children with physical or mental defects which significantly affect the quality of their lives. The problems involved in giving legal standing to the interests of persons not yet born has been much discussed in relation to abortion.[47] Since, however, the law has been prepared to allow that a child may have a right to sue for damage sustained prenatally (or even pre-conception),[48] there seems to be no cogent logical reason why it should not take account of the interests of children who might be born were compulsory sterilisation not carried out.[49] It seems doubtful however, that such considerations would be decisive, except in cases of severe physical or mental impairment predictable prior to conception.

However, to establish any test of 'fitness' for parenthood is incompatible with the idea of a human right to parenthood if the standard of 'fitness' goes above the barest minimum. For there to be a basic right to found a family, the opportunity to reproduce has to be much more than merely one consideration which courts should bear in mind when assessing a total situation. As a human right, it exercises some sort of exclusionary power over arguments based on public convenience and expense.

This means that the interests of the State are not in themselves sufficient to provide a justification for sterilisation without consent. Moreover, the human right to reproduce would appear to rule out any eugenic reasons for compulsory sterilisation which are based on the improvement of the human stock. However, since such rights can be waived (and effectively alienated in the case of the right to reproduce being waived by consenting to sterilisation), the existence of a human right does not in itself prevent proxy consent by suitably authorised persons in cases where the individual will never be in a position to consent on their own behalf.   The effect of the existence of a human right in such cases is to prevent such proxy consent being given on grounds other than the interests of the person to be sterilised.[50]   Trouble or expense caused to, for example, the State or parents, would not be relevant grounds for waiving human rights on behalf of others.

The problem remains however, as to who is the suitably authorised person to take such decisions.   Clearly, in Re D, supra, the court was unwilling to leave such a decision exclusively with the mother or with the medical profession.   Indeed, the court went so far as to say that although 'the jurisdiction to do what is considered necessary for the protection of an infant is to be exercised carefully and within limits',[51] nonetheless this was 'the very type of case where the court should throw some care' around the child.[52]

However, compulsory sterilisation of, for example, the insane or the recidivist, has been a feature of the development of the laws on this subject in the United States of America,[53] although never expressly legislated for in the United Kingdom.   The first sterilisation law successfully enacted in America was in 1907 in the State of Indiana, and although it was subsequently declared to be unconstitutional, it nonetheless formed the basis for other laws, which, according to Meyers:

> by 1950 had accounted for the sterilisation of over 50,000 persons in America, 20,000 in California alone.   By 1964 the accumulative total had reached 63,678.   Of these persons, 27,917 were sterilised on grounds of mental illness, 32,374 on grounds of mental deficiency and some 2,387 on other grounds.[54]

Although the incidence of compulsory sterilisation in the United States has decreased, nonetheless, there are still a few statutes in force permitting compulsory sterilisation of those who might be regarded as disadvantaged.   A common argument in favour of such legislation is the likelihood of the transmission of hereditary disease.   For example, in State v. Troutman,[55] a compulsory sterilisation statute was held to be valid and the court stated that:

> ....if there be any natural right for natively mental defectives to beget children, that right gives way to the police power of the State in protecting the common welfare, so far as it can be protected, against this hereditary type of feeble-mindedness.

In 1927 in the case of Buck v. Bell,[56] a compulsory sterilisation statute was challenged on due process grounds.   The case concerned an 18 year old feebleminded girl who had shortly before given birth to a feebleminded child and whose mother was also feebleminded.   The law provided that those in charge of the institution in which the feebleminded lived were in a position to arrange for the inmates to be sterilised, and the judgement reflects the prevailing attitude of the courts at that time in the United States.   The court said:

> We have seen more than once that the public welfare may call upon the best citizens for their lives.   It would be strange if it could not call upon those who already sap the strength of the State for these lesser sacrifices, often not felt to be such by those concerned, in order to avoid our being swamped with incompetence.   It is better for all the world, if instead of waiting to execute degenerate offspring for crime, or to let them starve for imbecility, society can

prevent those who are manifestly unfit from continuing their kind.[57]

Nor is it only the feeble-minded whose 'right to reproduce' has been threatened. In 1942 the case of Skinner v. Oklahoma,[58] challenged the law which provided for compulsory sterilisation of 'habitual' criminals, the basis of the challenge being the equal protection of the law guaranteed by the United States constitution. The challenge was successful on the basis that it did amount to unequal treatment and the court further raised the question of personal integrity by stating:

There are limits to the extent to which a legislatively represented majority may conduct biological experiments at the expense of the dignity and personality and natural power of a minority - even those who have been guilty of what the majority define as a crime.[59]

It is however accepted that some basic rights may be forfeited by criminals. The European Convention on Human Rights makes explicit provision for the abrogation of the right to life and the right to liberty in the case of duly convicted criminals,[60] although this abrogation is limited by the requirement that no-one be subject to inhuman or degrading treatment.[61] Assuming that compulsory sterilisation is not ruled out on these latter grounds, it seems that the Convention could allow sterilisation as a punishment, provided it is not carried out on arbitrarily selected individuals. However, the normal irreversibility of the operation and the harshness of compulsory sterilisation as a punishment, in the light of acknowledgement of the right to reproduce as a human right, would make it hard to justify in all but the most serious of crimes. Its use as a deterrent might be considered uncivilised, while its justification as a means of preventing the breeding of future criminals rests on highly dubious criminological and genetic theory.[62]

It would seem then, that the basis for compulsory sterilisation of this type is largely the interest of the State in not having to care for those who may be in some way disadvantaged or deviant. Appeals of this type to the public good are always suspect, and must be regarded as especially so in situations where prediction is particularly difficult. Meyers argues that since we do not understand sufficiently the nature of hereditary disease and its transmission it is an insufficient justification for sterilisation against peoples' will.[63] However, as genetic knowledge advances, it is clear that prediction may be made with some certainty as to the likelihood of the passing of a genetic disease or hereditary disorder.[64] Nonetheless, at least in this country, it has never been suggested that those who are likely to transmit such a disease should be prohibited from having children or should be forced to terminate such a pregnancy. The role of genetic counselling is largely to prepare parents to make such a choice and to help them with the consequences of any choice they may make.[65] However, as Meyers points out:

Compulsory sterilisation and castration will exist - blatantly and in their "voluntary" forms - so long as society prefers the concomitant invasion of bodily integrity and dignity (at least when not undertaken freely) to the added social burden and responsibility of confinement and care of those thought to be "unfit" to procreate. In man's present state of knowledge, it is submitted that such treatment of any individual is only medically and morally justified when carried out pursuant to his free, uncoerced request, once the full implications of the operation have been brought home to him or to those private persons closest to him and responsible for his welfare.[66]

While the moral basis for intervention by the State in these circumstances may be highly dubious, there is theoretically no reason why the law could not dispense with the requirement for consent in certain groups in the community unless this country is prepared to hold, in line with the attitude expressed in the 14th Amendment to the Constitution of the United States of America guaranteeing all citizens equality before the law, that such legislation or regulations would go against the fundamental freedoms guaranteed by law in the United Kingdom. Such a response would not affect the limited nature of any basic right which there may be to procreate, but would merely guarantee that no particular group was discriminated against.

Further problems may be caused for the doctor by those who are unable, temporarily to provide consent to the surgery. For example, the problem may arise where surgery is undertaken and the patient is under general anaesthetic, the nature of the surgery not implicity being concerned with sterilisation. Nonetheless the doctor may decide in the course of surgery that sterilisation may be beneficial to the particular patient. Normally, the clinical judgement of the doctor is jealously guarded both by the medical profession and by the law,[67] but as is pointed out in Re D, supra, decisions of this sort may be considered to be outwith the scope of clinical judgement.[68] In non-emergency surgery, consent is a prerequisite and any operation undertaken without consent would be regarded as a prima facie assault or perhaps, in line with recent trends, as a breach of duty leading to a claim in negligence.[69] This is not to suggest that a doctor who discovers in the course of surgery that there is a life-threatening situation which demands sterilisation would necessarily be at risk in performing the sterilisation. However, the recent case of Devi v. West Midland Regional Health Authority,[70] raised the question of the extent to which clinical discretion may be used in these circumstances. The patient in question was a married woman who already had four children but had hoped to have more. Her religious faith forbade sterilisation or contraception, but when she was admitted to hospital for a minor operation on her womb, the surgeons, discovering that the womb was ruptured and believing that a subsequent pregnancy would be dangerous, sterilised her. As a result of this sterilisation, the patient claimed she had suffered severe stress which affected her marriage and her libido. Damages were awarded, some part of them in compensation for the anxiety and stress, and some part for the loss of her ability to conceive. Situations of this sort serve to reinforce the assertion that there does exist some protectable human right to retain an existing capacity to procreate,[71] whether or not it is intended to use that capacity, unless the individual, or his fully authorised representative voluntarily chooses to alienate the right by giving it up, or, in certain circumstances, where the State has a right to intervene in matters of freedom to procreate.

S.A.M. McLean
T.D. Campbell.

185

NOTES.

1.   Gonzales, B., 'Voluntary Sterilization: Counseling as a prerequisite to Informed Consent', Proceedings of the 5th. World Congress on Medical Law, at p. 64 (1979).

2.   [1939] 1 K.B.687. This cáse preceded the Abortion Act 1967 which permits in s. 1, termination on these grounds amongst others.

3.   See Gordon, G., The Criminal Law of Scotland (1st Ed.), Edinburgh, W.Green & Son, 1967, 775.

4.   See Gordon, G., The Criminal Law of Scotland (2nd Ed.), Edinburgh, W.Green & Son, 1978, where the specific reference to sterilisation is removed, but an extensive discussion can be found at pp. 29-43 as to the likelihood of a new offence being created. Gordon points out (at p. 40), that the 'last example of declaring conduct criminal on the broad ground that it was contrary to morality and social order was Bernard Greenhuff [(1838) 2 Swin 236]' Williams, G., in Textbook of Criminal Law, London, Stevens & Sons, 1978, 524, appears to assume the legality of sterilisation performed with consent.

5.   Religious opposition to sterilisation sometimes stems from the assumption that there is a duty to procreate, but it is doubtful whether such a duty was an original element in the Judeo-Christian tradition and its incorporation into Jewish and Christian theology had more to do with political than with strictly religious exigencies.c.f. Daube, D., The Duty to Procreate, Edinburgh University Press, 1979.

6.   [1954] 3 All E.R. 59

7.   ibid., at p.68

8.   [1934] 2 K.B. 498. See also H.M.A. v. Rutherford 1947 J.C. 1.

9.   Rex v. Donovan, supra, at p. 507.

10.   For further discussion, see infra ch. 8.

11.   c.f. Jessin v. County of Shasta 79 Cal. Rptr. 359, 1969. For discussion see Meyers, D.W., The Human Body and the Law, Edinburgh University Press, 1970, ch.1.

12.   c.f. Cackett v. Cackett 1950 Prob. 253.; Baxter v. Baxter [1948] A.C. 274.

13.   c.f. R v. R [1952] 1 All E.R. 1194.

14.   c.f. L v. L 38 T.L.R. 697.

15.   Wilson, D.T. 'Voluntary Sterilisation: Legal and Ethical Aspects' 3 Leg. Med. Q. 13, at p.16 (1979). See also Murray v. Vandervander Oklahoma Court of Appeals, Div. No.1, No. 46, 159 (1975).

16.   The Royal Commission on Civil Liability and Compensation for Personal Injury, Cmnd 7054/1978 recommended the abolition of such actions in any event as being of 'little importance or relevance', paras. 445-447.

17.   Addison, P.H., 35 Med.-Leg. J. at p. 165 (1967).

18.   See Wesley Teo, 'Abortion:The Husband's Constitutional Rights', 85 Ethics, 337,(1975), at p. 340.

19.   See note 15, supra.

20.   Cackett v. Cackett, supra.

21.   Divorce (Scotland) Act 1976, s. 1, and the Matrimonial Causes Act 1973, s. 1. For a comprehensive discussion of the 1973 Act, see Cretney, S.M., Principles of Family Law, (3rd.Ed.),

London, Sweet & Maxwell, 1979 at pp. 98-155.

22. [1954] 3 All E.R. 59, at p. 62.
23. [1976] 1 All E.R. 326.
24. ibid., per Heilbron, J., at p. 332.
25. (1953), Article 12.
26. Lord Kilbrandon, 'The Comparative Law of Genetic Counseling',in Ethical Issues in Human Genetics, Hilton, B., Callahan, D., Harris, M., Condliffe, P. and Berkely, B., (eds), New York, Plenum Press, at p. 254.
27. Lord Kilbrandon further points out however, loc.cit., that the terms of the European Convention would probably preclude compulsory sterilisation 'if it were sought to be imposed on racial grounds, and it is probable that the same result would attend an attempt to sterilize, for example, habitual criminals....'
28. Thus, it has been suggested that, since parenthood is a skilled occupation, only those considered to be fit parents by the State should be permitted to procreate. See, Lafollette, H.,'Licensing Parents', 9 Philosophy and Public Affairs, 182 (1980).
29. For a general discussion of human rights see, Feinberg, J. Social Philosophy, Prentice-Hall, Englewood Cliffs, 1973, ch. 6.
30. Article 12. provides that 'Men and women of marriagable age have the right to marry and to found a family, according to the national laws governing the exercise of this right.' The Universal Declaration of Human Rights (1948), Article 16(1) states that 'Men and women of full age, without limitation due to race, nationality or religion, have the right to marry and to found a family. They are entitled to equal rights as to marriage, during marriage and its dissolution.'
31. For discussion of the universality of human rights see Cranston, M., 'Human Rights, Real and Supposed', in Raphael, D.D., (ed), Political Theory and The Rights of Man, London, Macmillan, 1967, at pp.43-53.
32. (1948), Article 16(3), which states that: 'The family is the natural and fundamental group unit of society and is entitled to protection by society and the State'.
33. This issue is discussed by Belliotti, R., 'Morality and In Vitro Fertilization', 2 Bioethics Quarterly, 6, (1980).
34. The problems of extending human rights to cover costly social and economic rights are discussed in Raphael, D.D., op.cit. at pp.43-53, 54-67,and 95-100.
35. See Feinberg, J., op.cit., at pp.86 et seq. For a discussion of what the law considers as amounting to real consent, see infra ch. 8. Legal capacity may be circumscribed by State rules regarding mental condition, age etc. Thus in Austria, consent to sterilisation can be given validly only where the person concerned is over the age of 25. For discussion, see Court Report in 1 International Journal of Medicine and Law, 371 et seq. (1979/80).
36. For discussion see Hoggett, B., Parents and Children, London, Sweet and Maxwell, 1977. For most purposes e.g. marriage, Marriage (Scotland) Act 1977), a child in Scotland is regarded as an adult at the age of 16. The Family Law Reform Act 1969 s. 8 (England and Wales), provides that a 16 year old can give consent to 'any surgical, medical or dental

treatment which, in the absence of consent, would constitute a trespass to his person' and expressly precludes the need to obtain parental consent in these circumstances. Thus it would seem that, at least over the age of 16, the parent or guardian will not be in a position to control the wishes of the child as to medical treatment.

37. Re D, supra, at p. 333.

38. For a discussion of the extent of the powers of a parent or guardian and of the extent of any consent which a child may be competent to give, see Cusine, D., 'To Sterilize or Not to Sterilize', 18 Med. Sci.& Law, (1978), 120.

39. The extent of parental powers is discussed in Walker, D.M., Principles of Scottish Private Law, (2nd.Ed.), Oxford, Clarendon Press, 1975, ch. 17.; see also, Cretney, op.cit., at p.430 et seq. Under the Guardianship Act 1973 s.1 (1) both mother and father have equal authority over the upbringing of a minor. Williams, op.cit., argues that although the situation regarding children is unclear, there does exist a limited authority in parents or guardians to consent on behalf of children but that 'When the child is above the ill-defined 'age of discretion', the ideal is to have the concurrent consent of parent and child. The position is unclear if the child, being old enough to consent, withholds consent...' at p.527.

40. Cusine, D., loc.cit., at p.123.

41. See Walker, op.cit., and Cretney, op.cit., at p. 430 et seq.

42. 'Focus', Journal of Medical Ethics, 1975, 1, 163, at p. 164.

43. s.1(1)(b) provides that a pregnancy may lawfully be terminated where it appears 'that there is a substantial risk that if the child were born it would suffer from such physical or mental abnormalities as to be seriously handicapped'.

44. For example the law does this by providing a right of action for those born suffering from congenital defects under common law in Scotland, and under the Congenital Disabilities (Civil Liability) Act 1976 in the rest of the United Kingdom. For discussion see infra, ch. 11. Equally, the Royal Commission on Civil Liability and Compensation for Personal Injury (Pearson Commission) Cmnd 7054/1978, recommended increased allowances for those born severely handicapped.(chs. 26 and 27).

45. See Dworkin, R., Taking Rights Seriously, London, Duckworth, 1977, at pp. 90-94.

46. See Feinberg, J., op.cit., at pp 94-97.

47. c.f. Hare, R.M., 'Abortion and the Golden Rule', 4 Philosophy and Public Affairs (1975), 201, and Tooley, M., 'Abortion and Infanticide', 2 Philosophy and Public Affairs, 37.

48. See infra, ch. 11.

49. Any such action might, however, be precluded since it may be seen as an action for 'wrongful life'. For discussion, see infra, chs. 6, 10 an 11. The problems inherent in this type of action are also discussed in Lovell, P.A., and Griffith-Jones, R.H., '"The Sins of the Fathers" - Tort Liability for Pre-Natal Injuries', 90 L.Q.R. 531 (1974), where they point out (at p. 558) that, '...the "wrongful life" suit, albeit inelegantly and inaccurately called, presents considerable difficulty. The argument "but for the

act complained of you would never have been born," can be overcome, but the real problems inherent are the practical ones of compensation determination and public policy. Disadvantaged birth is a social as well as a legal problem involving many more "victims" than the few who with luck might be able to gain from a law suit.   Alleviating a widespread social condition as opposed to the regulation of specific activities causing harm is not perhaps the province of the law of torts.'

50.   On the connection between rights and the interests of right-bearers, see Campbell, T.D., and McKay, A.J., 'Ante-Natal Injury and the Rights of the Foetus', 8 Philosophical Quarterly, Jan.1978, 17.

51.   Re D, supra, at p. 332.

52.   ibid., at p. 333.

53.   For discussion see Meyers, op.cit., ch 2.

54.   ibid., at p. 29.

55.   50 Idaho 763 (1931).

56.   274 U.S. 200 (1927).

57.   ibid., at p. 207.

58.   316 U.S. 535 (1942).

59.   ibid., at p. 546.

60.   The European Convention on Human Rights, Article 5 (1), 'Everyone has the right to liberty and security of person. No one shall be deprived of his liberty save in the following cases and in accordance with a procedure prescribed by law; a) the lawful detention of a person after conviction by a competent court...'.

61.   ibid., Article 3, 'No one shall be subjected to torture or to inhuman or degrading treatment or punishment.'

62.   See Meyers, op.cit., ch. 2; Bottomly, A.K., Criminology in Focus, Oxford, Martin Robertson, 1979, ch. 2.; Lombroso, C., L'Uomo Delinquente, Milan, Hoepli (5th Ed., Turin, Bocca), 1876.

63.   c.f. Meyers, op.cit., ch. 2.

64.   For discussion, see infra, ch. 10.   The scale of the problems of prediction should not, however, be underestimated.   As is pointed out in Emery, A., Elements of Medical Genetics, (5th Ed.), Edinburgh, Churchill Livingstone, 1979, 'most diseases which are inherited in a simple manner are very rare.   The common familial diseases usually follow no simple pattern of inheritance.', at p. 96.

65.   For further discussion, see infra ch. 10.

66.   Meyers, op.cit., at p.46.

67.   For discussion see McLean, S.A.M., 'Negligence-A Dagger at the Doctor's Back?', in Robson, P., and Watchman, P., (eds), Justice, Lord Denning and the Constitution, Gower Press, 1981.

68.   per Heilbron, J. 'I cannot believe...that a decision to carry out an operation of this nature performed for non-therapeutic purposes on a minor, can be held to be within the doctor's sole clinical judgement', at p. 335.

69.   see infra, chs. 7 and 8.

70.   [1980] 7 Current Law 44.

71.   This would seem to be the case even where the doctor anticipates danger to health if the ability to procreate is retained. Thus, in a case in 1969, a woman obtained damages

having been sterilised without her consent during a
caesarean, see (1969) 1 B.M.J. 456. For general discussion
of consent, see also infra, ch. 8.

14 Sane but Abnormal

G. Maher

The aim of this chapter is to consider the current law and practice within the United Kingdom relating to offenders who, though not insane in the legal sense of that term, are nevertheless considered by the law to be mentally 'abnormal'. The main group in this classification is that which falls within the framework of the defence of diminished responsibility, but also included are those covered by the defences (where applicable) of intoxication and automatism. The emphasis will be on discussion of some of the problems involved in the defence of automatism, though some mention will also be made of diminished responsibility. The argument will be advanced that the traditional understanding of the nature of criminal law and the appropriate powers for criminal courts have led to developments in legal doctrine which are far from satisfactory from the viewpoint of legal principle or social policy. Moreover, the law has moved towards certain classifications of mental abnormality which make only nonsense from the point of view of medical science. In order to understand why the law has moved in these ways, it is necessary to bear in mind some of the general features of the criminal law and powers of the criminal courts which are thought to be acceptable in a liberal society such as ours.

The traditionally held view is that criminal courts are there primarily to sift out the guilty from the innocent. Once the guilty have been identified, the courts are empowered to inflict upon the offenders measures which are, and are intended to be, in some way unpleasant, or more succinctly to punish them. More recently, it has become accepted that courts should also seek to deal with those guilty of breaking the law, in such a way as to reform or rehabilitate them. However, it is essential to appreciate that what justifies the courts in controlling the lives and liberties of people, whether for purely penal or for reformative purposes, is that such persons have been identified by law as persons fit for such treatment and this fitness is manifested by their already having infringed the norms of the criminal law. In other words, criminal courts have powers over offenders precisely because they _are_ offenders. The corollary of this point also holds in the general run of instances, that is that persons innocent of criminal offences (which in practice since everyone is presumed innocent means those accused of crime but not convicted), are free from control by the law.[1]

The most obvious exception to this rule is the case of persons compulsorily committed to hospital by criminal courts, who have been acquitted of offences on the grounds of insanity. Even here, however, it should be remembered that in English law from 1883 to 1964 the verdict was 'guilty but insane' which, whatever criticisms can be levelled at it as being illogical in terms of responsibility, does make a sort of sense when it is considered as a form of justification for the actions of the courts in controlling the future behaviour of an 'innocent' person.[2]

The situation then is as follows. Interference with the liberty of, or behaviour of, others is generally thought to be something which calls for justification. In the area of criminal law, what justifies, in a very general way, the courts in controlling the liberty of others is the very fact that some people are categorised as criminals.[3] General notions of criminal responsibility are intended to embody this justification. Within the framework of the criminal law, the only well-defined exception to this pattern is the case of acquittal, or at least avoidance of conviction in the technical sense, because of insanity. However it is possible to discern in the development of certain areas of criminal law a number of tensions within the general categories of legal doctrines and concepts, due, it is suggested, to the criminal courts themselves wishing to retain control over certain categories of persons, and doing so by means of conviction or, as the only alternative, acquittal on the grounds of insanity. However, before this thesis can be substantiated by examining the relevant areas of law, it will be useful to consider the existing powers which are available to the criminal courts.

POWERS OF THE CRIMINAL COURTS

In addition to their powers to deal with offenders in an overtly penal way (mainly by means of imposing fines and sentences of imprisonment) the criminal courts also have powers of disposal which are intended to avoid punishment as their aim.

1. The insanity defence. Where it is successfully argued that at the time of an offence the accused was 'insane',[4] a special verdict that the accused is not guilty by reason of insanity will be returned.[5] In Scotland, where it is found that the accused committed the act charged but was insane at the time, the special verdict will state this in express terms and go on to acquit him on the grounds of insanity.[6]

However any such finding of 'not guilty' or acquittal is in a sense purely nominal, for the courts must, after findings of this sort, commit the accused to such hospital as may be specified by the Secretary of State.[7] In Scotland, the committal is to the State Hospital at Carstairs or, if there are special reasons, to some other specified hospital.[8]

A similar process of compulsory committal exists for those persons who are found to be insane at the time of the trial and whose condition therefore gives rise to the finding that the accused is under a disability such that he is not fit to be tried,[9] or to a plea in bar of trial.[10] With this type of compulsory committal, it should be noted that there may not necessarily be grounds for convicting the accused in respect of the acts charged. Under English law in this situation the court has a discretion to postpone consideration of the issue of fitness to plead until the prosecution has presented its evidence, thereby postponing the issue of the disposal of the accused because of his unfitness to plead until it is shown that he in fact committed the acts in question.[11] Where an accused is found not to have committed these acts then the issue of unfitness to plead does not arise and the courts have no power to order committal.[12]

2. Hospital order. Where the offender is not within the terms of the insanity defence but nevertheless suffers from a mental disorder which requires or would benefit from special treatment, the court on

convicting him of an offence punishable by imprisonment (except where the penalty is fixed by law, which in effect means except the offence of murder) has power to make an order that he be admitted to, and detained in, a specified hospital for treatment.[13]   The court must be satisfied that the offender is suffering from the appropriate type of mental disorder[14] and that his mental condition warrants such an order being made.   For this purpose there must be written or oral evidence of two medical practitioners.   Furthermore, the court must be satisfied that in all the circumstances, including the nature of the offence and the character of the accused, such a method of disposal is the most suitable.   The making of a hospital order is an alternative to punishing the convicted person.   Thus where an order has been made the court may not pass a sentence of imprisonment or detention, impose a fine or make a probation order in respect of the offence.[15]

3.   Psychiatric probation orders.   A further power available to courts as an alternative to punishment in the disposal of offenders is the power to make probation orders.   These are used when the court is of the opinion that this method of proceeding is in all the circumstances of the case more suitable than passing a penal sentence.[16]   The general purpose and effect of a probation order is to place the offender under supervision for a period of between one and three years.

Where an offender is shown to be suffering from a mental condition which, although not warranting detention under a hospital order, requires and is susceptible to treatment , the court has power to make a probation order with a requirement for his treatment:

i.   as a resident patient at a hospital (but not a special or State Hospital) within the meaning of the Mental Health Acts or

ii.   as a non-resident patient at such a hospital or

iii. at the direction of a named qualified doctor.[17]

In such cases the supervision is carried out jointly by the doctor and probation officer.

Although probation orders are seen as alternatives to penal measures and thus, for example, are inconsistent with the making of compensation orders,[18] the power to make the orders arises usually only where the accused has been convicted of an offence.   However, in Scotland, where a court is satisfied that a person charged with a summary offence has committed the acts in question, it has power to make a probation order without convicting.[19]   In England, where a probation order has been made the finding of conviction is technical only, for it is a finding of conviction only as regards the particular proceedings but does not count as a previous conviction in any subsequent proceedings for another offence, unlike Scotland where the order does rank as a previous conviction.[20]   In both systems, however, dealing with an offender by means of probation order does not have the effect of 'full' conviction in that it does not lead to the imposition of any of the disqualifications or disabilities which attach to convicted persons in normal cases.

4.   Discharge.   A further power available to criminal courts in dealing with persons convicted of offences (unless the penalty is fixed) is that of absolute discharge.   Discharge by the court is appropriate where it is thought inexpedient to inflict punishment and where a probation order is inappropriate.[21]   In Scotland, where the

case is one tried summarily, the court may discharge absolutely without convicting the accused if satisfied that the person charged committed the acts in question.[22]

In England, the courts have the additional power to discharge a person in appropriate cases subject to the condition that he does not commit any offence during a specified period not exceeding three years. Any breach of such a condition has the consequence that the party discharged can be dealt with in respect of the original offence in any manner in which the court making the conditional discharge could have dealt with him.[23] In Scotland, courts lack the power to make conditional discharges; however, the practice of deferring sentence is adopted in many of the cases where in England conditional discharges are used.[24]

The effect of discharge, whether conditional or absolute, is similar to that of probation orders in relation to the finding of conviction, and so in Scotland, unlike England, an absolute discharge coupled with a conviction would rank as a previous conviction in later proceedings on other charges. However, a disqualification from driving under the Road Traffic Act 1972 may be imposed at the same time as a discharge.[25]

An illustration of the type of cases where absolute discharge is the appropriate method of disposal is the case of Farrell v. Stirling,[26] where a defence was raised to a number of charges under the Road Traffic Act 1972, that at the time of the incidents the accused was in a state of automatism due to hypoglycaemia. On examining the evidence the sheriff accepted this defence in relation to charges concerning the later but not the earlier of the incidents, as earlier the accused still had some control over his ability to drive. However, the sheriff took the view that as the accused, a diabetic on a regime of insulin, was not to blame for getting into the state of hypoglycaemia and would not have recognised the condition at its onset, he would convict the accused of the earlier charges but grant him an absolute discharge for the later ones.

5. Road Traffic disposals. As many of the cases where issues of mental abnormality arise relate to offences under the road traffic laws, the powers of courts to issue orders in such cases should be noted. Upon conviction of certain specified serious road traffic offences, the court must order the disqualification of the offender from driving and also endorse his licence (unless there are special reasons, which must relate to the offence rather than the circumstances of the offender, for not doing so). Where the offender is convicted of certain less serious offences under the road traffic legislation the court may, at its discretion, order disqualification but must endorse the offender's licence unless there are special reasons for not doing so.[27] Disqualification can also arise as a consequence of the 'totting-up' of previous endorsements of the licence.[28] The underlying rationale of the courts' powers to order disqualification from driving is not so much penal but rather to ensure road safety.[29]

It is also worth noting that where a person appears in court accused of an offence in respect of a motor vehicle, the court has a duty to inform the Secretary of State if it appears that the accused may be suffering from any disability in respect of holding a driving licence. This duty arises even if the accused is acquitted of the charge.[30] There is a similar obligation on motor insurers to notify the Secretary of State whenever they have refused to insure a driver on the ground that the driver's state of health was unsatisfactory.[31]

DIMINISHED RESPONSIBILITY

An illustration of the way in which the lack of a wide range of powers of disposal for criminal courts has resulted in a distortion of legal doctrine is the development of diminished responsibility. In briefest terms, where diminished responsibility is established it has the effect of being a defence to a charge of murder but allows conviction on the lesser charge of manslaughter (or culpable homicide). On the face of it the doctrine is illogical, for if the accused is responsible he can be convicted of murder; but if he is not responsible, the difficulty arises as to how he can still be convicted of manslaughter. That the criminal law should so openly admit a doctrine which apparently lacks coherence is to be explained only in terms of the limitations of the powers of the criminal courts, especially prior to the Mental Health Acts of 1959 and 1960.

The doctrine as an explicit part of the law relating to responsibility arose by means of case-law in Scotland in the nineteenth century. As Gordon has explained, the real basis of diminished responsibility is not the issue of liability but rather that of amount of punishment or type of disposal, a matter which arises only after the question of guilt has been decided.[32] As such, this was simply a reflection of the universal practice that mitigating circumstances, which would include as one but only one factor the mental condition of the accused, would lead to a reduction in the amount of punishment to be inflicted. Thus, 'diminished responsibility' was one of the factors considered by the judge in using his discretion in determining the sentence for a convicted person. Difficulty arose, however, whenever an offence carried a fixed penalty, for in such cases the judge had no discretion and could give no weight to any mitigating circumstances. The problem was particularly acute in relation to the crime of murder, where for long the fixed penalty was that of hanging, a penalty which might seem harsh when a convicted killer suffered from some mental defect but was not however insane in the legal sense. Accordingly, the doctrine developed from the general practice of taking into account mitigating or extenuating circumstances when sentencing. A successful plea of diminished responsibility gave rise to a reduction of the charge of murder to that to culpable homicide, a conviction for which would give the judge a wide range of discretion in disposal.

As a substantive doctrine, however, judges became wary of extending its scope, and in a number of cases stressed that the defence was applicable only where the accused's state of mind was in a condition very near to, though not amounting to, insanity.[33] One of the reasons for this judicial reaction against a doctrine of their own creation was that judges lacked powers to deal with mentally disordered offenders other than through the insanity defence, and in a number of cases it was stated that even where diminished responsibility was established, the element of protection of the public was to be borne in mind when deciding upon sentence.[34]

The doctrine of diminished responsibility, as a device for reducing a charge of murder to the lesser one of manslaughter, which allows for judicial discretion as regards sentence, was adopted by English law by means of the Homicide Act 1957, section 2 of which provides:

(1) Where a person kills or is a party to the killing of another he shall not be convicted of murder if he was suffering from such abnormality of mind (whether arising from a condition of arrested or retarded development of mind or any inherent causes or induced by disease or injury) as substantially impaired his mental responsibility for his acts and omissions in doing or being a party to the killing.

(3) A person who but for this section would be liable, whether as principal or as accessory, to be convicted of murder shall be liable instead to be convicted of manslaughter.

These provisions have been criticised as embodying not only the general logical error said to reside in the very notion of diminished responsibility, but also such matters as 'mental responsibility' which experts such as phychiatrists have to speak to although it is not obviously part of their expertise. However, in practice the doctrine works. The expression 'abnormality of mind' has been given a fairly extensive meaning and the defence is available in most cases where in some general sense the accused's condition was near to that of insanity as understood in the non-technical (i.e. non-McNaghten) sense. Thus it has been allowed in cases involving conditions of psychopathy, reactive depressions and dissociated states.[35]

However with the restriction of the death penalty for unlawful killing in the 1957 Act, and especially its total abolition in the Murder (Abolition of Death Penalty) Act 1965, the most forceful impetus for raising the defence has disappeared. Moreover, given the introduction of powers for the criminal courts to deal with mentally disordered offenders by the Mental Health Acts of 1959 and 1960 in cases of conviction of offences other than those with a fixed penalty, the sole function of the doctrine in current law is that it is 'a special device for, as it were, untying the hands of the judge in murder cases'.[36] In other words, the rationale behind the practice from which the doctrine of diminished responsibility emerged, namely the need to take into account all mitigating circumstances when deciding upon disposal, can be met in all cases other than murder, as the judge can decide to use hospital orders to deal with appropriate cases of mental disorder. The doctrine of diminished responsibility is accordingly needed in the present law only in relation to the crime of murder, as this is the sole offence which still carries a fixed sentence, the judge therefore lacking discretion in sentencing.

It should not be thought, however, that where diminished responsibility is successfully raised, then the result is always a lighter sentence. Indeed evidence suggests that periods of imprisonment, including in certain circumstances life imprisonment, can follow conviction after a successful plea of diminished responsibility.[37] The point is that the judge has more flexibility in dealing with a person convicted of unlawful killing when the defence has been successfully raised, so that disposal can be graded in terms of individual circumstances and varies from sentences of life imprisonment[38] to the other extreme of making of a probation order where the facts place the accused in a sympathetic light.[39]

It is no great surprise to find that most current debates on diminished responsibility concern not so much the details of the current law (though reforms have been suggested on such matters as the wording of the section of the 1957 Act, and the burden and onus of proof) but rather the whole future of the doctrine. The Committee on Mentally Abnormal Offenders,[40] (the Butler Committee), while suggesting a number of particular reforms, presented as its first option the abolition of the mandatory sentence for murder and with this change the abolition of the doctrine of diminished responsibility.[41] The Criminal Law Revision Committee in its 14th Report, while suggesting a number of alterations to the present law, was divided on the question of whether murder should retain a mandatory life sentence and made no recommendations on the matter.[42] Whatever the future of the plea of diminished responsibility, its development in the law as a substantive doctrine concerning legal responsibility can only be understood in terms of the powers of the courts to deal with cases of murder in the ways thought to be most appropriate to each case. And it is precisely this issue, namely that of appropriate disposal, which is at the centre of the debate about the current practice and the future of diminished responsibility.

AUTOMATISM[43]

An even more striking illustration of the way in which the criminal courts have caused a distortion of legal principle through a narrow construction and use of the range of powers available to them is the defence of automatism. This defence is by its very nature more radical than that of diminished responsibility which is limited in its application to charges of murder. The basis of the defence of automatism is that at the relevant time the accused was in such a condition that he could not be said to be acting or voluntarily acting at all; and, so goes the reasoning underlying the defence, if there is no question of the accused's having acted then no question of whether he acted in a criminal way can arise. Thus in principle, as indeed in practice, the defence is applicable in offences of strict liability, that is those offences which dispense with the usual requirement of mens rea.

As represented in case-law, a wide range of conditions has been put forward as the basis of the defence of automatism, including behaviour following on or during such conditions as sleepwalking[44]; concussion[45]; epilepsy[46]; hypoglycaemia[47]; inhalation of fumes[48]; taking an anaesthetic[49]; cerebral tumour[50]; and arteriosclerosis.[51]

The difficulty facing the courts in coming to terms with the defence of automatism is simply that, at the level of legal principle, the plea if established must lead to an outright acquittal. As against this, however, is the fact that the accused has already appeared in court as a result of prima facie criminal conduct, and the very basis of his defence is some condition which may well give rise to similar behaviour in the future. The present law on automatism is accordingly an attempt to balance the requirements of legal principle with the obvious policy consideration of public safety, but the actual course taken by the law can only be appreciated if we bear in mind the 'commit or convict' alternatives which the courts have tended to adopt in dealing with the defence.

In most legal systems the courts have adopted one (or both) of two tactics to limit the scope of the defence, with the effect that in some systems (including Scotland) there is no defence of automatism which leads to a straightforward acquittal. These tactics are:

1. where the cause of the automatism is a condition falling within the definition of the insanity defence, then the defence is to be treated as one of insanity only, and

2. where the accused is some way to 'blame' (without being necessarily negligent in the legal sense) for getting into the state of automatism, he will be convicted despite the lack of voluntary conduct while in that condition (the blameworthiness doctrine).

Whatever the policy motivations behind these two positions neither is entirely consistent with general legal principle.

Take first of all the proposition that where insanity and automatism are both raised, the issue of insanity takes priority. The distinction between insane and non-insane automatism which underlies this doctrine, is unknown to medical science.[52] Moreover there is an obvious lack of logic in this doctrine, for the issue of whether the accused was truly (voluntarily) acting has a logical precedence over the question of what was his state of mind at the time. Against this, however, it should be borne in mind that the policy underlying the whole insanity defence, which has the effect both of acquittal and compulsory committal, is sufficiently strong to allow the law to by-pass the mens rea doctrine. Indeed the insanity defence itself may be neutral as to whether or not the accused had the requisite mens rea at the time of the offence, and in practice any question of causal connection between the mental disorder and committing the act is simply assumed.[53]

However there is also to be found in some of the cases a further and more troublesome trend, namely that the concept of insanity for the purposes of this doctrine is given a wide definition. The classic illustration of this trend is the case of Bratty v. Attorney-General for Northern Ireland,[54] where the accused was charged with the murder of a girl whom he had strangled while in a condition which he described as a 'sort of blackness'. There was some evidence which suggested that he may have been undergoing an attack of psychomotor epilepsy at the time but his defence failed on the ground of the insufficiency of this evidence. The accused appealed to the (Northern Ireland) Court of Appeal and to the House of Lords, but the conviction was upheld. The House of Lords took the opportunity to make express the doctrine that where automatism was caused by a disease of the mind (the key expression used in the McNaghten Rules which form the basis of the insanity defence in English Law) then the defence was one of insanity not of automatism, which was a separate defence only where 'non-insane' in origin.

In the same case Lord Denning made the further comment:

It seems to me that any mental disorder which has manifested itself in violence and is prone to recur is a disease of the mind. At any rate it is the sort of disease for which a person should be detained in a hospital rather than be given an unqualified acquittal.[55] (emphasis added).

A similar approach was taken by the Scottish courts at about the same time. In H.M.A. v. Cunningham,[56] the accused was charged with a number of offences under road traffic legislation to which he raised a special defence that at the relevant time he 'suffered from temporary dissociation due to epileptic fugue'. The Court refused to entertain any such defence stating that:

Any mental or pathological condition short of insanity - any question of diminished responsibility owing to any cause, which does not involve insanity - is relevant only to the question of mitigating circumstances and sentence.[57]

The practical effect of this case is that non-insane automatism is not a defence at all in Scots law. The effect of the Court's observations as to the type of mental condition which does give rise to a defence of automatism (although its effect is acquittal by reason of insanity rather than on the grounds of the resulting automatism) is by no means clear, but it appears that any condition which results in a state of automatism must be deemed to be insanity in order to constitute a defence.[58] This approach has the same effect of that underlying Lord Denning's dictum in Bratty, supra, and is plainly motivated by the policy consideration that courts need to control the future behaviour of persons thought to constitute a threat to public safety.

It is not at all obvious, however, that so widening the concept of insanity to capture and indeed take over the automatism defence is the most appropriate way of satisfying this policy. Consider, for instance, the case of R. v. Quick[59] where the accused raised a defence of automatism, based on hypoglycaemia, to a charge of assault. The accused was an insulin-dependent diabetic who on the day of the assault had taken insulin as prescribed but had eaten little food during the day and had consumed some alcohol. The trial judge, acting consistently with the Denning dictum in Bratty, supra, ruled that the evidence supported a defence of insanity but not automatism. The accused then changed his plea to guilty but appealed to the Court of Appeal. The Court of Appeal expressed some disquiet about the extent to which the scope of insanity had been stretched in the context of automatism. Lawton L.J. put forward the general view that the expression 'defect of reason from disease of the mind' should not be given a meaning in law which would be regarded with incredulity outside a court and made the particular point that:

The difficulty arises as soon as the question is asked whether the accused should be detained in a mental hospital. No mental hospital would admit a diabetic merely because he had a low blood sugar reaction; and common sense is affronted by the prospect of a diabetic being sent to such a hospital, when in most cases the disordered mental condition can be rectified quickly by pushing a lump of sugar or a teaspoonful of glucose into the patient's mouth.[60]

It should be noted however, that although this case illustrates some of the problems inherent in moves to widen the notion of insanity to allow control over persons prone to bouts of automatism, it does not in itself provide much by way of qualification to it, and would still allow the label 'insanity' to be attached to persons suffering from conditions, such as diabetes, which might result in states of unconsciousness.[61]

The second tactic adopted by the courts to restrict the ambit of automatism as a complete defence is the 'blameworthiness' doctrine. Whereas the first tactic, the use of the insanity defence to include cases of automatism, served the general aim of control of (potential) offenders by widening the scope of the insanity defence and also extending the court's power of ordering committal, the blameworthiness doctrine seeks to do the same by securing the conviction of persons behaving in a state of automatism. But just as the first tactic is unsatisfactory in giving insanity too wide a scope, the second is equally, if not more, unsatisfactory by so extending the traditional doctrine of mens rea that elements of fiction are introduced into the law.

In essence the blameworthiness doctrine asserts that a person who behaves in a criminal way, but is in a state of automatism at the time, may nevertheless be liable to conviction if in some way he is to blame for getting into that state. This view in itself might be thought to accord with the intuition that moral responsibility attaches to persons who continue any conduct while aware that in so doing they may reach some condition in which they can no longer control their actions, and which might have dangerous consequences. But the force of this intuition is dependent upon the degrees of knowledge and forseeability of such consequences or the likelihood of entering the sate of automatism which can be ascribed to the person involved. However, the present law on the blameworthiness of automatism moves far beyond this moral intuition and constitutes a major inroad into the mens rea principle, concerned as this is with the state of mind of the accused at the time of the offence.

To appreciate that this is the case and to understand why the law has developed in such a way, it is necessary to study the context in which the case-law itself evolved. In a number of cases, usually involving charges such as dangerous driving or reckless driving, where a state of automatism was raised as the basis of a defence, the courts adopted the position that conviction was appropriate, even if the accused's mind was 'blank' at some stage of the driving, since at earlier stages he was getting into a condition of automatism. For instance, in Hill v. Baxter,[62] where one of the charges was dangerous driving, Pearson J. stated:

... suppose that the man in the driving seat falls asleep he is no longer driving but there was an earlier time at which he was falling asleep and therefore failing to perform the driver's elementary and essential duty of keeping himself awake and therefore he was driving dangerously. Similarly, in the case of a man who knows that he is liable to have an epileptic fit but, nevertheless, drives a vehicle on the road, there is a question of fact whether driving in these circumstances can properly be considered reckless or dangerous. The answer might depend to some extent on the degree of probability that an epileptic fit might come upon him.[63]

The crucial point in cases like these is that a person can be convicted of dangerous driving or reckless driving (or the like) because continuing to drive while becoming sleepy or while aware that a fit or coma is about to come on is in itself dangerous or reckless driving. In other words, the criminal conduct (actus reus) is located not at the time when the driver moving the vehicle is in a state of automatism but at the earlier stage when he was driving but should have stopped doing so because of the supervening disability. But this mode of reasoning cannot be applied when the actus reus of the offence does not lend itself to such backdating but refers to some specific time at which the automatism had already become established.

For instance, an offence such as assault (one of the charges in Quick, supra) requires proof of the requisite mens rea on the part of the accused at the time of the alleged assault itself. Even offences of strict liability, such as failing to comply with a traffic sign (one of the charges in Hill v. Baxter, supra) require proof of voluntary action by the accused at the time of the alleged incident. In cases like these it does not matter that at some earlier stage the accused, while getting into a state of automatism, could have desisted from what he was doing (but in fact did not do so), for at the time when the relevant conduct was taking place the automatism had already overtaken him.

One way of explaining the blameworthiness doctrine as consistent in general terms with the mens rea doctrine is to treat it as a form of the punishment of negligence in the criminal law. Although such may indeed be the effect of the blameworthiness doctrine, it is not at all apparent how it can be made to sit easily with the principles of mens rea. There is, in the first place, some debate on whether negligence in the criminal law can be taken as part of the general principles of responsibility which are embodied in the mens rea doctrine.[64] Secondly however, the problem still remains of how we can ascribe a state of mind to a person at a time when ex hypothesi he cannot be said to have one, even if he was negligent in bringing this condition into effect.

Williams[65] argues that prior to Quick, supra, the doctrine of blameworthiness or self-induced automatism had never been applied outside the special cases of road traffic offences such as dangerous driving or the like where the actus reus itself can be located at different stages during the course of the driving. This exception is, however, more apparent than real, for in back-dating the actus reus in such instances we can locate the appropriate (and real) mens rea. However, it is pure fiction to argue that we can find mens rea for some offence committed after a state of automatism has been reached, by asserting that the accused was somehow at fault for getting into that condition. Yet in Quick, supra, the Court took precisely that step, stating that:

A self-induced incapacity will not excuse (see R. v. Lipman [1970] 1 Q.B. 152), nor will one which could have been reasonably forseen as the result of either doing or omitting to do something, as, for example, taking alcohol against medical advice after using certain prescribed drugs or failing to have regular meals while taking insulin.[66]

A similar approach has for long been taken by the courts as regards the defence of intoxication which is no defence to any charge whose mens rea is a basic intent (as opposed to crimes of specific intent), no matter how extreme the state of intoxication. The illogicality of this rule and the degree of fiction it introduces into the law, have been openly admitted.[67]

The blameworthiness doctrine thus involves an element of fiction in its attempt to justify conviction, and thus control, of persons who at the time of the offence were in conditions of automatism. The general context of road traffic offences, in which many of the cases which support this doctrine have arisen, is misleading as some road traffic offences can be backdated to accommodate the principle that persons can be held to blame for not desisting from conduct while getting into a state of automatism. Moreover, the driving of motor vehicles is such an inherently dangerous activity that it is easier to impute or assume foresight or knowledge (even if the basis of liability is subjective) to persons who drive and are aware of being prone to blackouts. But there is an unsatisfactory degree of fiction in saying that a person is to blame for all consequences of his behaviour in a state of automatism where his condition is his own fault, no matter the nature of that behaviour or the extent of the consequences.[68]

CONCLUSION

The doctrines of diminished responsibility and automatism as defences to criminal charges illustrate, the one in an historical, the other in a more contemporary, context the way in which the courts' concern with the policy factor of public safety has influenced the development of legal principles, even to the extent of admitting into the law inconsistencies and fiction. Where courts have sought to ensure control of the future behaviour of (potential) offenders mainly by means of the alternative models of 'commit or convict', then such a development was perhaps inevitable. Diminished responsibility is said to attract an inherent illogicality in its operation, and its historical development in Scotland as well as its current operation in both England and Scotland can be appreciated only in terms of the courts' powers of disposal in respect of offenders.

The defence of automatism is perhaps of more significance at the present time, and it too presents a number of undesirable aspects in its current form. One approach to the defence is to throw the net of the insanity defence over it (and in Scotland this has had the effect of swallowing up the automatism defence entirely), but this has the unwelcome consequence of moving the legal definition of insanity far beyond the criteria recognised as appropriate by medical science. The other approach, that of convicting where automatism is blameworthy in origin, subverts the mens rea doctrine, either by extending the scope of negligence in the criminal law too widely or by introducing a degree of fiction into the search for the mental element. Moreover, there is the important fact that a degree of stigma attaches both to findings of conviction and of insanity, and the present problem is to find means to control persons prone to suffering bouts of automatism without sticking any such stigmatising label on them.

One method of achieving this aim is at the administrative level in relation to the issuing of licences for the driving of motor vehicles. The category of road traffic offences is hardly a major or significant one in terms of the general jurisprudence of the criminal law, but stricter control of the types of persons to whom licences are issued would be an important step in reducing the number of such offences. Moreover, driving is such an inherently dangerous activity that it should not be seen as too great a threat to personal freedom if high standards are required before a driving licence is to be issued. In this way, many persons who may be suffering from conditions rendering them liable e.g. to have blackouts can have the likelihood of their being involved in a road accident eliminated without having to be involved in criminal prosecution (though the sanction of the criminal law is a necessary back-up to any effective licencing system).

Indeed in the present law on the licensing of drivers of motor vehicles there exist ways of promoting this goal. The law already requires applicants for a driving licence to disclose any relevant disability or prospective disability, and the disabilities include liability to sudden attacks of giddiness or fainting.[69] The Secretary of State has power to refuse to grant a licence to persons suffering from such a disability or to issue a licence for a restricted period, unless the disability is properly controlled. Moreover persons already holding a licence are under an obligation to notify any disability or prospective disability which develops and the Secretary of State has power to revoke the licence or replace it with a restricted licence.[70]

However this mode of control is necessarily limited to road traffic cases and there is plainly need for the judiciary to be in a position to ensure future control in other cases without resorting to the polarised 'commit or convict' modes of disposal. Interestingly, there is a clear historical precedent for such a method in one of the earliest reported cases on automatism, the Scottish case of H.M.A. v. Simon Fraser.[71] Here the defence was raised to a charge of murdering his son that at the time the accused was asleep, i.e. that he was behaving while in a state of somnambulism. After being directed by the judge to that effect the jury returned the verdict that the accused was not responsible because he was in a state in which he was unconscious of what he was doing by reason of the somnambulism. The case ended with the accused giving an undertaking to sleep alone in the future and the Crown dropped all proceedings.[72]

The approach outlined in Fraser, supra, does point to one satisfactory method of dealing with many cases where the issue of the accused's state of mind is raised to the effect that he lacked mens rea for the offence (or that he did not act voluntarily) and where he does not warrant committal. Much of the difficulty about the actual course followed in Fraser, supra, lies in the lack of powers to enforce any such arrangement. However it was noted earlier that the criminal courts at present have the powers to impose a number of non-penal measures on offenders, which need not involve mandatory committal or the issuing of hospital orders. Greater use could be made of 'psychiatric' probation orders to ensure that persons receive medical supervision for the condition which leads to a state of automatism and the law should make it clear that mental conditions within the scope of such orders include temporary conditions which have some physical base.

The important point is that such control should be available to the courts without their having to convict the accused, at least in the sense of conviction which entails the existence of a full criminal record as well as civic disabilities and exclusions, and to which a greater type of stigma attaches as a convicted criminal. The courts in Scotland still have the power to make certain non-penal orders in summary cases without proceeding to convict the offender (as long as satisfied that he did the acts charged). A different, and perhaps more suitable, method would be to generalise the approach adopted when probation orders and discharges by the court are made by criminal courts in England: in such cases the accused is technically 'convicted' of the offence but the conviction does not count as a previous conviction and does not lead to civic disqualifications.

What is important is that the criminal courts move away from the position of seeing their alternative options as either convicting the accused or committing him as insane. The 'convict or commit' approach can be explained in terms of the courts seeking to gain control over persons whose mental condition renders them liable to behave in a criminal manner (at least prima facie), and so satisfy the policy goal of public safety. However it is an unsatisfactory method of control in several respects. First, many instances of 'non-insane' mental abnormality, such as blameless automatism, do not merit the stigma which follows from either conviction or committal. Moreover, the judges in adopting this approach have made serious inroads into the cardinal principle of mens rea and have added to that principle an unnecessary degree of fiction. Finally the widening of the scope of the insanity defence has moved legal definition far apart from current medical thought. If the courts, especially when dealing with cases of automatism, were to make greater use of their non-penal powers (in their existing or more generalised form) over persons 'convicted' only in a technical sense, then social policy could be satisfied and at the same time the basic principle of <u>mens</u> <u>rea</u> would not be undermined. In this way also, the criminal law would be in greater accord with medical science and the law would be able to reflect moral values in discriminating between those who are deserving of penal measures and those who are not.

G. Maher

NOTES.

1. Exceptions to this generalisation abound. The most obvious examples are cases of compulsory measures such as quarantine or compulsory committal to a mental hospital under civil proceedings: see Mental Health Act 1959, Part IV and the Mental Health (Scotland) Act 1960, Part IV.

2. See Trial of Lunatics Act 1883, s. 1. In some areas where control of potentially anti-social people is needed it is often convenient to by-pass the criminal process altogether, as in the case of children.

3. This is the case even where reformation rather than retribution is sought.

4. By whatever tests are used for this. Different tests are used in Scotland and England.

5. Criminal Procedure (Insanity) Act 1964, s. 1.

6. Criminal Procedure (Scotland) Act 1975, s. 174.

7. 1964 Act, s. 5(1) (a) & (c).

8. 1975 Act, s.175(3).

9. 1964 Act, s. 4 (England & Wales).

10. 1975 Act, ss.174; 375 (Scotland).

11. 1964 Act, s. 4(2). Similar proposals have been made for Scotland: see Criminal Procedure in Scotland (Second Report) (Thomson Report), Cmnd. 6218/1975, para. 52.18. For a case where the accused was detained as insane in bar of trial but was never shown to have committed the offence, see <u>H.M.A.</u> v. <u>Brown</u> (1907) 5 Adam 312, and comments by counsel in that case, Lord Macmillan, <u>A Man of Law's Tale</u>, London, Macmillan, 1952, at pp. 109-110.

12. The accused may, however, come within the civil provisions of the Mental Health legislation; see also Thomson Report, para. 52.08.

13. Mental Health Act 1959, s. 60; Criminal Procedure(Scotland) Act 1975, ss. 175: 376.

14. In England this covers the categories of mental illness, psychopathic disorder, subnormality and severe subnormality. In Scotland no such categorisation is provided by statute, the requirement referring to such mental disorder as would warrant admission under Part IV (civil proceedings) of the Mental Health (Scotland) Act 1960.

15. 1959 Act, s. 60(6); 1975 Act, ss. 175(7) & 376(10).

16. Powers of the Criminal Courts Act 1973, s. 2; 1975 Act, ss. 183 & 384. The offender must have had the effect of a probation order explained to him and must have expressed his

willingness to be put on probation.

17.   1973 Act, s. 3; 1975 Act, ss. 184 & 385. For discussion of the workings of psychiatric probation orders, see the Report of the Committee on Mentally Abnormal Offenders (Butler Report), Cmnd. 6244/1975, ch. 16; Thomson Report, ch. 59.

18.   1973 Act, s. 2(4).

19.   1975 Act, s. 384(1). This was the law in England by virtue of the Probation of Offenders Act 1907 but this provision was omitted from s. 3 of the Criminal Justice Act 1948.

20.   Contrast 1973 Act, s 13 with 1975 Act, ss. 191 & 392.

21.   1973 Act, s. 7; 1975 Act, ss. 182 & 383.

22.   1975 Act, s. 383.

23.   It thus differs from a suspended sentence which counts as a conviction and whose effect is that a fixed period of imprisonment is determined but not put into effect.

24.   Smith, A.D., 'Deferred Sentences in Scotland', 1968 S.L.T. (News) 153.

25.   Road Traffic Act 1972, ss. 102, 93 & 101.

26.   1975 S.L.T. (Sh. Ct.) 71.

27.   R.T.A. 1972, s. 93(1).

28.   R.T.A. 1972, s. 93(3) & (5).

29.   The Sentence of the Court, (3rd Ed.), London, H.M.S.O., 1978, para. 93.

30.   R.T.A. 1972, s. 92(1).

31.   R.T.A. 1972, s. 92(2).

32.   Gordon, G.H., The Criminal Law of Scotland, (2nd Ed.) Edinburgh, W.Green & Son, 1978, at pp. 380-386.

33.   H.M.A. v. Savage 1923 J.C. 49, at p. 51. It should be borne in mind that in Scotland the test for the insanity defence was never restricted to the M^CNaghten formula.

34.   See especially H.M.A. v. Kirkwood 1939 J.C. 36, where the court upheld a sentence of life imprisonment in a case where a plea of diminished responsibility had been accepted by the Crown.

35.   Butler Report, para. 19.5. The defence in English law covers a wider range of conditions than in Scots law.

36.   Butler Report, para. 19.8.

37.   ibid., para. 19.6.

38.   Such a sentence can be longer in duration than a sentence following conviction for murder: Butler Report, para. 19.6.

39.   See the cases discussed in Williams, G., Textbook of Criminal Law, London, Sweet & Maxwell, 1978, at pp. 628-629.

40.   Cmnd 6244/1975.

41.   Butler Report, paras, 19.8 - 19.16.

42.   C.L.R.C. 14th Report, Offences Against the Person, Cmnd. 7844/1980, paras. 42-61.

43.   The word automatism is used here as a legal term of art in the sense discussed in the text. In its medical sense automatism has a more restricted meaning and refers to a relatively rare aspect of epilepsy. See further Fenton, G.W., 'Epilepsy and Automatism', 7 Br. J. Hosp. Med. 57, (1972).

44.   H.M.A. v. Simon Fraser (1878) 4 Couper 70.

45.   R v. Bleta [1964] S.C.R. 561 (Canada).

46.   Bratty v. Attorney-General (Northern Ireland) [1963] A.C. 386; H.M.A. v. Cunningham 1963 J.C. 80 (defence rejected except as part of the insanity defence); R. v. Cottle [1958] N.Z.L.R. 999 (defence accepted).

47.   <u>Watmore</u> v. <u>Jenkins</u> [1962] 2 Q.B. 572; <u>R.</u> v. <u>Quick</u> [1973]
       Q.B. 910.
48.   <u>H.M.A.</u> v. <u>Ritchie</u> 1926 J.C. 45; <u>H.M.A.</u> v. <u>Murray</u> 1969
       S.L.T. (Notes) 85.
49.   <u>R.</u> v. <u>King</u> [1962] S.C.R. 747 (Canada).
50.   <u>R.</u> v. <u>Charlson</u> [1955] 1 W.L.R. 317.
51.   <u>R.</u> v. <u>Kemp</u> [1957] 1 Q.B. 399.
52.   c.f. Butler Report, para. 18.22.
53.   ibid., paras. 18.26 - 18.36.
54.   [1963] A.C. 386.
55.   ibid., at p.412.
56.   1963 J.C. 80.
57.   ibid., at p.84.
58.   An alternative interpretation of <u>Cunningham</u>, supra,is that
       automatism is relevant as a defence only where it is founded
       on insanity, and that the test for insanity is independent of
       the plea of automatism.   This interpretation is more in
       accord with recent pronouncements by the High Court of
       Justiciary on the insanity defence, especially in <u>H.M.A.</u> v.
       <u>Brennan</u> 1977 J.C. 38, where however <u>Cunningham</u> was not
       discussed. For further discussion, see Gordon, G.H.,
       'Automatism, Insanity and Intoxication', (1976), 21 <u>J. Law
       Soc. Scotland</u> 310, particularly at p.313.
59.   [1973] Q.B. 910.
60.   ibid., at p.918.
61.   Indeed the reasoning adopted by Lawton L.J. in <u>Quick</u>, supra,
       accepts, at least by implication, that the condition of
       diabetes can form the basis of the insanity defence.   Lawton
       L.J. accepted that the cause of the accused's hypoglycaemic
       episode was not his diabetes but the 'external' factor of the
       injected insulin, and it was only in this way that the
       insanity defence was avoided.
62.   [1958] 1 Q.B. 277.
63.   ibid., at p.286. Earlier (at p.282) Lord Goddard C.J. had
       said: 'That drivers do fall asleep is a not uncommon cause
       of serious road accidents, and it would be impossible as well
       as disastrous to hold that falling asleep at the wheel was
       any defence to a charge of dangerous driving. If a driver
       finds he is getting sleepy he must stop.'
64.   Hart, H.L.A., <u>Punishment and Responsibility</u>, Oxford,
       Clarendon Press, 1968, ch. 6.
65.   op.cit., at pp. 620 et seq.
66.   [1973] Q.B. 910, at p.922. Lawton L.J. took the view that
       the issue of the blameworthiness of the accused for getting
       into a state of automatism should have been put to the jury
       at the trial.   He mentioned a number of questions which this
       would have involved, such as to what extent the accused had
       brought about the hypoglycaemic episode by not following
       doctor's instructions about taking regular meals, and why, if
       he had been aware of the onset of hypoglycaemia, he had not
       eaten a lump of sugar as an antidote.
67.   <u>D.P.P.</u> v. <u>Majewski</u> [1977] A.C. 443, esp. at pp. 483 - 484
       (per Lord Salmon), and pp. 492-4 (per Lord Edmund-Davies). A
       different situation arises when a person has already planned
       some course of criminal conduct and takes alcohol or drugs to
       give him Dutch courage. This situation is treated more like
       that of backdating the <u>actus reus</u> rather than the <u>mens rea</u>.

68.   c.f. Gordon, G.H., op.cit., at p. 79: '.... legally relevant carelessness must relate to a fairly specific risk - the man who is liable to go into a coma is liable to do anything and it is not really plausible to say, for example, that a diabetic who sets fire while in a coma should be convicted of reckless fire-raising because he knew he was liable to blackouts.'

69.   R.T.A. 1972, s. 87 as amended; Motor Vehicle (Driving Licences) Regulations, S.I. 1976/1076.

70.   For a discussion of the present law in relation to the condition of diabetes, see Frier,B.M., et al, 'Driving and Insulin-Dependent Diabetes', The Lancet, 7 June 1980, at pp. 1232-1234.

71.   (1878) 4 Couper 70.

72.   This approach was followed in a later Scottish case, the Full Bench decision of H.M.A. v. Hayes (High Court, Oct. and Nov. 1949, unreported.), where the High Court advised that the accused, who raised the defence of dissociation due to epilepsy to a number of road traffic charges, should be discharged upon his giving an undertaking to surrender his driving licence and not to drive any vehicle again. See Gordon, G.H. op.cit., at p. 74; Gane, C.H.W., and Stoddart, C.N., A Casebook on Scottish Criminal Law, Edinburgh, W.Green & Son, 1980, at pp. 214 - 216.

15 The Expert Witness
G. H. Gordon

EVIDENCE IN GENERAL

Under British systems of law disputes are settled by a court (judge, or judge and jury) on the basis of facts spoken to by witnesses. In its pure form, so to speak, the system does not allow witnesses to express opinions or make inferences, since for them to do so would be to usurp the function of the court. In practice, however, such purity is impossible and has long since been departed from. Take the typical road accident: if the witness cannot say how many seconds elapsed while the car crossed the junction, he can only describe its speed by saying it went quickly, moderately, or slowly, i.e. by expressing an opinion. It is sometimes said that what is forbidden is the expression of an opinion on the issue which the court has to decide, expressions of opinion on other matters being admissible, or at least admissible where the person giving the opinion has some special qualification for doing so. But reliance on the 'fact in issue' as a criterion is unworkable. As the English Law Reform Committee pointed out, an answer like, 'There was nothing the driver could do to avoid the accident', is tantamount to answering the question the court has to decide: was the driver to blame?[1]

The important point is not that the witness may not express an opinion on what he saw, but that the court can disregard that opinion, since what matters is the court's assessment of blame and not the witness's. There are still, however, certain matters on which certain witnesses will not be allowed to give evidence at all, on which their evidence is incompetent. There is therefore an important distinction between evidence which is admissible, and which the court may accept or reject, in whole or in part, depending on the court's view of its weight; and evidence which is inadmissible and cannot be placed before the court at all.

The real, as against the formal or technical, limitations, on a non-expert witness's evidence are twofold. First, he may not give evidence of facts which are discoverable only by the exercise of skills or the application of experience which he does not possess. There may be areas of imprecision in the matching of evidence and skill, but the general principle is clear. Whether or not the fact that a witness is a driver entitles him to express an opinion on another man's driving skills, it does not entitle him to give evidence of a mechanical fault discoverable only by a skilled engineer. A traffic policeman will not be permitted to say the driver of a car was smoking cannabis resin, although an experienced member of the drugs squad might be; but neither would be permitted to say that the white powder in the driver's wallet was heroin.

Secondly, while he may express opinions or make inferences which are naturally involved in his account of what he observed, these are limited to inferences and opinion of a kind which require no special skill or experience and which relate directly to what he himself did observe. He can say, 'I saw A get his arm broken by an axe that he was hit with'; he cannot say, 'I saw A's broken arm, and it could have been caused by an axe'.[2]

EXPERT EVIDENCE

There are, as will be seen, differences between expert witnesses and other witnesses, but essentially they are the same. They are called by the parties and not by the court; they are exposed to cross-examination; their evidence is to be weighed by the court, and the final decision remains with the court. Where experts disagree, the court must choose between them.

In making this choice, as in coming to any other decision, the court is assisted by the legal rules regarding the burden and standard of proof. He who brings the action, be he prosecutor or civil claimant, must prove his case, but he need not do so in a scientific way or to any scientific standard. The prosecutor needs to prove his case only beyond reasonable doubt; the civil claimant will succeed normally if he shows that his case is more probably correct than that of his opponent, although recent cases have suggested that in order to succeed in a claim for medical negligence the claimant must prove that the facts disclose a high probability of negligence.[3]

TECHNICAL EVIDENCE

Some expert evidence is similar in kind to non-expert evidence of facts, the difference being that the facts are discoverable only by special techniques, and such evidence can be conveniently called technical evidence. Proof of such facts can be given only by experts, and disagreement is rare. Where there is disagreement, the court may require expert evidence of a more theoretical kind - opinion evidence - perhaps from the same witnesses, to assist in deciding on the reliability of the techniques used, so that the distinction between the two kinds of evidence, technical and opinion, is far from being hard and fast. Technical evidence can be exemplified by the analysis of blood for alcohol, or the testing of metal for resistance to stress, or the comparison of fingerprints - all direct evidence of things observed by the witness. Evidence, on the other hand, that fingerprints exhibiting a certain number of common characteristics were necessarily made by the same person, is opinion evidence, albeit it is never challenged. Its freedom from challenge has nothing to do with its being expert or opinion or technical evidence, but is due to the general acceptance of its reliablity. The exhibition to a jury of similarities in handwriting, and evidence of opinion that these are reliable indications of the identity of the witness, are, qua evidence, of the same kind as in the fingerprint case, but are much more likely to be challenged, to be met with by contrary evidence, or to be rejected by the jury. The differences here are differences of weight.

In the area of what is called forensic science we are approaching a position in criminal trials which is in some ways comparable to that which exists where there are court appointed experts, in that a certificate given by an officially recognised scientist will be regarded as sufficient evidence of the facts to which it speaks. That is to say, such evidence is bound to be accepted by the courts; but only if it is not challenged by the defence.[4] For the law still jealously guards the right of the accused to have his day in court, to cross-examine the Crown analyst and to call his own, or even just to ask the court to disregard the Crown analyst as unreliable.

OPINION EVIDENCE

Evidence of the kind so far discussed, technical evidence, is not essentially different from ordinary non-expert evidence, save perhaps that it is usually more precise and reliable, for the witness speaks to his own observations.   There is, however, another kind of expert evidence, which has been touched on previously, which does differ from non-expert evidence, and which is problematic - i.e.   opinion evidence.   The non-expert witness, as has been seen, is not allowed to given an opinion, or at least is not allowed to give an opinion which is not inextricably linked with his own observation.   The expert witness, on the other hand, is allowed to do this: this indeed is often thought of as the essential feature of expert evidence.   But this permission has to be contained within the principle that decisions are for the court.   The expert does not make the decision, he merely provides the court with what they lack - the necessary knowledge and experience - so that armed therewith they and not he can make the decision.   As Lord President Cooper said of expert witnesses in Davie v. Magistrates of Edinburgh[5]:

> Their duty is to furnish the judge or jury with the necessary scientific criteria for testing the accuracy of their conclusions, so as to enable the judge or jury to form their own independent judgement by the application of these criteria to the facts proved in evidence.[6]

From this concept of the place of the expert witness stem two results, relevant to competency and weight respectively: (a) the expert cannot supply the court with what it is already deemed to possess, i.e. ordinary common sense and experience of life, so that expert evidence is incompetent on matters not requiring special skill; and (b) the final decision remains that of the court who can, at least in theory, disregard expert opinion even where that opinion is competently before them, and can and must weigh the evidence against any other evidence in the case, as well as determining whether the witness is sufficiently expert to be relied on and whether his evidence carries sufficient conviction to be acted on.

The operation of (a) and (b) above in practice can be illustrated by the following cases.

(a) A common example of the incompetence of expert evidence on non-expert issues is to be found in the law of obscenity, where expert evidence on the corrupting effect of literature on the ordinary man is inadmissible   It is not just that the final decision rests with the court, but that the court cannot be guided by experts in coming to that decision.   As Lord Wilberforce put it in R. v. Jordan[7]:

> The jury consider the material for themselves....They cannot be told by psychologists or anyone else what the effect of the material on normal minds may be.

> The reason for this has sometimes been said to lie in the supposed common law rule excluding direct evidence as to the ultimate issue to be decided but I think that it (or this may be true of the rule itself) rests on ... the principle that since the decision has been given to the jury as representing the ordinary man, it follows that, at any rate as to matters affecting the ordinary man, the jury,as such, must make it.

> .... ordinary human nature, that of people at large, is not a subject of proof by evidence, whether supposedly expert or not.[8]

The one case which offers an exception to this rule about obscene publications itself illustrates the basis of the rule, and is truly an exception that proves the rule. It is D.P.P. v. A and BC Chewing Gum Ltd.,[9] which was a prosecution relating to allegedly obscene cards distributed with packets of chewing gum. Expert evidence was allowed on the likely effect of the cards on children, although not on whether what the children would be led to do was a sign of depravity or corruption. And the court repeated that the effect of articles on adult minds was something an adult jury could consider just as well as an expert witness.

(b) Davie v. Magistrates of Edinburgh, supra, was an action for damage allegedly done to houses as a result of blasting work carried out by the defender while constructing sewers. The factual evidence and the technical evidence of architects and engineers led to a 'well nigh irresistible inference' that the blasting caused the damage. As against that, the defenders led an expert witness who gave opinion evidence that the alleged causal connection was impossible. The trial judge found for the pursuers, and the question in the appeal was whether he was entitled to reject the expert evidence of impossibility. The appeal court held that he was, rejecting 'firmly' as 'contrary to the principle in accordance with which expert evidence is admitted', the argument that he was bound to accept the expert. Davie's case also dealt with the use of textbooks as sources of knowledge. The trial judge had referred not only to passages of a book which had been mentioned in evidence, but also to other passages, and it was held that he was not entitled to consider the latter:

Passages from a published work may be adopted by a witness and made part of his evidence or they may be put to the witness in cross-examination for his comment. But, except insofar as this is done, the court cannot ... rely upon such works for the purpose of displacing or criticising the witness's testimony.[10]

MEDICAL EVIDENCE

The medical witness is in the same position as any other expert witness, and his evidence often consists of a mixture of technical and opinion evidence. In the typical case of assault to severe injury and/or the danger of life the casualty surgeon will describe the wound and its treatment, and give his opinion on its likely future effect, on whether a knife or a bottle or a hammer or a brick could have caused it, and on whether it was severe or endangered life. Almost all of these matters touch upon the issue before the jury, but the only one that is likely to be dealt with specifically by the judge in his summing up is the last, and he will tell the jury that whether or not the wound was severe or dangerous is entirely a matter for them and not for the doctor; despite which, it is common practice to ask the doctor for his opinion. Nor is the answer confined to a description of the wound, the proximity to a vital organ, nor what would have happened but for surgical intervention, but extends to saying in terms whether or not it was severe or dangerous - and all without objection.

Medical evidence nowadays is rarely controversial, and often agreed by the parties; it is only in marginal cases where it deals with questions of value, such as the degree of severity of a wound, that the court has really to come to its own decision. This is because medicine has reached a stage at which it can often apply a body of accepted knowledge on which its practitioners agree and in relation to which its conclusions are accepted by the public: the doctor knows best.

Medical evidence in civil cases is often similar to that in criminal cases: it is directed to diagnosis and prognosis, to an opinion as to the likely cause of an injury and its likely effect on the patient. Very often nowadays these are the subject of agreed medical reports. Where, however, the medical evidence is not agreed, the court may reject some, and accept other parts of it. Although in practice expert disagreement will often lead to acquittal in criminal, and failure by the claimant in civil, cases this is not necessarily so. As Lord Widgery, C.J. said in R v. Sodo[11]:

> ...the proposition which one hears a great deal nowadays, that if experts differ there must be a reasonable doubt in the jury's mind which will lead to an acquittal...is heresy, and the more often it can be pointed to as heresy the better.[12]

One particularly delicate area for the expert witness is that of medical negligence claims. In such cases he will, of course, require to give the same kind of technical and opinion evidence as in other negligence cases. But in ordinary negligence cases the standard of negligence is that of the reasonable man, and so is not a matter for expert evidence. In cases of professional negligence, however, negligence consists in a certain degree of departure from accepted profesional practices, so that the court has to hear expert evidence on these practices. But the decision is still that of the court, and what counts as negligence is a legal question. In the case of doctors, for example, it is the law that there is no negligence unless the defender has acted in a way that no reputable doctor would act.[13] In particular, an error of clinical judgement does not constitute negligence.[14]

In medical negligence cases, therefore, the court will resolve any conflicts in the technical and diagnostic evidence in the same way as any other conflict in evidence, taking account not only of the expert witnesses, but also of the other facts in the case. So far as the question of negligence is concerned, this remains in the end a question for the court, which has to decide whether the claimant has proved negligence to a high degree of probability.[15] Here, as in other cases:

> Expert witnesses, however skilled or eminent, can give no more than evidence. They cannot usurp the functions of the jury or judge sitting as jury, any more than a technical assessor can substitute his advice for the judgement of the court.[16]

PSYCHIATRIC EVIDENCE

The advantages of agreement and acceptability which attach to most medical evidence do not attach to the same extent to psychiatric evidence, but such evidence is in the same position as any other expert evidence so far as it's competency is concerned. As Lord Parker, C.J. said in D.P.P. v. A and B.C. Chewing Gum, supra:

> No doubt when dealing with the effect of certain things on the mind science may still be less exact than evidence as to what effect some particular thing will have on the body, but

that ... is purely a question of weight.[17]
One must beware of exaggeration here. In most cases, at least in
Scotland, if two reputable psychiatrists say a person is insane or of
diminished responsibility, the Crown and the courts will accept their
opinion. But psychiatric evidence can still be problematic in a way
that does not apply to other kinds of expert evidence, and this is
only partly because lawyers still feel defensive about the now
burnt-out campaigns some psychiatrists used to seem to be waging to
take over the function of assessing responsibility and disposing of
offenders.

Psychiatric evidence faces two special difficulties, at the root
of which is the question whether much of the typical psychiatric
evidence is expert evidence at all. The first is connected with the
rule that opinion evidence as to matters not observed by the witness
is admissible only in areas involving special skill, although what is
such an area may itself be a matter for expert evidence. To put it
at its crudest, ordinary people know about drunks, but alcoholics are
a matter for experts; ordinary people know how jealous lovers behave,
but the behaviour of sufferers from paranoia is a matter for
experts.[18]

The second difficulty is more fundamental. The psychiatrist's
evidence is usually directed to the accused's responsibility for his
conduct, and responsibility is not a medical question, but a question
of law and morality[19]; indeed, it is the question which courts are
set up to decide, a question which is one for society as a whole and
therefore for the ordinary member of that society, both of whom are
deemed to be represented by the jury. If there is to be not merely
trial by jury rather than by experts, but government by the people and
not by psychiatrists, responsibility has to be a question for courts
and not for doctors, even if the doctors all agree.

The most the psychiatrist can do is give his opinion that certain
behaviour is the sign of a recognised mental or personality
disorder. At that stage two questions remain: is the disorder such
as to take the person out of the range of normality and so render
expert evidence about his conduct admissible?[20]; and if so does it
affect his responsibility for his actions? Whether a man is to be
described as a psychopath or as a violent, selfish, callous lout does
not affect the decision as to whether or not he is to blame for his
outrageous behaviour. What matters is whether or not he satisfies
the legal criteria for irresponsibility.

It is, of course, possible for the law to accept that anyone who
is insane or grossly ill mentally is ipso facto irresponsible.[21]
In that case the question of responsibility will become a medical
question, although the courts may have to adjudicate between different
expert opinions about the state of a particular person, or even
between different opinions as to whether a certain condition is a
state of mental illness or not.[22] However, once it is established
that there is severe mental illness, irresponsibility will follow.

This, however, is not the view currently taken in the English
speaking world. The law is still that responsibility is a legal and
not a medical question, and that being so, the courts' reluctance to
leave questions of responsibility to experts would remain even if
psychiatric evidence were as reliable as evidence of blood grouping,
and does remain even although in practice psychiatric evidence is
often accepted.

There are no experts in morals who are recognised by the law,
and if there were they would be theologians or philosophers and not

doctors. The doctor describes the patient's state, explains whether and why it is abnormal, gives an opinion on how it affected his behaviour, and perhaps on how it can be altered, and the court decides whether the person satisfies the legal criteria, whether these are expressed in terms of knowledge of the nature and quality of one's actions, or of capacity to appreciate what one is doing, or to control one's actions, or in terms of whether one's actions are a product of what the court accepts on the basis of medical evidence as being a mental illness.

The relationship between psychiatric testimony and legal questions of responsibility much exercised the courts of the District of Columbia in a series of cases between 1954 and 1972. In one such case the court said: 'Description and explanation of the origin, development and manifestations of the alleged disease are the chief functions of the expert witness'.[23] For the period in question the criterion of irresponsibility was the so-called 'product test'; i.e. was the act the product of mental disease,[24] and the court eventually went so far as to declare psychiatric evidence as to whether it was such a product to be incompetent.[25] The test was eventually abandoned because it 'gave the false impression that the question required a medical or scientific answer'. In the same case the court criticised the trial judge for failing to explain 'how medical experts can be expected to provide information about the impairment of free will, when free will would seem to be a philosophical and not a medical concept'.[26]

The difficulties are in a sense even greater where what is in issue is diminished responsibility, which is a plea in mitigation concerned with the extent of responsibility of someone who is admittedly responsible to some degree, and usually arising out of some personality defect rather than mental illness. But while this may be seen as even less a medical question than the question of responsibility, yea or nay, actual conflict may be reduced because of the absence of much clear legal guidance on what may or may not count as mitigation.[27]

It should be stressed, too, that while the philosophical and theoretical gulf between psychiatric abnormality and legal irresponsibility remains, it emerges as a practical problem only rarely in Britain where psychiatric evidence is much less controversial than in the United States. Whatever the weaknesses of psychiatric testimony, no-one will be found insane, and hardly anyone be found to be of diminished responsibility, except on the basis of such testimony, and in most cases the testimony will be unchallenged.[28]

GIVING EVIDENCE

Giving evidence in court may be something of an ordeal for persons unaccustomed to doing so, but it should be less of an ordeal for the expert, especially after he has been in the witness box once or twice. Even on his first appearance he has advantages over the ordinary witness: he is educated and articulate; he is usually in at least the same socio-economic group as is the lawyer examining him; he will be treated less aggressively in cross-examination; his convenience will be considered, and attempts will be made to take up as little of his time as possible; and he will be giving evidence about things with which he is very familiar. To say that he must

214

give his evidence impartially, that he appears as an independent witness and not as an advocate for the party who calls him, is true but rather insulting, since it applies to all witnesses. The only difference is that an expert who is giving opinion evidence cannot literally fulfil his oath to tell the truth etc., since only facts are true or false. He fulfils his oath by giving his opinion frankly and honestly, without minimising any difficulties it may cause or suppressing any doubts he has. He should give his evidence clearly, and he should bear in mind that he is talking to laymen and that if his evidence is to have any effect it must be made intelligible to them, must be expressed in language they can understand and must display reasoning which they will find convincing. The court has to be persuaded of the cogency of his opinion and impressed by the authority with which he gives it, an authority which will depend largely on his qualifications but can be affected by the way he gives evidence. The expert is expected to express his opinions, but he may lose persuasiveness if he appears opinionated or blinkered.

The expert witness's relationship with the party's legal advisers is as important as, if not more important than, his skill in giving evidence in court. He must know what it is they want from him, and they must know what to expect from him. He should direct his evidence to the factual and legal issues in the case, and so, when, for example, giving psychiatric evidence in a criminal trial he should know what the legal problems are to whose solution his evidence is directed. Where there are certain statutory requirements, as in the case of pre-sentencing reports on the appropriateness of a hospital order, he should make sure that his report includes the required information about things like his own qualifications, the accused's disorder, and whether or not he is dangerous.

It is also important that he makes the legal advisers aware of any qualifications or limitations on his opinion. Nothing more annoys lawyers than an expert who gives a firm opinion in his report or at a consultation, and then waters it down under cross-examination until it becomes useless. The lawyer does not want the expert to be dishonest, but he does want to know what he is likely to say before he decides whether or not to call him as a witness.[29]

It is also important for the expert witness to distinguish between opinion and fact, and to make clear on what facts his opinion is based. This is particularly important in psychiatric evidence where the witness must distinguish between an opinion based on the fact that the patient said something to him, and an opinion based on the truth of what the patient said. For the latter opinion is useless unless what the patient said was true, and it will be for the lawyer to lead evidence of its truth. There is no use giving evidence that a man is mentally ill because he has delusions that his wife is unfaithful if it turns out that she is unfaithful, or even that there are circumstances making belief in her infidelity quite a reasonable one.[30]

PRIVILEGE

The privilege of confidentiality, i.e. the right to refuse to answer questions in the witness box, belongs only to lawyers. Although the doctor-patient relationship is a confidential one, and a doctor may in certain circumstances be sued by his patient for breach of confidence, the doctor is not entitled to refuse to disclose information in the witness box. However, any such disclosure is itself of course privileged, and cannot give any ground for an action of breach of confidence.[31] There are not many modern cases on medical confidentiality, but the rule is clear.

In Hunter v. Mann,[32] a doctor was convicted of failing to give information as to the identity of the driver of a stolen car who was suspected of reckless driving, contrary to s.168(2)(b) of the Road Traffic Act 1972. It was held that the doctor was not entitled to an acquittal on the ground that the offence consisted in failure to give information which it was in the accused's power to give, on the ground that as a doctor he had no power to give information obtained from a patient.

The only live question on medical privilege, and it applies equally to journalists, is whether and to what extent the judge has a discretion to allow the doctor to give evidence. In Hunter v. Mann, supra, Lord Widgery, C.J. said:

... if a doctor is asked a question which he finds embarrassing because it involves him talking about things which he would normally regard as confidential, he can seek the protection of the judge and ask the judge if it is necessary for him to answer. The judge, by virtue of an overriding authority to control his court which all English judges have, can, if he thinks fit, tell the doctor that he need not answer the question. Whether or not the judge would take that line, of course, depends largely on the importance of the potential answer to the issues being tried.[33]

The statutory duty under s. 168, however, cannot be affected by judicial discretion, since the question is put by a policemen and, on the authority of Hunter v. Mann, supra, must be answered on pain of conviction for the statutory offence.

The nature and extent of judicial discretion has been discussed recently in two cases concerning journalists. In A-G v. Mulholland; A-G v. Foster,[34] a case arising out of the Vassal Tribunal, Lord Denning, M.R. said that neither the clergyman, the banker nor the medical man was entitled to refuse to answer when directed by the judge but that the judge 'will respect the confidence which each member of these honourable professions receives in the course of it', and will order an answer only where the question is 'a proper and indeed a necessary question' to be put and answered. It was for the judge to weigh the conflicting interests of the respect due to professional confidence and the ultimate interest of the community in justice being done.[35] Donovan, L.J. took the same view, saying that the question must be one the answer to which will serve a useful purpose in relation to the proceedings in hand. If the judge thought more harm than good would result from compelling disclosure, he could exercise his discretion not to order the witness to answer. The judge was not bound hand and foot to require an answer.[36]

In H.M. Advocate v. Airs[37] the Scottish High Court seem to have taken a slightly harder line. A journalist refused to identify the accused as a person with whom he had had a conversation. Two other witnesses had identified him, and the accused's counsel conceded the question of identification before beginning to cross-examine the journalist. In these circumstances it was argued that the journalist's refusal to answer did not put him in contempt, because the answer was not necessary. The court held that in fact it was necessary, since the journalist was a witness of obvious credit and the jury might accept his evidence while having doubts as to the reliability of the other witnesses. It was, said the court, hard to figure any circumstances in which a relevant question could be judged unnecessary or not useful. If such circumstances arose, they would not lead to the witness having a right to refuse to answer, but could be dealt with by 'a residual discretion in the court to excuse' him from answering on grounds of conscience.

It is not altogether clear from Airs, supra, whether this discretion is limited to cases where the answer would not be necessary or useful, but it is probably not so limited, and there is one recorded case of a priest being allowed not to breach the secret of the confessional, where the evidence was necessary and useful.[38] The court is, however, less likely to be so ready to accord the same privilege to a doctor.

The question of judicial discretion was discussed in the House of Lords in D. v. N.S.P.C.C.,[39] where their Lordships referred to a passage in the Law Reform Committee's Report on Privilege in Civil Proceedings.[40] The Committee's view was that the propriety of allowing a witness to refuse to answer must depend upon all the circumstances of the case, and that it was best left to the trial judge 'to hold the balance fairly between the Hippocratic oath and the witness's oath to tell the truth'. Some of their Lordships approved the Committee's approach, and in particular their general view that the policy of the law was to limit privilege to a minimum, but accord the judge a wide discretion where disclosure would be a breach of some ethical or social value and secrecy would be unlikely to result in serious injustice.[41] Lord Simon of Glaisdale, however, said that all the judge could do was exercise 'a considerable moral authority on the course of a trial', by, for example, asking counsel if he really wanted to press the witness. 'But', he went on, 'it is far from the exercise of a formal discretion and if it comes to the forensic crunch, ... it must be law, not discretion, which is in command'.[42]

The most that can safely be said is that where a doctor feels that to answer a question would be a breach of confidence he should say so, and ask the judge to permit him to refuse. If the judge nonetheless directs him to answer, he must do so, or face punishment for contempt of court. An appeal court is unlikely to overturn the trial judge's exercise of his discretion either on general grounds, or (at any rate in Scotland) on the ground that the evidence was unnecessary or unhelpful.

Where a doctor examines a prisoner awaiting trial in order to report on his mental state, that examination is not confidential. Where one such a prisoner eventually raised a defence of automatism it was held that the Crown could elicit evidence from the doctor that he had not suggested this at the time of his examination and indeed that it was inconsistent with what he had told the doctor about the circumstances of the offence.[43]

G.H. Gordon

NOTES.

1.   Evidence of Opinion and Expert Evidence: Cmnd 4489/1970. See also Criminal Law Revision Committee, 11th. Report, Cmnd 4991/1972, paras. 266 to 270; Scottish Law Commission

memorandum No. 46: The Law of Evidence (1980), paras. R.01 to R.05.

2.   c.f. R. v. Davies [1962] 1 W.L.R. 1111, where a witness who was himself a driver but had not seen the accused driving was allowed to express an opinion that the accused was drunk, but not that he was unfit to drive.

3.   c.f. Hucks v. Cole & Another 'The Times' 9 May, 1968; Whitehouse v. Jordan [1981] 1 All E.R. 267. For a more general discussion of the standard and burden of proof in medical negligence cases see, McLean, S.A.M., 'Negligence - a Dagger at the Doctor's Back?', in Robson, P., and Watchman, P., (eds), Justice, Lord Denning and the Constitution, Gower Publishing Co. Ltd. 1981; see also infra, ch. 7.

4.   e.g. Road Traffic Act 1972, s.10: Criminal Justice (Scotland) Act 1980, s.26.

5.   1953 S.C. 34.

6.   ibid., at p. 40.

7.   [1977] A.C. 699: see also Galletly v. Laird 1953 J.C. 16.

8.   R v. Jordan, supra, at pp. 717 - 718.

9.   [1968] 1 Q.B. 159.

10.   per Lord President Cooper at p. 41.

11.   [1975] R.T.R. 357; See also R v. Jennion [1962] 1 W.L.R. 317.

12.   R v. Sodo, supra, at p. 360.

13.   see Hunter v. Hanley 1955 S.C. 200; S.L.T. 213.

14.   Whitehouse v. Jordan, supra; Hucks v. Cole, supra.

15.   Whitehouse v. Jordan, supra.

16.   Davie, supra, per Lord President Cooper at p. 40.

17.   ibid.,at p. 164.

18.   c.f. R v. Turner [1975] 1 Q.B. 834: R v. Chard (1971) 56 Cr. App. R. 260. It is also accepted that non-experts can give evidence involving testamentary capacity. Where what is relied on is the testator's eccentricity and his correspondence there is no room for medical evidence: see Morrison v. MacLean's Trustees (1862) 24 D. 625; McNaughton v. Smith 1949 S.L.T. (Notes) 53.

19.   For further discussion, see infra ch. 14.

20.   Similarly, expert evidence as to the reliability of a witness is admissible where a) that reliability is attacked on the grounds that the witness is abnormal, and b) non-expert evidence would be admissible to attack it if he were normal: Lavery v. R.[1974] A.C. 85; R v. Turner, supra: R v. Toohey [1965] A.C. 595; R v. Bracewell (1978) 68 Cr. App. R. 44.

21.   See Report of the Committee on Mentally Abnormal Offenders, Cmnd 6244/1975 (Butler Report), paras. 18.17, 18.18. It is the law in e.g. Norway.

22.   In one famous case the staff of a mental hospital in Washington D.C. held a meeting between the trial of a case and the hearing of the appeal. At the meeting they decided that 'sociopathic personality disturbance' which had formerly not been a mental illness should now be so described, thus changing the law and necessitating a retrial: Blocker v. U.S. 288 F. 2d 853 (1961).

23.   Carter v. U.S. 252 F. 2d 608 (1957).

24.   Durham v. U.S. 214 F. 2d 862 (1954).

25.   Washington v. U.S., 390 G. 2d 444 (1967).

26.   U.S. v. Brawner, 471 F. 2d 969 (1972).

27.   But see Brennan v. H.M. Advocate, 1977 J.C. 38; S.L.T. 151.

28. Where the only evidence in the case is expert opinion
     evidence pointing one way, e.g. that the accused is of
     diminished responsibility, a verdict rejecting that opinion
     may be quashed on appeal as not being 'a true verdict
     according to the evidence' even where the burden of proof is
     on the appellant: R v. Mathieson [1958] 1 W.L.R. 474; R v.
     Bailey [1961] Crim.L.R. 828.   But such an unusual result
     will happen only where the expert evidence itself is highly
     cogent and there is no other evidence of any kind to cast
     doubt on it: Walton v. R [1978] A.C. 788.
29. On the other hand where the lawyers on both sides prepare an
     agreed joint report, their respective experts should ensure
     that that report actually represents their views, and that
     the latter have not been modified in order to reach a
     compromise: Whitehouse v. Jordan [1980] 1 All E.R. 650
     (C.A.), Lord Denning M.R. at p.655.
30. c.f. R v. Ahmed Din [1962] 1 W.L.R. 680; R v. Bathurst
     [1968] 2 Q.B. 99; Whitehouse v. Jordan, supra.
31. For a brief discussion of confidentiality, see infra pp.
     19-22.
32. [1974] 1 Q.B. 767.
33. at p. 775.
34. [1963] 2 Q.B. 477.
35. ibid., at pp. 489-490.
36. ibid., at p.492.
37. [1975] J.C. 64.
38. Henry Daniels, Glasgow High Court, 1960, a trial for culpable
     homicide: see Beltrami, J.: The Defender, Edinburgh, 1980.
     Chap.10.
39. [1975] A.C. 171.
40. Cmnd 3472/1967, para. 51.
41. ibid., para. 1.
42. at p. 239.
43. R v. Smith (Stanley) [1979] 1 W.L.R. 1445.   It was held in R
     v. Payne [1963] 1 W.L.R. 637, that where a driver consented
     to medical examination on being told that it was to check for
     any disability and the doctor would not consider his fitness
     to drive, the judge should exercise his discretion not to
     allow the doctor to give evidence related to his fitness.
     That case, however, depended on general principles as to the
     admission of unfairly obtained evidence, and had nothing to
     do with confidentiality, and must now be read in the light of
     R v. Sang [1980] A.C. 402.

5 —